AMERICAN PROTESTANTISM
and a JEWISH STATE

AMERICAN PROTESTANTISM
and a
JEWISH STATE

by
HERTZEL FISHMAN

Wayne State University Press, Detroit, 1973

Published simultaneously in Canada
by the Copp Clark Publishing Company
517 Wellington Street, West
Toronto 2B, Canada.

Library of Congress Cataloging in Publication Data

Fishman, Hertzel, 1921-
     American Protestantism and a Jewish state.
     Bibliography: p.

     1. Protestantism and Zionism. 2. Israel—
Foreign opinion, American. I. Title.
DS149.F52 1972   956.94'001   72-3746
ISBN 0-8143-1481-3

Grateful acknowledgment is made to the Morris and Emma Schaver Fund
for financial assistance in the publication of this volume.

To the memory of my parents
Shmuel and Leah
whose love for Zion and humanity
was imbued in their children
through enlightened precept and personal example.

contents

acknowledgments

The author is indebted to his children, David, Leora and Talya, whose persistent urging moved him to complete this book, and to his talented wife, Priscilla, who helped prepare it for publication.

introduction

The purpose of this book is to record and analyze the attitudes of American liberal Protestantism toward the emergence of a Jewish state in Palestine. These attitudes have perplexed Jews and Gentiles alike. While Protestant support for a Jewish state is rooted in the millennarian tradition of Christendom, the interpretation of this tradition by most American liberal Protestant leaders militated against strong church support for the establishment of such a state. Within the leadership councils of the American Protestant establishment, particularly the Federal Council of Churches and its successor, the National Council of Churches, there has been a sharp division on the subject. This was especially apparent between those whose background stemmed from foreign missionary families or institutional affiliations, and those who were not committed to missionary goals.

As the question of a Jewish state in Palestine merged in the minds of Protestant spokesmen with the subject of Jewish nationalism and Jewish ethnicity, the theme of anti-Semitism became linked with the topic. Jews were increasingly confused by the dichotomy in the attitudes of the American Protestant establishment. American liberal Protestants expressed general dismay at the persecution of Jews, but at the same time they ignored and often obstructed practical measures to alleviate collective Jewish suffering and homelessness. Jews were equally bewildered by Protestantism's espousal of the concept of justice for the Arabs, and its neglect of the practical implications of this doctrine as it affected justice for the Jews. They were heartened by the clarifying moral perceptions of Reinhold Niebuhr, but were aware that he and his pragmatic-moralistic school of thought did not represent the mainstream of American liberal Protestantism.

The period selected for this study is 1937 to 1967, from the year in which a British royal commission recommended the partitioning of Palestine into Jewish and Arab states through the period of the Six-Day War in June 1967 between Israel and her Arab neighbors. This thirty-year span coincides with the most dramatic era in modern Jewish history, during which six million Jews were decimated in the Nazi holocaust of World War II and a sovereign Jewish state was reestablished in Palestine after two millennia.

The reaction of American Protestantism to these events provides the substance of this book. American Protestantism here refers to some thirty-four national Protestant groups, having a membership of over 42 million, which are represented in the National Council of Churches.[1] While not necessarily speaking for American Protestants as individuals, or even for their respective memberships, the representatives of these groups closely reflect the institutions and theology of liberal Protestantism.

The spokesmen for American Protestantism on the subjects of Jewry and a Jewish state have been clergymen and laymen who have played prominent roles either in the affairs of the council, in its component organizations, or in ad hoc groups especially concerned with these topics. Their views have been reflected in resolutions and publications of the Federal Council of Churches and the National Council of Churches, of the World Council of Churches, in the proceedings and pronouncements of ad hoc groups, and to a lesser degree in the policy statements and the periodicals of their own denominations. Above all, they have expressed their attitudes in editorials, articles, letters, and book reviews appearing primarily in two independent Protestant journals of opinion, the *Christian Century* and *Christianity and Crisis*.

The *Christian Century*, first published in 1884, has the largest number of subscribers of any Protestant weekly, about 40,000.[2] While continuing to enjoy its status as the only nondenominational Protestant weekly in the United States, its earlier virtual monopoly as the only periodical representing liberal Protestant views was broken in 1941 with the appearance of the nondenominational biweekly *Christianity and Crisis*. In the opinion of one authority, the latter periodical, with an approximate circulation of 10,000, has greater public influence than denominational magazines with many more readers.[3]

In addition to these two publications, this study will incorporate selectively the views of the monthly *International Review of Missions,* first published in 1912, and of the biweekly *Christianity Today,* launched in 1951. Both periodicals cut across American Protestant denominations, and each one reflects the attitudes of a distinctive segment of American Protestantism. The *International Review of Missions* represents the attitudes of the missionary movement, which has had a strong bearing on the subject of Jewish statehood. *Christianity Today* reflects a conservative, neo-evangelical point of view. While in the author's view neither of these magazines is as critically reflective or as open to divergent opinions as are the *Christian Century* and *Christianity and Crisis,* incorporating their statements at appropriate points in the analysis will enhance the value of the study by making it more broadly representative of American Protestantism.

In the absence of an official, regularly published organ representing the authoritative viewpoints or even a reasonable consensus of American Protestantism, the *Christian Century* and *Christianity and Crisis* have provided a forum reflecting liberal Protestant attitudes on a wide range of contemporary issues, including the question of Jewish statehood. The two publications have made their pages available to a broad spectrum of Protestant leaders who have expressed themselves repeatedly on the topic. While Protestant denominational publications have commented infrequently on the issue of Jewish statehood, these two journals, especially the *Christian Century,* have devoted many columns and pages to the subject as a newsworthy topic.

To the extent that Jewry and Jewish statehood were at all of concern to American Protestantism, this interest was most systematically expressed in the pages of the *Christian Century.* During the thirty-year period under discussion, some two thousand separate entries appeared in the *Christian Century* on these subjects. Because of the larger number of pages per issue and the greater frequency of publication, this independent journal kept the topic alive in its weekly columns and dealt with it more extensively than its competitor, the biweekly *Christianity and Crisis.* Because of its privileged position as the only American Protestant independent weekly concerned with reporting and analyzing contemporary affairs, the *Christian Century* not only presented the views of American Protestantism, but also helped mold these opinions and attitudes.

The stance of American Protestantism toward a restored Jewish state can best be understood by looking first at its theological perception of this subject and at its missionary role in the Middle East before 1930. The first chapter will provide a selective overview of this background.

1

Early American Protestant Views of Zion

THOUGH THE AMERICAN PURITANS, LIKE THEIR English counterparts, were strongly influenced by the Old Testament, they did not interpret the biblical concept of Zion as a restored Jewish state in the Holy Land.[1] While originally intending to transpose a design of scriptural Zion onto American soil in the form of a Holy Commonwealth, the American Puritans settled instead for a much more restricted meaning of Zion—the church militant itself.[2] In doing so, they reverted to Augustine's insistence in the fifth century that the triumphant Christian church was the de facto Millennium and that all earlier millennial hopes, expressed or implied by New Testament writers and church fathers, were to be ignored.[3]

Despite Augustine's teachings, the hope for the Millennium did not evaporate from Christian thought.[4] For hundreds of years, while the church reigned supreme in Europe, masses of Christians acknowledged its unrivaled hegemony and teachings, voluntarily or under coercion. Periodically, however, a bold voice would challenge church policies and doctrines, including those pertaining to the Millennium. Such deviant challengers were forerunners of the Reformation period. In its turn the Reformation made the Bible available to the Christian masses and allowed them to read scriptural prophecies and eschatological visions directly, without mediator or censor.[5] The Pope was replaced by the Bible as the Reformation's final spiritual authority. It enabled Protestants to be their own biblical interpreters. It permitted Christians once again to believe in the Millennium of the future.

In England by the end of the sixteenth century the Bible had become the Englishman's book of books. A new millennarian trend was advanced by a growing number of British theologians. If the Bible was to be taken seriously, Old Testament prophecy regarding

Jewish restoration to the Holy Land had to find a place in Protestant theology.[6] That this development took place in a country where almost no professing Jews had lived since their expulsion in 1290 was a paradox. But more than in any other Protestant country, the notion of the restoration of the Jews to the Holy Land took root in England and clearly affected later British policy with respect to the Jewish national home in Palestine.[7]

Still another novel element was discernible in the Protestant millennarian spirit of England. Leading English Protestants foresaw the possibility of the Millennium actually taking place on English soil. Stirred by the biblical portrayal of the Jewish people's struggle for the Promised Land, the Puritans seeking the Kingdom of God saw themselves treading a similar road and began to identify themselves with ancient Israel. To them Jerusalem represented not a geographical entity in the Near East but an ideal society for mankind. Zion became the symbol of their own national future, later expressed in William Blake's *Milton*:

> I will not cease from mental fight,
> Nor shall my sword sleep in my hand,
> Till we have built Jerusalem
> In England's green and pleasant land.

America: The New Jerusalem

It is little wonder, therefore, that the early American Puritans and their successors viewed New England as the site of a new Jerusalem—the territorial symbol of religious faith and exemplary virtue.[8] "Protestants were assuredly not people to whom things happened, but people who made things happen, and they tried to make them happen according to a divine plan operative in history."[9] In due course, the initial millennarian thrust of Puritanism became interwoven with America's national faith of manifest destiny.

H. Richard Niebuhr has held that belief in the Kingdom of God on Earth has been the distinctive note of American Christianity, differentiating it from Christianity in other lands.[10] For the great majority of American Protestants, the notion of a new Jerusalem evolving gradually on American soil, rather than through a sudden supernatural apocalypse, was a distinct possibility. This concept served to deemphasize the other-worldly thinking of European

Protestantism, favoring instead a theology of social gospel and, in more recent times, of social action.

This optimistic outlook toward achieving a paradise-on-earth did not prevail universally or consistently throughout American Protestantism. Faith in an earthly Millennium was never unequivocal. Theologically, the sinfulness of man necessitated a belief in an eschatological earthly transformation, while pragmatically, daily hardships and tribulations were ameliorated by hope for a new life on earth under a future dispensation.[11] Alongside the optimists whose this-worldly messianic beliefs were at best teleological, there always existed groups who hoped and believed in the imminent Second Coming of Christ and the cataclysmic commencement of the Millennium. Such religious groups were typically constituted by "the disinherited, in final despair of obtaining through social processes the benefits they seek."[12] In their view, the church's duty was not to reform the social order, but to prepare a "true Church," a comparatively small body of saints, for membership in the coming kingdom. Though these "pessimistic" denominations did not reflect the majority of American Protestantism, their intense devotion to the singular Adventist outlook toward Christ's Second Coming, has won them a notable place in American religious history. They have given the millennarian concept persistent emphasis within American Protestantism.[13]

How did these two principal divisions in American Protestantism—the mainstream pseudo-optimists of a gradual millennial bent and the fundamentalist, literal millennarians—view the place of the Jews in their respective messianic outlooks?

We have already noted that at the beginning of the Puritan experience in America, scriptural prophecy concerning Jerusalem's redemption and Zion's restoration was interpreted to apply to the church itself. As in England and elsewhere in the Protestant world, millennarian expectations in the American churches related directly to the Jews in one way only: their conversion to Christianity would accelerate the messianic advent.[14] In fact, the religious fervor expended in missionary work among the American Indians was in large measure due to a belief that they were the ten lost tribes of Israel,[15] and that the Messiah would not arrive until "all Israel would be saved."[16] Within American Protestantism, the Jews were still a mysterious component in God's scheme, for the "old" Israel had ceased to exist with the emergence of the Christian church, the "new"

Israel.[17] American Protestants, like Christians all over the world, retained a sentimental association with the "land of Israel," the country of Jesus' earthly drama. In usage, the term was applied symbolically, but not practically. It was a metaphysical and metaphorical term connoting a distant past or a vague theological future, not a viable present. It had little to do with the nationalist strivings of the contemporary Jewish people.[18]

The early nineteenth century marked a turning point in the attitudes of American Protestants toward the Jewish people and Palestine. Leading Americans began to speak out on the subject of the Jews and a Jewish homeland, largely as a result of Jewish persecution abroad.[19] Furthermore, a millennarian fervor began to influence American Protestants, especially those of the smaller, fundamentalist denominations. In 1816, Hezekiah Niles of Baltimore, publisher of the important *Weekly Register*, recognized the plight of European Jewry in the aftermath of Napoleon's defeat, and wondered why wealthy Jews could not exploit Turkish weaknesses to secure Palestine as a homeland.[20] Mordecai Manuel Noah, a former United States consul to Tunis and a figure in New York City politics, visited the Levant and, upon his return, began to agitate for a political haven of refuge for persecuted Jews. When John Adams was asked to respond to a proto-Zionist speech delivered by Noah in April 1818, dedicating the new Shearith Israel Synagogue in New York City, the former President declared: "I really wish the Jews again in Judea, an independent nation. For, as I believe, the most enlightened men of it have participated in the amelioration of the philosophy of the age. Once restored to an independent government, and no longer persecuted, they would soon wear away some of the asperities and peculiarities of their character."[21]

Dispensationalism

Adams may have been ahead of his time with respect to advocacy of Jewish political restoration to Palestine, but not by much. By the mid-nineteenth century Protestant America began to feel the impact of theological Dispensationalism—which viewed God as dispensing or administering periods of history in accordance with specific revelations.[22] Dispensationalism permeated smaller Adventist church groups and influenced members of major denominations as well. In fact, this theology viewed itself as cutting across denomination boundaries and deliberately avoided being trapped in a specific organized church mold. It was concerned with a spiritual fellowship of individual Christians who appreciated Scripture more literally than did the "modernists" who viewed it symbolically, spiritually, or critically.

American Dispensationalism broke with the age-old Christian tradition which had refused to recognize the viable existence of the Jewish people. Whereas classical Christendom held that only the church was the acknowledged "new" Israel, and that "old" Israel had theologically withered away with the first advent of Jesus and the destruction of the Temple,[23] Dispensationalism kept Israel and the church in two distinct categories. One authority on Dispensationalism put it this way: "the basic premise of Dispensationalism is two purposes of God expressed in the formation of two peoples who maintain their distinction throughout eternity."[24] Unlike the mainstream of Christian tradition, Dispensationalism understood Paul's prayer for "natural" Israel to be a clear reference to Israel as a national people, distinct from and outside the church.[25]

This understanding, plus the literal interpretation of Scripture, readily leads to the literal fulfillment of Old Testament prophecies— the basic tenet of millennial eschatology.

In the Millennium, the church will reign as "the bride of Christ," while the people of Israel will be restored to their ancestral land and will inherit the earthly kingdom forecast by the prophets.[26] Some American Dispensationalists began to take on the prophetic role of predicting the imminent Second Coming of Christ as the next major event in history before God's final judgment of the world and the emergence of the ultimate dispensation, the Millennium.[27] One such Dispensationalist was William E. Blackstone, whose book *Jesus is Coming* (written in the 1880s) passed through several revised editions.[28]

Blackstone, for example, interprets the word "generation" in the New Testament verse "This generation shall not pass away till all be fulfilled" (Luke 21:32) to mean the Jewish people.[29] He quotes profusely from Old Testament sources prophesying Israel's restoration.[30] In the 1908 edition of his book he is able to point to the organized Zionist movement, launched in 1897, as a sure sign of Jesus' imminent advent.[31] Naturally, the Dispensationalists, like all other millennarians, believed that the Jews would become converts to Christianity after passing through a period of tribulation, but the first stage in this drama of salvation would be their physical restoration to Palestine. In March 1891 a petition organized by Blackstone was presented to President Benjamin Harrison on behalf of 413 prominent Christians and Jews. Reacting to the wave of pogroms initiated by the Russian Government in the 1880s against its Jewish nationals, the petition's opening sentence asks: "What shall be done for the Russian Jews?" The memorial proceeds to answer: "Why not give Palestine back to them again? According to God's distribution of nations, it is their home, an inalienable possession, from which they were expelled by force. . . . Let us now restore them to the land of which they were so cruelly despoiled by our Roman ancestors."[32]

It is readily explainable why the humanitarian motivation to help the Jews of Russia would have awakened the conscience of Christian leaders in American public life, prompting them to lend their names to the Blackstone petition. Both the discrimination against American Jews in Russia by the Czar's government and the persecutions of Russian Jews were ample reasons to arouse the American public.[33] However, the growing notion among responsible American Christian leaders and molders of public opinion that Palestine could become an answer to the problem of Russian Jewry was a matter transcending mere humanitarian sentiment. It is also possible to attribute this thinking primarily to a strong religious motivation which developed in the United States as a result of the millennarian spirit affecting all of nineteenth century American Protestantism. Ernest R. Sandeen, an authority on millennarianism, reports that beginning in the 1860s, the editorial board of *Prophetic Times*, a monthly periodical propagating the millennarian doctrines, included distinguished clergymen from the ranks of the Lutheran, Episcopal, Presbyterian, Dutch Reformed, and Baptist denominations.[34] These represented a significant element in American Protestantism.

Though millennarianism did not capture the thinking of most members of large Protestant denominations, with the exception of the Southern Baptists, it came to dominate the beliefs of some of the smaller Protestant churches.

The Mormons

Among the latter, the Mormons were not atypical. In 1830, Joseph Smith published *The Book of Mormon* which was offered as the interpretive record, by professed divine inspiration, of a Jewish settlement in ancient America, dating from the destruction of the first Jewish Temple in 586 B.C.E.[35] The people with whom it purported to deal were described as "a lonesome and solemn people, wanderers, cast out from Jerusalem," who yearned for the eventual restoration of the House of Israel. The Mormon prophet, however, distinguished between two Houses of Israel, that of the Jews and that of the Gentiles. While the former indeed were to be restored to Palestine, the latter's gathering place was to be in American Zion, specifically, Jackson County, Missouri. Both of these restorations were necessary preludes to the Second Coming of the Christian Messiah.

In 1845, a year after Smith was killed by a mob, the Mormon Council of Twelve under the leadership of Smith's successor, Brigham Young, published a proclamation addressed to the mortal rulers of the world. Among other things, the declaration stated: "And we further testify that the Jews among all nations are hereby commanded, in the name of the Messiah, to prepare to return to Jerusalem in Palestine . . . and also to organize and establish their own political government." The manifesto concluded with the admonition to the Jews that the Mormons "now hold the keys of the priesthood and kingdom" which will be restored to them after they repent and "prepare to obey the ordinances of God." The Church of Jesus Christ of Latter Day Saints—the Mormons—has persistently related its own religious goals to those of Jewish restoration to Palestine, viewing the ingathering of Jews to the Holy Land both as a prelude to the latter's conversion to Christianity and as a sign of Christ's imminent Second Coming.[36]

American Bible Romanticists

The Mormons were not alone in their spiritual proximity to the Holy Land. The view that, aside from the Protestant missionaries, there was little interest in the Middle East on the part of Americans until well into the present century is inaccurate.[37]

Edward Robinson, the pioneer and dean of American archeologists in the Holy Land, explained in 1838 why he and subsequently other Americans were irresistibly drawn to their Palestinian explorations:

As in the case of most of my countrymen, especially in New England, the scenes of the Bible had made a deep impression upon my mind from the earliest childhood. . . . Indeed in no country in the world, perhaps, is such a feeling more widely diffused than in New England; in no country are the Scriptures better known, or more highly prized. From his earliest years the child is there accustomed not only to read the Bible for himself, but he reads or listens to it in the morning or evening devotions of the family, and in the daily village school, in the Sunday school and Bible class, and in the weekly ministrations of the sanctuary.[38]

Robinson's comments about the Bible-loving New England environment in which he and his generation were raised can be appreciated more readily if we recall that until 1827 the clergy in Massachusetts were charged by law to inspect and license schools and teachers. Many of the teachers were, in fact, clergymen. Until 1834, everyone was required by law to contribute to the churches' support. Nine-tenths of all college presidents were ministers, as were most members of the faculties.[39] It is not difficult to understand why so many New Englanders gave thought to the Holy Land, if not to its relationship to the viable Jewish people.

In 1838, Edward Robinson, assisted by his former student at Andover, Eli Smith, crisscrossed Palestine diligently for more than six weeks. He spent the next two years in Europe writing his famous three volume work,[40] on which his greatest competitor, the Swiss scholar Titus Tobler, commented: "The works of Robinson and Smith alone surpass the total of all previous contributions to Palestinian geography from the time of Eusebius and Jerome to the early nineteenth century."[41] Except for a return trip to the Middle East in 1852 to amplify his earlier work, Robinson taught at Union Theological Seminary in New York City, almost until his death in 1863.

One can detect the persistence of a romantic strain in Protestant religious interest in Palestine. The Holy Land had been the object of eighteen centuries of Christian pilgrimages. Even an admittedly nonpracticing Protestant like John Lloyd Stephens, whom Van Wyck Brooks designated as "the greatest of American travel writers," was seized with awe in the mid-1830s when visiting the actual places associated with the life of Jesus.[42]

Another example of an American Protestant steeped in Old Testament lore and romanticism was U.S. Navy Lieutenant William F. Lynch, who in 1847 persuaded the U.S. Secretary of the Navy to allow him to mount an official expedition to navigate the Jordan

River and the Dead Sea. His journal shows that his self-appointed mission to explore these two bodies of water in the Holy Land was the result of combining a pioneering spirit with religious sentiment.[43]

United States Missionaries in the Near East

The principal pragmatic interest of American Protestants in the Near East has been closely related to the activities and attitudes of the Protestant missionaries in the region.[44] In the first twenty-five years of missionary work, which began in 1819, about sixty missionaries were sent to the Middle East from the United States, all but a few by the American Board of Commissioners for Foreign Missions.[45] Their original objective was to establish local Protestant churches with native pastors, but their success was largely achieved in secular educational endeavors.

The work of American Protestant missionaries in the Near East created two important conditions which have continued to influence the attitudes of American Protestants toward the area. First, it secured the position of Protestants in the Ottoman Empire. Until the missionaries arrived on the scene, Christian influence in the region had been dominated by the Catholic and Eastern Orthodox religious groups. By the mid-1840's, however, the United States minister in Constantinople could tell the American consul in Beirut that American missionaries had the full backing of their government. He said: "The missionaries themselves know that I will protect them to the full extent of my power, not only through you, but if need be, by calling the whole of the American Squadron in the Mediterranean to Beyrout."[46]

The intrusion of American missionaries, along with their Anglican and Lutheran (German) counterparts, into the Near East undoubtedly contributed to involving their respective governments in the region's problems.

Although the American Protestant missionaries in Syria and Palestine could count only some thirty new converts to Protestantism by 1856,[47] their impact upon the area was felt in a more significant way, through a small network of elementary and secondary missionary schools. Their influence became increasingly widespread through the introduction of an Arabic printing press, the publication of an Arabic edition of the Protestant Bible in 1864, and the founding of

23

the American University of Beirut (Syrian Protestant College) in 1866,[48] perhaps the most important Protestant-sponsored institution in the region.[49]

Though the missionaries failed in their principal aim of converting large numbers of Arab Muslims to Christianity, "they succeeded better than they knew in accomplishing a regeneration in the spirit of the people."[50] In particular, this spirit was directed into channels of an Arab cultural revival and helped lay the groundwork for modern Arab nationalism. A prominent Arab academician has already observed that the principal difference between the American University and the French Université de Saint Josef at Beirut lay in the former's role as an intellectual center of Arab nationalism, while the latter fostered distrust of Arab nationalism and placed greater concentration on classical, academic studies.[51] Inevitably, the missionary sponsorship of the University of Beirut led, in time, to the identification of American Protestant missionary interests with Arab nationalist interests.

The non-Arab, American Protestant officials and faculty members of the American University of Beirut consistently supported the cause of Arab nationalism. In pursuing this policy, the American University leaders were determined to spread the Wilsonian concept of self-determination in the Near East, as well as to strengthen the role and influence of American Protestant-supported institutions in the region.[52] The post-World War I peace conferences proved to be appropriate international forums for demonstrating their political leverage.

Protestant Influence at Peace Conferences

At the Paris Peace Conference, the most important role on behalf of American Protestantism was played by Dr. Howard Bliss, president of the American University of Beirut. In one historian's estimation, "Bliss was the most influential American in the Near East."[53] He was markedly anti-French in his political views and resented the French occupation and influence in Syria.[54]

At Paris, Bliss urged a mixed-nationality commission of the Allies to investigate the true political will of the Syrians, and on January 28, 1919 he advised the American delegation what it would find: a universal desire for a united Syria, to include Palestine, under an American protectorate.[55] Bliss was attempting to forestall the establishment of a separate Jewish national homeland in Palestine, as promised by the Balfour Declaration.[56]

On February 13, 1919, Dr. Bliss appeared before the Big Ten Powers. He formally requested the appointment of a commission to investigate the political wishes of the Syrian population whose views, he charged, had hitherto been suppressed by French censorship. After Bliss finished his presentation, C. Gamen, chief representative of the Central Syrian Committee, also pleaded for a greater Syria, but he incorporated a plan for an autonomous Jewish Palestine, connected to Syria by ties of federation.

Bliss repeated his plea to the American delegation on February 26. The Americans in turn prevailed upon the French and British delegates, on March 20, 1919, to send a mixed team representing the three major powers.[57] At French insistence, however, the Big Three agreed that the team would investigate the political preferences not only of Syria's inhabitants, but of those in all former Turkish territories, including Palestine.[58]

Within a few days, President Wilson had selected his two commissioners: the president of Protestant-sponsored Oberlin College in Ohio, Henry C. King, who had been a religious director for the American Expeditionary Forces, and Charles Crane, a former Chicago manufacturer and vice-chairman of the Democratic Party's finance committee in the 1912 campaign.[59] The British chose two Near Eastern experts, but when the French withdrew from the agreement, anticipating the anti-French reception awaiting the commission in Syria, so did the British. Consequently, the investigatory group as finally constituted was exclusively American. Its secretary was Albert Lybyer, a former teacher at the Protestant-supported Robert College in Constantinople. He later became identified with the Institute of Arab American Affairs in Washington.[60]

In the last days of May 1919, the King-Crane Commission set out for its six-week inquiry in the Near East. On June 20, the commissioners telegraphed from Jerusalem to the American delegation in Paris their first conclusions regarding the Palestine situation. They were against Jewish immigration to Palestine and the Balfour Declaration because it caused Arab unrest and would require the support of a large army. A second telegram of July 12 from Beirut expressed great sympathy for a united Arab kingdom under Faisal, preferably as an American protectorate. The commissioners stressed Faisal's deep love for Christians, especially for Americans. As one telling argument on his behalf, they reported his seeming willingness to allow the establishment of an American women's college in forbidden Mecca. One scholar of the period sums up the missionary bias of the commission as follows: "No zealous missionary could have asked for more. If the Holy of Holies were thus open to them, then they could foresee the whole of the Arab world coming under their spiritual wing. With the French and the Vatican beaten, and the Jews out of the way, their missions would flower in the desert under American protection."[61]

The commissioners maintained that Faisal, "a real great lover of Christians," longed to reconcile Christianity and Islam. He could effectively do so because of his prestige in the Moslem world. "Given proper sympathy and surroundings," they telegraphed, "no danger of his getting adrift or taking big step without Anglo-Saxon approval."[62]

The final King-Crane Report, presented to the American delegation on August 28, 1919, was blatantly against a Jewish state in Palestine:

> . . . with a deep sense of sympathy for the Jewish cause, the Commission feels bound to recommend that . . . Jewish immigration should be definitely limited, and that the project for making Palestine distinctly a Jewish Commonwealth should be given up. There would then be no reason why Palestine could not be included in a united Syrian state, just as other portions of the country, the Holy Places being cared for by an international and interreligious commission. . . . The Jews, of course, would have representation upon this commission.[63]

The King-Crane Report was never acted upon officially by the American delegation, probably due to the report's outspoken hostility to France and Britain. It was kept secret until 1922, when it was revealed by Russian sources.[64]

Two officials of the American Board of Commissioners for Foreign Missions represented the Federal Council of Protestant Churches in the United States at the Lausanne Conference held from November 1922 to February 1923. At this conference, Ottoman rights to Arab lands were officially renounced by the Turks. The role of the Protestant representatives was to ensure that missionary interests in the former Ottoman Empire were kept intact.[65] The same motivation underlay their concern with the Anglo-American Treaty of 1924 on Palestine. Thus, article five of the Anglo-American Treaty, protecting mission rights in Palestine, could not be modified without the express consent of the United States.[66] On the other hand, the State Department's hostility to the pro-Zionist component in the treaty was so manifest that the Balfour Declaration was mentioned in the preamble only when Britain actually forced the department to accept it by referring to the Joint Congressional Resolution of September 11, 1922 applauding the declaration.[67]

The missionary influence upon American Protestant attitudes towards a Jewish state in Palestine will be more fully assessed in the following chapters. Here it may be pointed out that the missionary impact at various echelons of the United States Department of State was not negligible. The direct organizational pressures applied by Protestant missionaries, and the influence of their politically and financially important lay backers, were not ignored by the executive branch. Perhaps even more significant is the fact that their views were reflected through individuals occupying positions of authority in the Department of State, especially in the Middle East division, who were children or grandchildren of Near Eastern missionaries or who grew up or went to school in the Arab Near East.

The Christian Century's Position

In contrast to the active concern of missionary circles with the problems of the Middle East, the Palestine question was not a subject of vital interest to Protestant churches in America following World War I. In keeping with the isolationist spirit of American society in general, the churches were not overly concerned with international affairs other than through their missions and overseas relief operations.[68] Their main postwar emphasis was on reconstructing and strengthening their own denominations in America. As the prominent Protestant independent weekly, the *Christian Century*, editorialized during the Versailles Peace Conference, "The Zion of our faith is now to be rebuilt."[69]

Britain's assumption of the Palestine mandate was welcomed by American Protestant circles. When General Allenby took Jerusalem from the Turkish infidels in December 1917, there was much rejoicing.[70] In fact, in listing the religious sites which were now to be supervised by a Christian power, a leading American Protestant theologian, Professor H. L. Willett of the University of Chicago, simply forgot to include the Western Wall in Jerusalem, considered to be the site of the ancient Jewish Temple. While he did mention a few Muslim sites, the Christian places were the focus of his attention. When an earthquake hit the Holy Land in 1927, the *Christian Century* reminded its American readers not to forget the equally important earthshaking event: "the Holy Land again was under a Christian government! Palestine is still the Holy Land and such it will always be, not because it is holier than other lands in which the spirit of God is working out great purposes, but because of its association with the most impressive group of men, prophets and apostles, the world has ever seen, and because it is the land 'over whose acres walked those holy feet which twenty centuries ago were nailed for our advantage to the bitter cross.' "[71]

In the month following the publication of the Balfour Declaration in November 1917, the *Christian Century* had warned against taking seriously the millennarians who were euphoric with "Second Coming propaganda."[72] While acknowledging "the wide vogue which pre-millennialism has attained in the Church today," the paper felt it was harmful to "a truly spiritual religion," and urged that the Protestant churches "show convincingly the better way of reading the Scripture." The periodical remained consistent in its negative theological attitude towards Jewish restoration to Palestine. While expressing misgivings about Great Britain's policy of encouraging "aggressive Jews to claim the country as a 'homeland' for their people" —for "historically the Jew has never been in possession of Palestine"[73]— the journal insisted that "it is the conviction of most modern biblical scholars that the Old Testament contains no anticipation of the restoration of Israel to its ancient homeland which can apply to the Jewish people and the present age."[74]

The *Christian Century* did not favor Jewish nationalism and the intrusion of Zionist pioneers upon the status quo of Palestine's native Arab population. It applauded the British commission's report on the 1929 Palestine riots, which recommended stopping land sales to the Jews and curtailing Jewish immigration to Palestine. It considered the report as the death knoll of the Balfour Declaration, labeling the latter "a mischievous and ambiguous promise" which would allow for Jewish nationalistic ambitions that "could not be realized consistently with justice to other elements of the population."[75]

One of the principal arguments of the *Christian Century* against a Jewish state in Palestine was the contention that large numbers of Jews did not in fact support such a venture. The great majority of Jews in the world were either uninterested in a Jewish state, or "are more or less opposed to it."[76] Editorializing at the end of 1929, the *Christian Century* stated:

> As long as the Jews were the victims of persecution and outrage in any of the lands of their occupation, it was inevitable that they should dream of a homeland where they might be at peace and work out their cultural and religious ideals. But the new world of today is open to them with growing freedom and opportunity. The Jew is respected and honored in all the regions where he has exhibited his powers in the fields of industry, commerce, politics, art and literature. Does he really desire to emigrate to a small, poverty stricken and unresourceful land like Palestine? Some of his people do. . . . But for the most part, the Jews are a practical people, perhaps the most practical in the world. Is the remaking of Palestine a practicable enterprise? Perhaps it is. It is a question for them to decide.[77]

This attitude, then, was the prevailing one in American Protestant circles until the advent of Hitler. The impact of millennarianism waned considerably after the First World War, due both to the growth of liberalism and of isolationist nationalism in Protestant churches, as well as to the demise of prominent millennarian leaders.[78] While individual American Protestant leaders would periodically report in the *Christian Century* on their trips to Palestine, the question of a Jewish state was usually skirted. Rather they related either their impressions of the Holy Land itself, as an object of Christian admiration or criticism,[79] or their favorable reactions to the accomplishments of the young Jewish pioneers.[80]

The rise of Nazism violently upset this passive Protestant attitude towards the Palestine problem.

2

The Apparition of Jewish Nationalism

IN THE 1930s, THE CHRISTIAN CENTURY WAS THE only independent, nondenominational Protestant weekly in the United States. It was most effective in molding and reflecting liberal Protestant opinion on current public issues, including the subject of Jewish nationalism. It maintained a clear editorial policy on current events, but its columns were open to divergent viewpoints. It devoted considerable attention to the subject of Jewish nationalism, in marked contrast to the Protestant denominational press which had little of significance to say about the subject. The *Christian Century* may be considered as the most significant source for ascertaining the attitudes of American Protestantism during this period.

The Christian Century's Critique of American Judaism

The *Christian Century* was consistently opposed to Jewish nationalism. This opposition was compounded by the journal's view of American nationalism in which the melting pot theory played a major part. Any ethnic or religious group within American society that professed cultural pluralism was, in the publication's opinion, clearly out of step with the best interests of the nation.[1]

Quite objectively, the Jews were the one discernible ethnic-religious group within the American body politic which, from the time its members arrived in the United States, seemed to deviate blatantly from the melting pot norm. Whereas other immigrant groups would gradually give up more and more of their unique ethnic characteristics, and even modify some of their "old country" religious beliefs and practices to suit their new American environment, American Jews by and large continued to view themselves as a religious and ethnic group—a faith and a culture—apart from the great majority of Americans. They wished to achieve equal rights and opportunities as individuals, but continued to perpetuate their group identity. Not all Jews were able to define the nature of their collectivity, but most of them continued to maintain an emotional and psychological, if not practical, relationship with it.[2]

The *Christian Century* clearly did not understand the unique nature of American Jewry. During the 1930s, it vigorously upheld the melting pot theory, and the principal target of its indignation was the Jews. When the Jews exercised their distinctive patterns of faith and culture outside the purview of the majority populace, they were, in the paper's view, violating a cardinal democratic principle of "majority rule."

> Can democracy suffer a hereditary minority to perpetuate itself as a permanent minority with its own distinctive culture, sanctioned by its own distinctive cult forms? . . . They have no right *in a democracy* to remove their faith from the normal influences of the democratic process by insulating it behind the walls of a racial and cultural solidarity.[3]

It would appear that the *Christian Century*'s view of American nationalism confused the democratic political process with majority rule in matters of faith and culture. Yet, this conclusion seems to be ambivalent. While not denying the right of American Jews to practice Judaism—in fact, while applauding their right to do so—the paper would have liked them to practice *its* notion of Judaism. It hoped for a diminution of distinctive Jewish beliefs and practices, and an adoption by American Judaism of some distinctive Christian beliefs and practices which the *Christian Century* equated with authentic American nationalism. In this manner, Judaism would increasingly melt into the American Christian melting pot. Such melting was not to be accomplished by force or even by Christian proselytizing.[4] It would be implemented by the open competition between Judaism and Christianity, and by the mutual effects of one faith upon the other.

This contest, however, did not imply that both religions were equally valid: "Not for a moment do we consent to be misunderstood with those whose creed asserts that one religion is as good as another, your religion for you, mine for me."[5] It merely allowed the "separatist" Judaic religion to encounter the "universalistic" Christian religion in an open market, and to induce the former to become more universalistic. In this way, Judaism might become attuned to what the paper considered to be America's democratic environment. "The Jewish religion, or any other religion, is an alien element in American democracy unless it proclaims itself as a universal faith and proceeds upon such a conviction to persuade us all to be Jews."[6] The genius of American democracy was to provide an ongoing public forum for both Judaism and Christianity to engage in open "conflict looking toward a higher integration."[7]

It is little wonder, therefore, that when, in 1946, The Jewish Theological Seminary of America announced a $15 million campaign to strengthen American Judaism's distinctiveness, the *Christian Century* criticized this policy because "if the process of social assimilation is really speeding up, we cannot regard that as anything but a gain for the American future."[8]

The *Christian Century* did not comprehend the character of Judaism nor did it recognize the place of religious minorities in American society. Yet its erudite editors and its educated readers surely were not unaware of *both* the separatist and the universalist tendencies of Judaism, originating in Pentateuchal and Prophetic sources of the Bible. The laws of social justice in the Five Books of Moses were explicitly directed not only to Jews, nor did Amos and Isaiah pronounce their visions of international peace other than to a universal humanity. Still, American Jews were expected, by the American Protestant ethos, to surrender their particularistic patterns and to concentrate more potently on the universalistic elements of Judaism, in the hope of accelerating a "higher integration of social relationships" in the United States.[9] To American Protestantism, America's greatness lay in its homogeneity, not in its heterogeneity. Cultural pluralism, which contributed distinct racial, cultural, and religious strains to a common melting pot, was tolerable only until the unsettling 1930s. But such a philosophy could not be tolerated as a permanent feature of American democracy. "America's hospitality [to cultural pluralism] has already imperiled its democracy. Carried too far, this hospitality results in a society so heterogeneous that it cannot be a community: too many communities can destroy the community."[10]

The *Christian Century*'s attack on cultural pluralism was an open attack on the American Jewish community. It wrote: "When the doctrine of cultural pluralism is taken to mean religious pluralism

—"Judaism is true for the Jew and Christianity is true for the Christian"—it sets itself in direct opposition to the Christian faith which cannot exist at all except on the presumption of its universality."[11] Other ethnic, religious, and racial communities in the United States proceeded to practice their unique patterns of behavior without consistent reminders of their melting pot obligations. It was taken for granted that sooner or later they would melt into the majority culture. Although the Catholic community was always considered suspect by Protestantism for its alleged dependence on Papal authority, it was still part of a universalistic Christian framework. The American-German community was not castigated for perpetuating its distinctive cultural practices. The American Negroes were not criticized for their separatist racial patterns of expression and behavior. Only American Jews were singled out for all three offenses: they retained a distinctive culture, they felt a common solidarity of peoplehood or race, and their religion was essentially separatist rather than primarily universalist.

The *Christian Century* argued that, by championing these distinctive characteristics, American Jews were perpetuating and strengthening the forces of anti-Semitism in the United States. In its view, this thesis was tantamount to a self-fulfilling prophecy: "Democracy cannot guarantee our American Jewish brethren against the emergence of a crisis in which the prejudice and anger generated by their long resistance to the democratic process will flame up to their great hurt."[12]

The periodical was clearly interested in trying to influence American Jewry to alter its pattern of religious-ethnic uniqueness. What twenty centuries of anti-Semitism and brutal physical persecution could not compel the Jews to do, the modern American Protestant weekly would have them do in a single generation. In its articles and editorials, the *Christian Century* warned the insecure Jews during the Depression that they would not be tolerated by American society if they continued to retain their unique ethnic-religious attributes. Judaism should divest itself of its "cultural fatalism"[13] and freely encourage the devotees of one religion to cross over to another. With remarkable lack of subtlety it asserted that, should Judaism remain obstinate and not allow itself to reach "a higher synthesis," the Protestant's "spirit of tolerance would shrivel up."[14]

This enforced religious liberalism was characteristic of American Protestantism until the early 1950s. Either the other religious groups in the United States were to toe the mark of liberal religion as defined by the Protestant churches, or they would be harassed and sniped at by the Protestant establishment. Either the other religions were to take on more common characteristics of a "civic," white Anglo-Saxon Protestant ethos, or they could not be acknowledged as partners in the American religious arena.[15]

The starting point for the Jewish religious group to begin its melting process into the spiritual mainstream of America could be the incorporation by Judaism of the teachings of Jesus into its liturgy and preachments.[16] "A simple gesture of [this] recognition would be the unconstrained observance of Jesus' birthday." To be sure, his place in Judaism did not have to be the same as that which is accorded him in the Christian church. Neither should Judaism feel, so the periodical said, that its interaction with Christianity must be a one-way movement in which Christianity did all the giving and Judaism all the receiving. "If the religion of Judaism is good for the Jews, it is also good for gentiles," proclaimed the *Christian Century*. "If it is not good for gentiles, it is not the best religion for Jews."[17] Whatever this simplistic and deceptive statement was meant to convey, the periodical felt it was "not fair to democracy to cherish a religious faith which provides a sanction for racial or cultural or any other form of separation."[18]

A more accurate statement of the journal's viewpoint, on the subject of who was to influence whom in the interplay between Judaism and Christianity, was explicated several years later when it quoted from a study about intermarriage. The study indicated that the total number of conversions to Judaism was relatively small. Approving this small number of converts, the paper hoped the finding "would clear away such misunderstandings as have grown out of a widespread belief that the purpose of many synagogues and rabbis has been to employ Judaism to block the normal assimilative processes of American life."[19] It was clearly the policy of the periodical to advocate assimilation, and rabbis who fought this homogenizing tendency while seeking to strengthen Jewish loyalties, were viewed as reactionary forces in America.[20]

This view prevailed in American Protestantism until the post–World War II era, when a new mutual pluralistic tolerance began to emerge among religions in America.[21] Furthermore, the international campaign to establish a Jewish state after the war substantially muted American Protestantism's aggressive advocacy of Jewish religious assimilation in the United States by diverting its anti-Jewish thrust from the purely religious to the political arena.

Objections to Jewish Nationalism

Despite the sharpness of the *Christian Century's* critique of Judaism as a religion, it was mild when compared to the paper's criticism of Judaism as a way of life of a particular people. The "peoplehood" concept of American Jewry was a disturbing factor in the orderly design of American social groupings. One could grasp the meaning of a religious group, an ethnic collective entity, or even a "nationality" which was somehow associated with a modern nation. The Jews, however, were the only large group in America which was more than a religious or ethnic entity, and still less than a nationality. They had no sovereign political state, an essential prerequisite of modern nationhood.[22] Furthermore, since World War I American Jews had blended increasingly into the American political and social fabric. They were Americans by nationality. What then *were* the Jews?

While some writers have called them a 'race,' the latter term has been appropriated by social scientists to describe a group's visible, physical characteristics (Caucasian, Negroid, Mongoloid). The term most approximating Jewish group practices, values, and ideals—incorporating many aspects of religion, ethnicity, and even nationality—is peoplehood. The Jews are a "people," in Hebrew: '*am*, a connotation applied to them from Bible times. Some modern Jewish writers specifically add the adjective "religious" before "people," while others use the term "religious civilization" to indicate the rubric of religious peoplehood.[23]

This complicated analysis of the nature of the Jewish group disturbed the *Christian Century*. Encouraged by a very small number of Jewish Reform rabbis and laymen in the United States, who fought the concept of Judaism denoting anything more than a religion, the periodical persisted in attacking the notion of Jewish peoplehood and its nationalist manifestation, Zionism. One can detect several strains in the anti–Jewish nationalist stance of American Protestantism.

One objection to Jewish nationalism lay in its possible conflict with other nationalisms, in the United States and elsewhere. Before the establishment of the state of Israel, the sheer advocacy by Jews of such a state implied, in the eyes of the *Christian Century*, a clash of national loyalties—Jewish vs. other.

When, early in 1942, there was clamor for the formation of a separate Jewish army unit to fight against the Nazis, to be composed mostly of Palestinian Jews and European refugees, the periodical objected lest "such an army would dramatize and make official the segregation of the Jew. It might, as claimed, increase his sense of separate nationality."[24] Acknowledging its anti-Zionist bias, the *Christian Century* could not refrain from stating, "at the risk of further misunderstanding," that the formation of such an army would do world Jewry far more harm than good.[25] Three years later, it strongly advised Jews to reach a decision "whether they are an integral part of the nations in which they live or members of a Levantine nation dwelling in exile."[26]

When a representative national conference of American Jewish organizations meeting in Pittsburgh at the end of 1944 called on the United Nations to seat representatives of the Jewish people on the board of the United Nations Relief and Rehabilitation Agency, the *Christian Century* was angry.

> No single factor has done more to render insecure the position of the modern Jew than the charge that he is not completely, wholeheartedly, first, last and all the time a citizen of the country in which he resides, but that he attempts to hold a dual citizenship, which in actuality works out in a divided loyalty, with his primary loyalty given to an allegiance other than the land in which he lives. We do not believe that this is true for the overwhelming majority of Jews in this and other countries. But the resolutions adopted by the Pittsburgh Convention are well calculated to revive this ancient charge.[27]

The periodical accused American Zionist organizations of operating "under the cloak of religious liberty" when in fact they were "parts of a government operating outside the law of nations."[28] In its obsessive denunciation of Jewish nationalism, the *Christian Century* even suggested insidious comparisons between German nationalism and Jewish nationalism. In June 1937 it editorialized:

> The Jewish position in American democracy may be visualized in principle by imagining five million Germans held together in racial and cultural unity by the Hitler doctrine of the folkic soul, trans-

ported to America, established in our democratic land as the Jews now are, and determined to maintain their racial doctrine and their racial separateness.[29]

After the Nazis were defeated in 1945, the *Christian Century* expressed the hope that the German people would not develop a martyr complex and "become another Jewry; they have not lived long enough with their ideology of a unique and privileged race."[30] This implication that the Jews have a "privileged race" mentality analogous to the Nazi superior race ideology was challenged in the periodical by the director of the Chicago chapter of the National Conference on Christians and Jews. "I was shocked beyond words," he wrote, "and could hardly believe my eyes when I came across this sentence."[31] The periodical did not see fit to comment on his criticism.

How can one assess the almost hysterical policy against Jewish nationalism on the part of the *Christian Century*? It appears that the Protestant attitude towards the concept of Jewish nationalism was based fundamentally on theological grounds. In May 1933, after the rise of Nazism, the *Christian Century*, in a long, penetrating editorial, openly admitted that

> The Christian mind has never allowed itself to feel the same human concern for Jewish sufferings that it has felt for the cruelties visited upon Armenians, the Boers, the people of India, American slaves, or the Congo blacks under Leopold imperialism. Christian indifference to Jewish suffering has for centuries been rationalized by the tenable belief that such sufferings were the judgment of God upon the Jewish people for their rejection of Jesus.[32]

The editorial proceeded to urge its readers to distinguish between Jews as Jews and Jews as nationalists. It was not the former who were guilty of Jesus's death. Jews as Jews should not be despised by the Christian world. His crucifixion was brought about by the "nationalist" Jews.

> He was crucified because he had a program for Israel which ran counter to the cherished nationalism of Israel's leaders—political and priestly. He opposed their nationalism with the universalism of God's love and God's kingdom. . . . In the eyes of the Jewish rulers, he was a seditious person, a menace to their fantastic nationalism and to their vested rights and prestige. . . . It was nationalism that crucified Jesus. . . . It was because he threatened by his teaching to

upset their cherished ambition to make Israel and Israel's God the dominant power of the world that he came into collision with Israel's rulers.[33]

Here then, one finds the major source of Protestant hostility to modern Jewish nationalism. By juxtaposing modern Jewish nationalism to the Jewish nationalists of the first century, the *Christian Century* took upon itself to exonerate "Jews as Jews" from the crime of the crucifixion, even as it directed the anger of its Protestant readers against modern Jewish nationalists. It is not important here to dispute the *Christian Century's* interpretation of the events leading to Jesus' crucifixion, as did a few published letters in a subsequent issue,[34] or other analyses of the event.[35] What is important is the revelation of the theological underpinning for its contemporary anti–Jewish nationalism crusade.

The editorial draws an ironic conclusion: "Jewish nationalism crucified Christ, and Christian nationalism is now, and for centuries has been, engaged in crucifying the Jews. . . . Let the Jews see themselves as suffering from the same cause as that which put Jesus of Nazareth to death."[36]

The pages of the *Christian Century* carried little criticism with regard to other nationalist groups. American nationalism is applauded, and the nationalist aspirations of colonially held societies are respected. Only Nazi nationalism and Jewish nationalism are put in the same category.[37]

The truculent attitude of American Protestantism towards Jewish nationalism in the 1930s may also be understood in implicit theological terms. As indicated in the first chapter, great numbers of Christians believed that "old Israel" had ceased to exist as a collective national entity with the birth of Christ, its place taken by the church, the "new Israel." While liberal Protestantism sought to explain away anti-Semitism in religious, psychological, and sociological terms,[38] it never faced up to the obvious embarrassment that "old Israel," though considered theologically deceased, was nonetheless very much alive. Its descendants were promoting its resurrection as a modern sovereign nation in its ancient land of Israel. To modern Protestantism, Jewish nationalism was not just any "nationalism." It contradicted the centuries-old Christian theological myth of Jewish national demise. The apparition of "old Israel" warranted theological concern, if not outright opposition from Protestants.

The Jew: Enemy of Isolationism

As mentioned earlier, the *Christian Century*'s sharp bias against Jewish nationalism was compounded by its own concept of authentic Americanism. The periodical's notion of Americanism was not universally held by American Protestants, but it undoubtedly reflected the attitudes of large numbers of Protestants. In essence, the idea of American nationalism advocated by the paper was isolationism. To be sure, the *Christian Century* was not pro-German during the period of Nazism's rise, nor did it actively desire a German victory when war broke out in 1939. Along with other American groups and periodicals, it merely wanted the United States to keep out of the war.[39] Any group advocating United States intervention was severely criticized by the publication and, of course, American Jewry, as a collective entity identified with intervention, was a frequent target of its wrath.

During the crucial year of 1941, before America actually entered the war, the *Christian Century* was especially hostile to those who sought to influence American intervention. In early January of that year, it rejected the "doctrinaire dogma that Hitler is anti-Christ" and advised Jews "not to declare that those who are not with us in these theories are against us."[40] In June 1941, it reported the death in the House of Representatives of a Jewish Congressman from New York City who died of a heart attack after replying to a speech in which a Mississippi Congressman had charged that "Wall Street and a little group of our international Jewish brethren" were behind a prointerventionist meeting in New York City.

Ignoring the probability that American Jewry was indeed overwhelmingly for United States entry into the war on the side of the Allies, as were other ethnic groups in America, the *Christian Century* nonetheless expressed the belief "that there are plenty of Jews in the United States who are decidedly against intervention. . . . The trouble is that, with the exception of those who are Communists or members of other left-wing groups, they have generally kept silent."[41] This Protestant periodical found it inconceivable that American Jewry, like other American groups, felt that democracy was gravely threatened, or that America's best interests lay with a victory over Germany. It blatantly warned American Jewry "to keep silent no longer" if it wished to protect the American nation against the possibility of "a future racial tragedy" which was bound to make scapegoats of Jews during the projected disillusionment following the peace.[42] In September 1941, the periodical, obviously frustrated by its inability to influence American Jewry to side with its non-interventionist stand, flatly stated that

> Despite all the attempts to gloss over and to conceal the tension between Jew and gentile in this land of freedom, the simple truth is that the spirit of tolerance is hardly more than skin deep. . . . The reason is that anti-Semitism . . . is an irrational passion which . . . cannot be controlled in the interest of any rational public policy. . . . The Jewish problem is not primarily a religious problem. It is a racial and social problem. . . . Its explosive possibilities do not inhere in any conflict of religious forms or creeds, but in a tragic social unassimilability.[43]

3

Early Opposition to a Jewish State: The 1930s

IF THEOLOGY PLAYED A ROLE IN SHAPING THE NEGA-
tive attitudes of American Protestantism toward Jewish nationalism,
it inevitably influenced Protestant views regarding a sovereign Jewish state. Furthermore, if the *Christian Century's* objections to Jewish nationalism were compounded by its own brand of American
nationalism, the periodical's approach to a Jewish state in Palestine
was further complicated by its responses both to Arab nationalism
and to the growing pressure from Jewish refugees in Europe.

When, by late 1933, the need for Jewish emigration from
Germany to Palestine began to be recognized, the journal maintained
that transporting "masses of these persecuted people to Palestine"
would engage the British Mandatory Forces in the Holy Land in a
military campaign "involving the slaughter of hordes of Arabs."[1] To
offset this possibility, the *Christian Century* advised American Jews
to consider whether in the long run they would not do better to
bring pressures on Germany, in order to make it possible for Jews
to live there, than to stake their hopes on any "chimerical scheme"
in Palestine.[2]

Indeed, we noted in an earlier chapter that the *Christian Century* had maintained that the majority of world Jewry was either
uninterested in pushing for the Zionist solution or was opposed to
it.[3] It had also asserted then that, on theological grounds, most modern Bible scholars did not believe that the Old Testament anticipated
the restoration of the modern Jewish people to its ancient homeland.
On practical grounds, it argued, Zionists were deceiving themselves
about Palestine's absorptive capacity.

Taking its cue from the report of the 1929 British investigating
commission headed by Sir John Hope Simpson, the periodical criticized Zionist policy giving employment preference in Palestine to

Jews over Arabs "as most unjust to the majority of the inhabitants."[4] The *Christian Century*, reflecting the attitudes of American Protestantism, could not bring itself to the realization—as it did subsequently with regard to the development of other nationalisms—that the Jewish return to Palestine, whether brought about by persecutions or by idealism, was an authentic expression of Jewish nationalism and not merely a migration of individual Jews to a neutral haven of refuge. If the Jewish homeland was to make possible the development of a modern Jewish nation from an amorphous body of Jewish refugees, it would have to cultivate the elementary characteristics of nationhood, of which a Jewish labor force was an indispensable component.

The Jews of Palestine were not against the employment of Arabs, and indeed a great many Arabs were engaged by Jewish agricultural and industrial concerns. But it was Zionist policy to strengthen the concept of the dignity of Jewish labor, both because Jews were not accustomed to engage in agricultural and manual work in the Diaspora and because the Zionist leaders realized that no healthy national society could be built on the hard work and good will of others. Jewish manpower, Jewish schools, institutions of self-government, and other instruments for nation-building were either expressed or implied in the Palestine Mandate. The growth of the Jewish community in Palestine after World War I was largely determined by the degree to which these goals were attained.

That the Jewish nationalist goal clashed with Arab nationalist aspirations in Palestine is a matter of record. But the *Christian Century* could not refrain from the self-fulfilling prediction that in choosing between the Zionists and the Arab world, the British government ultimately would have to side with the latter, because of its heavy involvement in the Middle East.[5]

In the meantime Germany was inadvertently helping to develop and strengthen Jewish nationalism in Palestine by pressing for the emigration of its Jewish citizens. In the 1930s, however, few countries were ready to receive them.[6] The Jewish national home in Palestine, sanctioned by the League of Nations, grew more significant than ever as a haven of refuge. Whereas in 1932, a year before Hitler's rise to power, the number of Jewish immigrants to Palestine numbered only 13,500, the following four years witnessed a Jewish immigration of 38,600, 42,800, 65,100 and 21,200 respectively.[7] A large proportion of the immigrants came from Germany. By the end of 1936, there were 404,000 Jews in Palestine, totaling close to 30% of the overall population.[8]

The 1936-37 Riots in Palestine

In April 1936 an Arab campaign of terror was launched against the Jewish community in Palestine. Its purposes were threefold: to end Jewish immigration, to forbid land purchases by Jews from Arabs, and to replace the mandatory regime by a national government responsible to a representative council.[9] The following month, the British government advised Parliament that a royal commission would be appointed to investigate the causes of the unrest in the Holy Land after order was restored there.[10]

The British Royal Commission, headed by Earl Peel, former secretary of state for India, arrived in Palestine in November and conducted hearings until the end of January 1937. The royal commission was charged "to ascertain whether upon a proper construction of . . . the Mandate, either the Arabs or the Jews have any legitimate grievances," and if any complaints were valid, "to make recommendations for their removal and for the prevention of their recurrence."[11]

It was not until the very end of the commission's stay in Palestine that official spokesmen for either Arabs or Christians appeared publicly to offer testimony. The only official spokesman of a Christian group, representing the Greek Catholic Church in Palestine, the Melkites, addressed the commission on January 18, 1937, at its very last public meeting. Said Msgr. Hajjar, Galilean bishop of the church: "Judaism looks to this country as the Land of Promise. According to Christianity, we are the new Israelites, we are the new people of God, we are the descendants of the sons of Abraham, and as such we replace the Jews of old."[12]

No other Christian spokesman, either Catholic or Protestant, testified publicly before the commission. Yet the testimony of other witnesses included inevitable references to the religious interests of Christianity, Judaism, and Islam in the Holy Land. In fact, however, the primary parties to the Palestine problem were the last two religions, and this point was not overlooked by the members of the commission, all Christians. The commission reported in its final document to Parliament:

The attention of the world has been concentrated on the issue as between the Moslem Arabs and the Jews in Palestine to the practical exclusion of the Christian communities. And yet the religious stake of the Christians in the Holy Places is just as great as that of the Jews or Moslems. The Christian communities constitute between seven and eight percent of the population. The five hundred million Christians in the world cannot be indifferent to the position and well-being of their co-religionists in the Holy Land.[13]

While the Jews and Arabs—most of the latter were Muslims—were engaged in a clear-cut nationalist struggle for political control in Palestine, the Christian interests in the Holy Land, at least from the public viewpoint of world Christendom, were largely religious or ecclesiastical in nature.

It is little wonder, therefore, that in proposing the partition of Palestine into 1) an Arab state, 2) a Jewish state (comprising about twenty percent of the country's territory), and 3) a British mandatory zone, the commission incorporated the major religious sites of the three faiths in the latter area. It proposed that the new British mandatory jurisdiction keep "the sanctity of Jerusalem and Bethlehem inviolate," and ensure free and safe access to them for all the world.[14] Furthermore, the commission felt "it would accord with Christian sentiment in the world at large" if Nazareth and the Sea of Galilee were also covered by this new mandate.[15]

The commission believed that its recommendations were a fair compromise between the "irreconcilable" interests of the Arabs and the Jews, and that the mounting needs of Jewish immigration to Palestine could now be met. The Palestine Arabs, in turn, could achieve their national independence and be able to join neighboring Arab states, on an equal footing, in the cause of Arab unity. The commission discreetly avoided mentioning the political and military advantages to the British government, but clearly, peace in Palestine would have relieved the United Kingdom of the responsibility and cost of maintaining large garrisons there. Its strategic interests would be kept intact through military alliances with both the Arab and Jewish states, and through direct control of the ports of Haifa and Aqaba.

In a White Paper issued simultaneously with the commission's report, the British government expressed general agreement with the recommendations.[16] Parliament, however, refused to endorse them.[17]

The Partition Report

How did American Protestantism react to the Royal Commission's report on partition? As long as the Holy Land was viewed largely in sentimental-religious terms, Protestantism had been unconcerned with the Arab-Jewish conflict in Palestine. For generations the country had been subject neither to Arab nor Jewish sovereignty, and the Holy Places were under the de facto influence of Christian powers. But the growing phenomenon of clashing Arab-Jewish nationalist interests, plus the increased pressures for Jewish immigration from Europe, brought the Palestine question into sharper world focus, compelling American Protestantism to react to this new set of circumstances.

The *Christian Century* was against partition.[18] Its arguments were varied but it would appear that the basic reason, again, was theological in nature. The notion of a sovereign Jewish state was simply too unpalatable to digest. The idea of a resurrected "old Israel" was too radical to accept.

The periodical expressed its opposition to a sovereign Jewish state by turning back the clock of history some twenty years and protesting the issuance of the Balfour Declaration in 1917. No progress could be made in Palestine until Great Britain gave an "honest and unequivocal interpretation" of its wartime pledges to both the Jews and the Arabs.[19] While acknowledging the royal commission's impartiality and concurring with its report that the pledges to the Jews and Arabs were "incompatible," the Protestant periodical nonetheless refused to accept the recommendation of partition. While admitting that "most Americans" might favor the plan, the *Christian Century* believed that partition was simply a British strategem to "divide and rule." It asked bluntly: "Can the Arab, convinced that he has been betrayed by all that Britain and the League have done up to now, be persuaded that this new proposal offers him justice? We doubt it."

The periodical did not discuss the question of the right of the Jews to protest the partition recommendation, nor did it question Britain's increasingly restrictive immigration policies with respect to Palestine. It ignored the explicit pro-Jewish homeland terms of the Palestine mandate,[20] and the repeated criticisms of the Permanent Mandate Commission of the League of Nations with regard to their weak implementation. When the *Christian Century*, therefore, asked for an "honest and unequivocal" interpretation of the conflicting British wartime promises to the Arabs and the Jews, it obviously wanted sanction for its own interpretation, which denied the Jews any hope of a sovereign state. The journal was against the very purposes of the mandate, whose preamble incorporated the Balfour Declaration. To support its subtle anti-Zionist bias, it referred to, but did not identify, "a great body of Jewish opinion which does not insist on the policy of unrestricted immigration to attain a Jewish majority."[21]

The journal felt that the most appropriate solution to the problem would be "a compromise between Arabs and Jews which would indeed amend, or reinterpret, the Mandate under which Palestine is governed, but would stop short of partition."[22]

During the decade of the 1930s, American Protestantism's repugnance to the concept of a Jewish state was only partly shared by the Protestant missionary movement. Primarily concerned with the interests of Christian Arabs, the *International Review of Missions* was apprehensive. If several Galilean Christian villages and the Lake of Galilee's western shore should be included in the projected small Jewish state, it would be "a bitter shock to Christian sentiment."[23] The periodical rejoiced in having Jerusalem under Christian tutelage, while rationalizing that the amputation of Jerusalem from the Jewish state would not be offensive to Jewish sentiment. It noted that "the most godly elements of Judaism," the extreme Orthodox Jews of Jerusalem, "would be happier in a Christian controlled Jerusalem than in a secular, commercial Jewish state."[24]

The missionary periodical was partially correct. The ultra-Orthodox Jews of Jerusalem were not Zionists. They did not see themselves as agents of God in helping to rebuild the Jewish state. On the contrary, they viewed the Zionists as usurpers of God's prerogative in doing so. Redemption would come not from man's struggle but from God's supernatural design. They viewed the Holy City not in a political framework, but as a religious center of Jewish orthodoxy. They were content merely to live in Jerusalem, to receive charitable contributions from abroad, and to be left alone to study classical religious texts and pray for the miraculous coming of the Jewish Messiah at the Western Wall, the sentimental relic of the ancient Jewish Temple. To them Judaism was exclusively a religious movement, not a nationalist movement in pursuit of a sovereign Jewish state. In this they sharply differed from the religious Zionists who believed that Judaism was both religion and nationalism, and that it was their religious obligation not to await Jewish national redemption passively, but to expedite the advent of the messianic era. They could do this by reconstituting a Jewish state.

The *International Review of Missions* could not support the latter viewpoint, for it did not recognize the legitimacy of the Jewish "religion." Christianity alone was the valid religion. However, unlike the *Christian Century*, it did not actively oppose the establishment of a small secular Jewish state. When the partition plan excluded Jerusalem from the jurisdiction of the proposed Jewish state, the missionary movement, as we shall see shortly, even expressed mild sympathy for a Jewish state.

Why did the world missionary movement—apart from its American component—not attack the concept of a Jewish state? It is only possible to surmise the reasoning behind this attitude. The missionary spokesmen may have believed that Jews living in part of Palestine, as members of a restricted Jewish political entity, could conceivably retain their Jewishness ethnically or even nationalistically, while adopting Christianity someday as their religion. To the missionaries, the notion of a Hebrew Christian was not paradoxical. Indeed, the term was cultivated in some missionary circles with much fervor. Once Jerusalem was placed outside the jurisdiction of a Jewish state, a principal psychological obstacle for missionary acceptance of a Jewish sovereign entity was muted, if not removed.

Furthermore, the *International Review of Missions*, while receptive to the views of American Protestant missions, primarily reflected the thinking of many Protestant groups from Europe. It would appear that European, and especially British, Protestants did not share, by and large, the strong anti-Zionist views of their American counterparts. While European Protestants undoubtedly hoped for the eventual conversion of Jews to Christianity, they were influenced by millennial theology with its component of Jewish national restoration. Unlike American missionaries who concentrated their efforts in other areas of the Arab world and not in Palestine, European missionaries were active largely in the Holy Land. To European Protestants, a "Jewish National Homeland" did not preclude a sovereign Jewish state in Palestine. As long as Christian interests were safeguarded in the Holy Land, a small, secular Jewish state there did not greatly upset European Protestants. Being ambivalent about the matter, European Protestant denominations neither advocated such a state, nor did they actively oppose it on theological or nationalist grounds. "For twenty years," concluded the *International Review of Missions,* "we have had a Holy Land that was unholy because it was untrue, unreal. Now we are offered . . . two non-Christian states which will be real, and a new chance to make the Holy City what it ought to be: a focus of religion, Christian, Muslim and Jewish, under an administration that ought to be Christian enough to develop the best in all of them."[25]

The *Christian Century*'s most cogent reason for opposing the partition plan was its concern for some 225,000 Arabs who would be transferred from their homes in the area of the projected Jewish state to the Arab state. Though the plan provided for substantial funds from both Jewish and British government sources to implement this resettlement scheme, the journal remained skeptical.[26] On the other hand, it was not completely oblivious to Jewish needs, if not to Jewish rights. One of its Palestinian correspondents advocated numerical parity between Arabs and Jews, if partition were to be ruled out.[27] The editors themselves, in sharp reaction to the renewed Arab terrorism in Jerusalem, recognized that while Arab grievances were real, "so are the needs and rights of the Jews. . . . To such a complex problem as this, there is no solution that is entirely right."[28] Had the periodical really pursued this even-handed attitude, it would undoubtedly have changed its anti-Zionist policy. But this was not the case. It merely expressed a softer attitude towards the Zionists when the Arabs were threatening Christian interests in Palestine. It was also more sensitive to Zionist claims when Arabs engaged in systematic violence against Palestinian Jews, or when the plight of European Jews became so desperate that the journal felt duty-bound to proclaim pious sympathy for them, and to allude with great reluctance to Palestine as a possible haven of refuge.

Limited Jewish Immigration Recognized

Several years earlier, for example, after the Arab riots of 1929, the *Christian Century* had recognized that the attacks would not fully frustrate Jewish resettlement plans. Nevertheless it had seen fit to remind its readers that Palestine was a predominantly non-Jewish land. "What ever Jewish culture is developed there, it will have to make terms with a non-Jewish environment, just as truly as in England or the United States."[29] Jewish immigration into Palestine was not objectionable to the periodical as long as Jews would understand that they were not to establish a society in which they might become the majority, but rather were to melt into the predominant culture.

Following the infamous "Night of the Broken Glass" (*Kristalnacht*) in Germany, on November 9, 1938, when thousands of Jewish shops and synagogues were looted or destroyed and some twenty thousand Jews were arrested and taken to concentration camps,[30] the *Christian Century* recognized the world's strong sympathies for the Jewish victims. At the same time it was relieved that the partition plan had been abandoned by the British government.[31] Said the periodical: "They will have strong backing in their demand for increased immigration to Palestine, or at least to certain parts of it, if they do not insist that the Balfour Declaration . . . guarantees them possession of the whole country regardless of its other inhabitants."[32]

The paper's anti-Jewish nationalism policy invariably was couched in moralistic terms. Despite the resolution of the Zionist Congress to accept partition in principle, but to seek an adjustment of the area designated as the Jewish state, the *Christian Century* waved the flag of Jewish "possession of the whole country regardless of its other inhabitants" as reason for its opposition even to a restricted Jewish sovereign state. Limited immigration, yes; Jewish sovereignty, no.

The editors of the *Christian Century* were reflecting the views of American Protestantism on the subject of Palestine. Naturally, not all American Protestant leaders agreed with this point of view. But until the end of the 1930s, no representative of a major organized body of American Protestants took issue publicly with the paper's views, which leads to the conclusion that American Protestantism either approved of the *Christian Century*'s attitude, or was indifferent to the entire subject of a Jewish state. If we accept the latter premise, we may conclude that the *Christian Century* was merely expressing the bias of its own editors. It is more correct, however, to accept the first premise, that the paper was expressing the views of Protestantism on the subject of Palestine, because we find support for this anti-Zionist policy in other Protestant sources. Such sources while perhaps reflecting only a small segment of American Protestantism, nonetheless represented the most persistent and articulate Protestant spokesmen on the subject of Palestine. Above all, they appeared to be self-motivated and not induced by outside pressure groups. In most cases, they involved individuals and religious institutions with close ties to the Arabs of the Near East.

One such typical spokesman among American Protestant leaders was the Reverend Daniel Bliss, whose missionary family had made major contributions to the Arab cultural revival at the American University of Beirut.[33] Dr. Bliss, who was raised in the Middle East as a child, was an influential Congregational minister. His speeches and articles about the Palestine question were respected in Protestant circles.

One outstanding feature of Dr. Bliss's approach to Jewish nationalism was an ostensible reasonableness which sought to avoid any overt extremism likely to antagonize his readers or listeners.[34] Writing in the *Christian Century* in January 1939, Dr. Bliss sought "a peaceful way out of this muddled and dangerous situation."[35] He felt compromises should be made "all around." Great Britain should repudiate its World War I promises to both Jews and Arabs; the Arabs should withdraw their claims for immediate independence in Palestine, while their eventual independence would depend largely on their ability to control their extremist elements and "on their record of good behaviour." The Zionists "would have to pay for peace" by withdrawing their political and national goals. "There is plenty of room for the nonpolitical Jews in Palestine," he noted, and then added that it was Britain's "solemn duty to protect and safeguard the permanent Jewish minority."

Dr. Bliss' intermediate-range plan was conditioned, however, on an immediate "essential step": Great Britain would have to "stop Jewish and Arab immigration into Palestine immediately. . . ." Such a move would remove the cause of Arab terrorism and relieve the Arabs of the "desperate sense of insecurity that Jewish immigration creates. . . ."[36]

The final thrust of the *Christian Century* against an independent sovereign Jewish state is represented by its endorsement of a binational state. Impressed by the spiritual and cultural Zionism of Judah Magnes and Martin Buber,[37] in contrast to political Zionism which sought a sovereign Jewish state, the Protestant periodical, during the debate on the Peel partition plan, applauded the views of those Jews "accused of being naive in their faith in the possibility of a bi-national state."[38] Such Jews, it maintained, "may well be

more realistic than their critics in their understanding of the diffi-
culties in the way of a successful working out of the Partition Plan."[39]
It even spoke optimistically of Arab moderates in Palestine who
favored Viscount Herbert Samuel's suggestion that autonomous Jewish cantons would "represent a permanent Jewish minority within
an Arab state."[40]

While a few leading Zionists, and even fewer Arab nationalists,
continued to promote the concept of a binational state in Palestine,
their numbers dwindled considerably when the pressures for Jewish
immigration to Palestine increased as a result of the expanding Nazi
rule in Europe. A mood of despair seized the Jewish people. The
idealistic binational concept became increasingly unrealistic. Zionists
worked all the harder for greater Jewish immigration into Palestine,
while Arab nationalists organized more militantly against this process. For the *Christian Century* to continue raising the prospect of
binationalism in the face of political unreality was tantamount to
offering deceptive platitudes instead of hard solutions.

On May 17, 1939, the British government issued its White Paper[41] which unequivocally ruled out a Jewish state by drastically
limiting Jewish immigration during a five-year period, and subjecting
Jewish immigration thereafter to Arab consent. In its response to
this event, the Protestant periodical consoled the Zionists in these
words:

> What today looks to many Zionists like black defeat, will in the light
> of history, turn out to be glorious victory. . . . The ambition to make
> Palestine a Jewish state must be dropped but there is no reason why
> under the new British proposal it cannot still become a cultural and
> spiritual center for world Jewry. . . . If Jewish devotion can . . . make
> of Zionism a demonstration of the universal values in Judaism, social
> as well as religious, the great blow which has fallen on Jewish hopes
> with the publication of the British White Paper may turn out to be
> a blessing in disguise.[42]

These comforting words were not at all clear to the Zionists.
What was the "blessing in disguise"? How could Judaism best demonstrate its universal values—whatever they were—in a Palestinian
cultural and spiritual center, if Jews had no political control over
their own destiny? Zionists, while surely concerned with universal
values, were even more concerned with the priority of group survival, for without such collective Jewish security, how could modern
Judaism be assured of demonstrating anything? The solace offered

by the *Christian Century* did not seem very sincere in Zionist eyes. Without a Jewish state, the future of both Jewry and Judaism was bleak.

4

The Impact of the Holocaust on the "Christian Century"

WHEN HITLER BEGAN HIS BRUTAL CAMPAIGN AGAINST German Jewry in March 1933, the *Christian Century* simply refused to believe it. Though daily news reports by competent and highly respected United States correspondents in Germany had been filling the columns of American newspapers for almost a month, the Protestant periodical felt there was need for further investigation before passing judgment. It expressed the hope that "all thoughtful persons, Jews as well as Christians, will put . . . tighter curbs upon their emotions until the facts are beyond dispute."[1]

Stephen Wise's "Exaggerations"

This cool, wait-and-see attitude of the *Christian Century* towards the subject of Jewish persecution in Europe persisted, even through the end of 1942 after the general press had widely featured the first horror stories of the "final solution" policy of the Nazis.[2] Though the American government had already known in August of the mass deportations and killings of Jews, both through its own European agents and through information provided by Rabbi Stephen Wise, president of the World Jewish Congress, it preferred to remain silent until the reports could be more fully substantiated. Finally, at the end of November, when Under-Secretary of State Sumner Welles confirmed them to Wise, the rabbi told the gruesome story to the press.

The *Christian Century* immediately questioned "whether any good purpose" was served by Dr. Wise's charges.[3] It gave four reasons for its skepticism. First, the State Department had "conspicuously refrained" from issuing any public confirmation. Secondly, Dr.

Wise's figures on the number of Jews killed differed radically from those given out on the same day by the Polish government-in-exile. Whereas Dr. Wise charged that Hitler had ordered all Jews in Nazi-ruled Europe killed by the end of the year, the exiled Polish government claimed "only that orders have been issued for the extermination of half the Jews in Poland by the end of the year," and that 250,000 had been killed up to the end of September. Thirdly, a Polish underground leader, Dr. Stasburger, whose figures were used to support Rabbi Wise's charges, was "the same Polish leader who is campaigning in this country for the complete destruction of Germany." And, finally, the periodical was outraged at Dr. Wise's allegation that Hitler was paying twenty dollars each for Jewish corpses to be processed into soap fats and fertilizer. Such an allegation, concluded the *Christian Century*, was "unpleasantly reminiscent of the 'cadaver factory' lie which was one of the propaganda triumphs of the First World War." Such was the reaction of the country's leading independent Protestant journal to the first news of the holocaust.

Needless to say, such a reaction elicited several responses, and in a later issue, the *Christian Century* printed a letter of protest written by Rabbi Theodore Lewis of Brooklyn, New York. He described the editorial as "a heartless and unpardonable comment,"[4] and felt that the journal concentrated its criticism not against Hitler's proven diabolical actions, but against Wise's alleged exaggerations. He wrote: "Suppose the figures of Dr. Wise on the number of Jews killed do differ radically from those given by the Polish Government in Exile. Is this the real issue? Is it not rather the fact of the massacre which is beyond question, and which is continuing daily, and which if not halted will result in the actual and complete annihilation of European Jewry? Just where is your Christian conscience?"

The periodical did not comment on the letter. Instead, in its subsequent issue it applauded the statement issued by the governments of the eleven allied nations on December 17, in which they reaffirmed their resolve to punish those responsible for the crimes.[5] But its tone of approval carried little moral outrage. Said the *Christian Century*:

> It is well to exercise some rhetorical restraint in speaking of a crime so vast and foul that language is bankrupt in attempting to characterize it adequately. The calm tone of the [allied] pronouncement does not reflect an absence of emotion, but the presence of a cold determination not to expend in vain outcry one unit of emotional

energy which can be better employed in bringing the war to such a conclusion that this gigantic crime can be stopped and the criminals punished. The right response to the Polish horror is a few straight words to say that it has been entered in the books, and then redoubled action on the [war] fronts and on the production lines.

In January 1943 the *Christian Century* printed a letter from Rabbi Stephen Wise.[6] He advised the paper that the State Department not only authorized the publication of the statement that he had made, but for months had been seeking, with the help of the World Jewish Congress, to make sure of the accuracy of the events surrounding the mass slaughter of Jews. Wise continued: "*Christian Century* almost uniformly takes a frankly or disguisedly anti-Jewish attitude whenever it deals with Jewish subjects. Whether this is merely the reflection of a personal Judeophobia on the part of the editor [C. C. Morrison], or whether it conveys the considered attitude of the editorial board of the *Christian Century* is not for me to say."

Without reacting to Wise's accusation, the paper's editor responded that the journal had inquired of the State Department, which stated that its reply was "not for publication," and that the protested editorial was written in the light of the confidential reply.[7] At any rate, the journal maintained that the government's reply did not support Dr. Wise's contention.[8]

The *Christian Century* persisted in its restrained reaction to the massacre of Jews. In May 1943 it finally acknowledged the "stupendous slaughter" of two million Jews in the Nazi-dominated countries of Europe. It arrived at this conclusion thanks to "accurate statistics" published in April in the *Information Service* bulletin of the Federal Council of Churches.[9] In September 1944 it editorialized about the "alleged killing of a million and a half persons" at the German concentration camp near Lublin, Poland.[10] Though this sophisticated Protestant periodical presumably knew who these "persons" were, the editorial does not mention the name "Jew." To add insult to injury, the cautious voice of American Protestant opinion again reminded its readers that "the parallel between this story and the 'corpse factory' atrocity tale of the First World War is too striking to be overlooked. That story started in 1917, and was not finally discredited until 1925."

As the war was drawing to a close, the *Christian Century* "gazed into the pit" of the liberated concentration camps and reluctantly repented:[11]

> We have found it hard to believe that the reports from the Nazi con-
> centration camps could be true. Almost desperately we have tried
> to think that they must be widely exaggerated . . . or perhaps they
> were just mere atrocity mongering. . . . But such puny barricades
> cannot stand up against the terrible facts. The evidence is too con-
> clusive. . . . It will be a long long time before we can forget what
> scores of honorable, competent observers tell us they have seen with
> their own eyes. The thing is well-nigh incredible. But it hap-
> pened. . . . The foul stench of the concentration camps should bur-
> den the Christian conscience until Christian men cannot resist.

Why did it take "scores of honorable, competent observers" to convince the Protestant journal that the "exaggerated" stories of Dr. Wise and his colleagues were no exaggerations at all? A clue to this attitude may be found in an article published towards the end of the war by a Protestant professor of religious literature at Chicago's Theological Seminary. Responding to an article by Arthur Koestler, in which the latter portrayed himself screaming for help in the midst of a nightmare, while the crowd walks past laughing and chatting, the professor candidly admits:

> I am probably a typical member of the crowd he thinks indiffer-
> ent. . . . What . . . are the reasons for our not stopping our work and
> for not joining the screamers? . . . The screamers do not tell us spe-
> cifically what they want us to do. . . . If the war isn't a big enough
> fight, just how much bigger would they make it? . . . What are the
> chances of obtaining [peace] if we approach the task emotionally
> exhausted, and mentally confused by months or years of scream-
> ing? . . .[12]

Jewish history indicates that the Jews had been "screaming" for generations, without appreciable Christian response. Even the twentieth century holocaust did not make a significant difference. Feingold asserts categorically that earlier, before the "final solution" policy had been decided upon by the Nazi leaders on January 20, 1942, Jews could have been saved from death, had the Christian countries desired it.[13] The callous attitudes of Christian governments at the refugee conferences at Evian in 1938 and at Bermuda in 1943 have been described in detail.[14] The anti-Jewish bias and hostility of key Christian officials in the United States and other governments have been documented.[15] The Jew, apparently, was dispensable. As the *Christian Century* aptly characterized the pathetic voyage of the S.S. *St. Louis*, crowded in June 1939 with 907 Jews in flight "from a place where they are not wanted to other places where they are not wanted": "Everything . . . about this hapless voyage was symbolic—not least of all the identity and situation of the voyagers."[16] The myth of the wandering Jew was really no myth at all.

Against Immigration to the United States

More specifically, how did American Protestantism respond to the problem of Jewish refugees from Europe? The *Christian Century* "liked" the United States government's March 22, 1938 invitation to thirty-three governments, suggesting that an international committee facilitate the reception of political refugees from Austria and Germany "without altering immigration laws."[17] The Federal Council of Churches of Christ in America "hailed with appreciation" this United States proposal.[18]

After the futile Evian conference of July 1938, the periodical "refuse[d] to believe that even in a time of general economic depression, the world is either so poor or so heartless that it cannot do what it knows it ought to do for these innocent victims of racial fanaticism. . . ."[19] Nonetheless, only a month earlier, it had found the Evian decision to establish a permanent organization to deal with the refugee problem "a more significant outcome than would have been the making of immediate arrangements for the relief of a few thousand expatriots."[20]

Following the brutal November 10 *Kristalnacht* in Germany, the periodical veered, if only once, from its restrained, proper stance, by not only revealing a modicum of sympathy for a Palestinian haven of refuge, but by suggesting:

> It does not seem a violent assumption to suppose that somewhere there must be a point beyond which a nation, or the government of a nation, cannot be allowed to go on in its treatment of the people within its borders without evoking protest or even possibly provoking preventive measures from its neighbors. Has that point been reached? Suppose that, instead of merely subjecting the Jews to economic and social disadvantages, Nazi Germany should decide to massacre them. . . . Is there an end to the world's tolerance? And

if there is, what will it do when the end is reached? That question
we cannot answer.[21]

How beautifully are these sentiments expressed! But how valid
do they appear, when placed in the perspective of *Christian Century* policies with regard to isolationism and the Jewish problem?
Only a week later the periodical raised the possibility of distributing
Jewish refugees among receiving countries on the basis of an internationally-agreed quota system.[22] It acknowledged that the United
States could absorb "100,000 or so of Jewish immigrants . . . without
difficulty," but then proceeded to disclose that the "evils" of such
a proposal would be "as great as those which it is designed to cure."
The Protestant journal listed a number of considerations which made
it "highly inadvisable to let down our immigration barriers." One
was the economic condition of the country with its large unemployed
population. If "an appreciable number of Jews" were to enter the
United States, it would cause anti-Semitism. In fact, opined the
paper, "it would be a tragic disservice to the Jews in America to
increase their number by substantial immigration." For, according
to the weekly, the Jewish problem in America, while having its own
unique aspects, was part of a larger social problem affecting the
social integration of America's varied nationalities and races. "Many"
such groupings were obstructing the American "democratic process"
which could be salvaged only by freezing the country's ethnic status
quo. Said the *Christian Century*:

> There is no ethical principle that requires either an individual person or a nation to expose itself to a condition sure to involve a moral
> overstrain. . . . Our immigration laws . . . should be maintained and
> even further strengthened. Christian and other high minded citizens
> have no need to feel apologetic for the limitations upon immigration
> into the country.[23]

The *Christian Century* made no attempt to disguise its "bafflement" with respect to the specific Jewish problem "created by German inhumanity." But, it asserted, democracy could not solve the
deeper problem of anti-Semitism; "perhaps religion can" after undergoing "a drastic revolution in the Christian attitude to the Jewish
faith."[24] The journal did not bother to explain the nature of the
revolution.

The truly baffling attitudes of the most prestigious American

Protestant weekly towards the Jewish refugee problem are further revealed in other editorials.[25] During the prewar period, while expressing interest in finding homes for Hitler's victims, the journal commented on Britain's Prime Minister Chamberlain's offhand suggestion, that the refugees consider Tanganyika as a haven, with a snide statement that the British were "spiking down" that colony so that it could not be returned to Germany. "Certainly there would be a tremendous popular opposition to handing back to Germany a colony newly populated with German refugees."[26] If Jewish lives could be saved in Tanganyika, as a result of which Britain might strengthen her political position there vis-à-vis Germany, then perhaps it would be better to examine the motivations behind such offers before rushing to save Jewish lives.

American Protestant attitudes towards Jewish refugees are also depicted in their approach to Palestine as a haven of refuge. The *Christian Century*'s views on the subject were ambivalent. When a dramatic emergency arose with respect to the refugees, it expressed reluctant sympathy for their need to enter Palestine. In the main, however, it consistently sought to sever any connection between the needs of Jewish refugees and the role of Palestine as a natural haven of refuge for them.

The Politics of Piety

As Europe increasingly came under the influence of Hitler's Germany, the *Christian Century* began to realize that Jews could no longer remain in the lands of their birth.[27] This represented a sharp break with the old line it had taken about Jews melting into the cultures of their respective countries. When other countries refused to extend a welcome to Jewish refugees, the periodical, while continuing to insist that the problem of the refugees and that of Palestine were "separate and independent," nonetheless rebuked the Arabs for demanding "such a stringent limitation upon immigration and land transfers."[28] Begrudgingly, it seemed to recognize the principle that Palestine serve as a legitimate sanctuary for Jewish immigrants. But in the same editorial the periodical remained true to its consistent anti-Zionist bias. It urged Zionist supporters in England and America to advise their Palestinian cohorts not to resist the British government—as "unbiased an arbitrator as could be found"—once the British declared their new policy with regard to Palestine in the 1939 White Paper.

While the *Christian Century* was thus trying to demonstrate its own brand of even-handedness, it challenged the Zionist claims with increasing vigor. When an American National Zionist Conference, held in Washington in January, 1939, adopted a resolution calling for the immigration of 100,000 German Jews to Palestine during a single year, the periodical labelled the action "provocative" and questioned whether that "portion of American Jewry which supports political Zionism" really wants peace in Palestine.[29] "Can it be that it would be glad to see Great Britain involved in an endless campaign there to suppress the Arabs by bloodshed?"

The periodical, realizing nonetheless that Palestine was the only country capable of receiving Jewish refugees, tried to play down that country's role as a haven of refuge. No matter how wide open the gates of Palestine might be thrown, it declared, "only a meager fraction of the Jewish victims of the Nazi terror" would enter therein, "and most of them do not want to . . . ."[30] It would appear that the Protestant journal was putting words in the mouths of helpless Jewish victims, while callously and reprehensibly playing with their lives.

Though the *Christian Century* insisted that Jews keep the issue of refugees and the issue of Palestine separate, it violated its own separatist admonition frequently, by dealing with them simultaneously, even in the same editorial. When it did so, it would apply two principles. The first principle, "the consent of the governed," was applied to the Arabs of Palestine and the second, "the common responsibility of all civilized and justice-loving peoples of the earth," was applied to refugee Jews—in that order of priority.[31] While the first principle was invoked to offset the possibility of the Jews ever becoming a majority of the population and thereby creating a sovereign Jewish state, the second principle was a general call to an inchoate humanity to become suddenly humane to Jewish refugees. The periodical, fully aware of the lack of cooperation from all states for the purpose of saving Jewish lives, undoubtedly knew all along that its pious call would be ineffectual. Yet it continued to play the role of a disturbed religious conscience, realizing fully that its target audience, "all civilized and justice-loving peoples," was intangible, inattentive, and diffuse.

Writing in the *Christian Century* in January 1939, before the promulgation of the Palestine White Paper, but when war clouds were already hovering above Europe, Dr. Daniel Bliss reflected the ambivalence towards the plight of Jewish refugees by reiterating the American Protestant formula of separating politics from humanitarian concern:

> Let no one imagine that a proposal to keep all but a limited number of Jews out of Palestine is just one more indication of a world wide anti-Semitic campaign. . . . This is not an attempt to settle the Jewish problem but only the controversy in Palestine. . . . [The former] must be determined elsewhere. . . . We certainly can sympathize with the Jews as they grope for a straw of security in a pagan and unchristian world that apparently wants them not. But this is not a time simply for sympathy, but for intelligent statesmanship in the interests primarily of peace.[32]

"Sympathy" seems to connote a religious term void of substantive meaning when applied to Jews. It seems to indicate a pious expression of an uneasy conscience, not a resolve to save human lives. This conclusion may also be reached upon reviewing the pages of the *Federal Council Bulletin,* the official monthly publication of the Federal Council of Churches of Christ (the forerunner of the National Council of Churches). Reflecting the views of the policy coordinating body of American Protestantism, the *Federal Council Bulletin* offered continual sympathy for the victims of Nazism and condemned anti-Semitism. But during the prewar period it found it necessary in practically all its sympathy-for-Nazi-victims editorials to remind its readers that about half of the sufferers were of "Jewish blood" but of "Christian faith."[33] One may ask, were not Jews of the "Jewish faith" a sufficiently worthy category of human beings to warrant unqualified Christian compassion, though it was apparent that they were Hitler's principal target?

Only at its biannual meeting in December 1942, after Hitler's "final solution" policy had become undeniable, did the Federal Council conclude "that something like a policy of deliberate extermination of the Jews in Europe is being carried out," but it had nothing to say about attempting to rescue those who survived. With one offhand exception, no mention of Palestine as a possible haven of refuge appears anywhere in the *Federal Council Bulletin* before or during the entire war period. Instead, the 1942 Federal Council policy statement called for ensuring a "respected place . . . in Western civilization" for the Jews in the postwar era and "immigration opportunities . . . in this and other lands" for those who will be obliged "to emigrate from the war-ridden lands of Europe."[34]

At its March 1943 executive committee meeting, the Federal Council at last designated Sunday, May 2, a separate day of compassion for the suffering Jews of Europe.[35] It assessed the event as a success,[36] but at least one Protestant minister deemed it "a complete fiasco."[37]

The formula of expressing formal piety towards the plight of European Jews was pursued by the *Christian Century* after the outbreak of the war. By the fall of 1942, however, the periodical expressed genuine doubt whether the overwhelming majority of Jews in European countries would be able to resume life as normal citizens. "Large scale immigration, unjust and cruel as it may be, is not only the lesser evil, but the only permanent solution."[38] Despite this logic, as knowledge of the holocaust became more widespread and Jewish militancy in Palestine against Britain's policy increased, the *Christian Century* adopted an even stronger anti-Zionist attitude while continuing to pay lip-service sympathy to the Nazi victims. When in February 1943 the British government announced that it agreed to allow 35,000 Jews, mostly children, to enter Palestine from the Balkans, the Protestant periodical wondered why it should be assumed

> that all the Jews who are snatched from the grasp of Hitler and his tortures must be taken to Palestine. Surely not even the most convinced Zionist would want the lives of these helpless ones to be used to prejudice the future adjudication of the Palestine question. . . . There are many other temporary places of refuge available, in Russia, in the Near East and in North Africa. At a pinch, perhaps even the United States.[39]

It is difficult to reconcile this attitude with a sensitive Christian conscience.

The periodical continued to discover new and amazing reasons to justify its militant anti-Zionism. Quoting from a letter written by an Orthodox Jew from Boston, protesting several policies of the Jewish Agency in Palestine toward some religious Jewish immigrants, the editor of the *Christian Century* explained: "We print this letter as an indication of one of the elements which make the Palestine problem almost insoluble."[40]

By September 1943, however, the journal apparently recognized the enormity of European Jewry's plight. The *Christian Century* declared that it behooved the world policy makers to "provide places of asylum and escape for those who can get away, with special consideration of the admission of more refugees to the United States and to Palestine."[41] In May 1944, after several millions of Jews had been exterminated, it even proposed that temporary "free ports" be set up in the United States for refugees.[42]

One might conclude that the periodical felt the survivors would surely not be numerous enough to upset the economic and social patterns of the United States. And "free ports," after all, did not imply permanent refuge.

5

American Protestant Pro-Zionist Sentiment

War II, the *Christian Century* was the only independent, nondenominational American Protestant weekly written for an intellectual audience. In the absence of serious discussion of the Palestine question in any of the Protestant denominational periodicals, it presented the only articulate voice of American Protestantism regarding Jewry and Zionism.

Its anti-Zionist policy, however, did not win the approval of all Protestant organizations or leading churchmen. There were Protestants who, as individuals or in relatively small groups, supported the Zionist position on Palestine. The Fundamentalist church groups were inherently, though vaguely, committed theologically to the return of the Jews to the Holy Land as a prelude to the Second Coming.[1] Liberal Protestant leaders, like John Haynes Holmes of the Unitarian Community Church in New York, were impressed with the self-sacrificing idealism of the Jewish pioneers in Palestine, and felt that they should be encouraged in their efforts to establish a "new" society. As Hitler's militant anti-Jewish policies spread over Europe, increasing numbers of American Protestant leaders shook off their apathy towards Jewish suffering and, in the absence of any realistic alternative for Jewish refugees, related the latter's possible survival to an open-door policy in Palestine.

It would seem, however, that in the great majority of cases where American Protestant leaders or groups publicly identified themselves with the plight of European Jewry and with the place of Palestine in the physical salvation of the Jews, the initiative and motivation for this pro-Zionist sentiment came from the presence and pressures of American Jews, especially those, then relatively few, who considered themselves Zionists. The pro-Zionist public expressions of American Protestantism did not arise spontaneously. They were deliberately cultivated and even channelled organizationally by American Zionists.

Pro-Palestine Federation

Even before the rise of Hitler there were two small groups of American Christians, mostly Protestants, who openly supported Jewish national aspirations in Palestine. One was the Pro-Palestine Federation of America, officially launched in New York City in January 1930, in response to the urging of Judge Julian Mack of Chicago, a noted Zionist, and directed by Aaron B. Elias, a committed Jew and Zionist who became the secretary (and only Jewish member) of the organization. In 1937, the group's membership numbered three hundred.

In an early issue of its publication, The *Pro-Palestine Herald*, the federation's secretary discussed the organization's origins:

> As a result of the Arab riots in Palestine in 1929, and the subsequent assault upon the rights of the Jewish people contained in the Mandate, through the Passfield White Paper, leading Christian Americans, ministers of the Gospel, college professors, professional men, and eminent statesmen formed the Pro-Palestine Federation of America. This organization, embodying the finest Christian principles, is dedicated to the task of encouraging closer cooperation between Jew and Gentile, and also to the defense of the Jewish national home cause as defined in the Mandate for Palestine.[2]

The second Christian group which supported Jewish nationalist aims was the American Palestine Committee, organized in May 1932, apparently at the initiative of the Zionist Organization of America. In contrast to the Pro-Palestine Federation which largely attracted clergymen and Christian educators, the committee concentrated on political figures. Its initial membership included ten senators, eighteen representatives, and several Cabinet and sub-Cabinet officials. Headed by a Mormon, Senator William King of Utah, the committee's honorary chairmen were Vice President Charles Curtis; Senator William E. Borah, chairman of the Senate Foreign Affairs Committee; and Senator Claude E. Swanson, ranking member of the same committee.[3] The American Palestine Committee was not active, reflecting the weak leadership of the Zionist Organization of America (ZOA) in the early 1930s.[4] The committee did not fulfill any meaningful purpose until it was reactivated almost a decade later.

The Pro-Palestine Federation, on the other hand, was moved almost singlehandedly by the determination of its Jewish secretary, whose "methods of procedure" did not sit well with the American Zionist establishment.[5] Though its work was considered "negligible" by the ZOA president, it proceeded independently to take such actions as it deemed fit to strengthen the Zionist position in Palestine.[6]

The most prominent Christian member of the Pro-Palestine Federation was, undoubtedly, John Haynes Holmes. A nondenominational Protestant fighter for liberal causes and a pacifist, Holmes personified a Christian conscience rooted in the peace and social justice themes of the Old Testament. He marvelled at the "romance and adventure" which Jewish pioneers were experiencing in Palestine.[7] Having visited the Holy Land in 1929, under the sponsorship of Nathan Straus, Holmes viewed the Zionist enterprise there as "an opportunity to the Jews to build not only for themselves but for all the world an ideal society."[8] Holmes was particularly impressed with the communal settlements in Palestine. To him, these colonies approximated the model social laboratories to be emulated by other countries throughout the world.[9] He acknowledged that the political struggle with the Arabs (who, in his estimation, were direct beneficiaries of the Zionist venture) had hampered the vision of a peaceful Zion. "The ideal Zion seems not so easy today as it did a dozen or score of years ago. But the faith is there."[10]

As Palestine assumed increasing significance as a haven for Nazi victims, Holmes wrote Elias in November 1933: "Thousands of German Jews, especially the younger men and women, are looking to Palestine this day with eager longing as the solution of their present problem and as their future hope. We should all now unite to secure at the hands of the British Government a relaxation of immigration restrictions. . . . I join not only gladly but eagerly in any organized work for the accomplishment of this great end."[11]

In May 1936 the Pro-Palestine Federation addressed Great Britain's Prime Minister Stanley Baldwin in the name of "the consensus of enlightened Christian American opinion," to open widely the gates of Palestine to receive the victimized Jews escaping from Germany. The signatories reiterated their steadfast support of the Jewish national homeland by declaring that the "restoration of the Land of Israel to the Children of Israel is the guiding star in this

great struggle for a better world and a better humanity."[12] The sign-
ers included James F. Freeman, Episcopal bishop of Washington,
S. Parkes Cadman, president of the Union of Congregational
Churches in America, and Ivan Lee Holt, president of the Federal
Council of Churches of Christ in America.

Later in 1936 the Pro-Palestine Federation convened an American Christian Conference on the Jewish Problem, in New York City.
Because of the inactivity of the American Palestine Committee, the
conference sponsored by the Pro-Palestine Federation included state
governors, university presidents, United States senators, as well as
leading clergymen.[13] The conference protested against the persecution of Jews in Germany, Poland, and Rumania, and declared that
"if Christian people in those countries are unable to stop these hor-
rors," then "civilized communities" should help "the victims of bar-
barism" to "reach a land where their lives and inalienable rights may
be reasonably secure. Their natural place of refuge is Palestine."[14]

After the British royal commission in 1937 had recommended
the partition of Palestine into Arab and Jewish states, Dr. Holmes
expressed his opposition to such a plan and advocated instead a
"bi-racial, bi-religious" society. He wrote: "If the Jews do not thus
present united opposition [to the partition plan] then the Christians
must take up the fight. For the partition of Palestine is as gross an
outrage upon Christian traditions as upon Jewish hopes. The Holy
Land is one, and must be kept one, as the sacred symbol of the one-
ness of mankind."[15]

Holmes's statement also revealed his own vision of the Jewish
national home, which was not in line with official Zionist policy.
He was not for an independent sovereign Jewish state, but rather
for a binational community. Earlier, in appraising his 1929 trip to
Palestine,[16] he enthusiastically endorsed the concept of a cultural
and spiritual home for the Jewish people, but warned the Zionists
not to seek a political state with its trappings of power. Unlike the
editors of the *Christian Century*, he acknowledged the national existence of a Jewish people, but to him Jewish nationalism was to find
its ultimate expression in a higher collective ethic, rather than in
greater physical security for the nation based on political sovereignty. In his extreme idealism if not naivete, Holmes believed that
Jewish Palestine should divorce itself of British mandatory protection and join the Palestinian Arabs in a shared community of highly
public-spirited and ethical citizens.[17] Though he did uphold the
right of Jewish immigration, Holmes avoided the key questions con-

cerning who was to regulate that immigration and who was to govern the community. He viewed Palestine as a noble social experiment, but did not bother to explore the political means by which it would develop or fail. He was against political statehood for either Jews or Arabs, because to him such a framework meant power, and ultimately, war. He preferred instead an inchoate model of a binational state.[18]

The Pro-Palestine Federation, though a small group, supplemented the weak public relations work of the official American Zionist organizations in the United States during the 1930s. It held a series of public meetings during that decade which endorsed the Zionist demands of unlimited immigration to Palestine and kept Christian pro-Zionist sentiment in the public eye.[19]

Despite its small membership, the Pro-Palestine Federation could not be ignored by those Christian groups who were opposed in principle to the Zionist position. In December 1936 the *Christian Century* took sharp issue with the deliberations and resolutions of the American Christian Conference on the Jewish Problem that had been convened by the Pro-Palestine Federation. The periodical felt that the conference tended toward "American entanglement in a political situation that is not properly our problem."[20] In its view, the religious leaders who voted for the conference resolutions did not "speak the profound conviction of Christian America," because though the mass of American Christians may have sympathy for the Jews, they have no adequate information about the meaning of the Balfour Declaration. However, the journal maintained, even if American opinion were far more unanimous than it is on the subject, "good Christians who are also good citizens must consider, as they exercise their moral enthusiasms, that their undoubted right to do this does not override their responsibility both to maintain the spirit of democracy at home, and to refrain from creating embarrassing complications abroad." Clearly the conference's interpretation of the Balfour Declaration was not that of the *Christian Century*, nor did the conference views, which were contrary to those of the periodical, reflect "the spirit of democracy at home."

Reinhold Niebuhr's Pro-Zionism

The isolationist and restrictive "democratic" outlook of the *Christian Century* did not go unchallenged by Protestant leaders who viewed the world responsibilities of the United States and democracy in a much more active light. Perhaps the most outstanding representative of the latter group, recognized "without question" even by the *Christian Century* as "the most vital personal force in American theology," was Reinhold Niebuhr, professor of social ethics at Union Theological Seminary.[21]

In February 1942, Dr. Niebuhr expressed his basic attitude on the Palestine question and Jewish nationalism in a two-part article published in the *Nation*.[22] Upholding the right of the Jews to survive as a people, and as such having a moral right to collective survival, Niebuhr took issue with "modern liberalism." He held that its "individualist and universalist presuppositions and illusions have prevented it from seeing some rather obvious facts in man's collective life. . . . a collective survival impulse is as legitimate a right as an individual one. Justice, in history, is concerned with collective as well as with individual rights."[23]

Niebuhr felt that those who sought to solve the Jewish problem by religious universalism were pursuing a "false" goal. He said: "It is just as false as if the command 'Thou shalt love thy neighbor as thyself' were interpreted to mean that I must destroy myself so that no friction may arise between my neighbor and myself." He regarded those who did not take ethnic factors into consideration guilty of "a premature universalism or a conscious or unconscious ethnic imperialism." He accused the liberal-democratic society of "implicitly making collective extinction the price of its provisional tolerance."[24]

Following Justice Louis Brandeis's thesis that American Jews should be considered a "nationality" like all other ethnic groups in the United States,[25] Niebuhr suggested that the American Finns, for example, "need not seek to perpetuate themselves in America, for their collective will is expressed in Finland," while Jews, as a nationality, were scattered among all nations.[26] The Jews, therefore, required a homeland which would express this collective will.

As a moral pragmatist, Niebuhr felt that a Jewish homeland was needed because the most generous immigration laws of Western democracies did not permit the dispossessed Jews of Europe to find a haven. He reproached his fellow liberals who maintained "a conspiracy of silence on this point." They did not dare to work for liberal immigration laws, he claimed, because, fearful of political repercussions, they "tacitly acknowledge[d] that their theories do not square with the actual facts."[27]

At the same time, Niebuhr cautioned Zionists to stop arguing that their demands in Palestine entailed no injustice to the Arab population. He said: "It is absurd to expect any people to regard the restriction of their sovereignty over a traditional possession as 'just' no matter how many other benefits accrue from that abridgement."[28]

The Impact of American Zionist Militancy

As the ravages of World War II exacerbated Jewish suffering in Europe, the need to open Palestine's doors to Jewish immigration, despite the restrictive 1939 British White Paper, became more acute. The activist element in American Zionism began to take over the leadership of the movement and inaugurated an intensive political campaign not only to win over American public opinion to the Zionist cause, but to persuade the United States government to influence its British ally with respect to the future of Palestine. The 1930s had been an especially disheartening decade among American Zionists. As reported by Moshe Sharett (then Shertok) to David Ben-Gurion, before the latter set out from Palestine to visit the United States in the spring of 1940: "The Zionist Organization of America is at a low ebb. It is rent by internal dissension and disrupted by personal and factional rivalries. . . . We have never yet got as far as the application of strong public pressure in America, by using means which count in modern politics."[29]

By early 1941, the tides of caution and restraint began to shift in American Zionist circles. The National Conference for Palestine, meeting in New York City on January 25-26, 1941, heard Rabbi Abba Hillel Silver of Cleveland sound the call for a Jewish commonwealth in Palestine and for an end to Jewish silence on the issue lest it embarrass the United States government.

Silver's maximalist Zionist position was applauded by the delegates, but not by the American Zionist leadership which still preferred quiet diplomacy. However, the latter had to give way to the new militancy, not only because the American Zionist membership largely followed Silver's views, but because the Palestinian Zionist leadership insisted that a more active political policy be adopted by American Zionists.

Already in 1939, in response to the British White Paper, the various Zionist groups in the United States had agreed to organize a new propaganda unit, subsequently known as the American Zionist Emergency Council (AZEC). This council at first coordinated the public relations activities of the four principal American Zionist groups—whose total membership was then some 171,000.[30] But in 1941 it began to extend its activities to the arena of American political life.

In the spring of 1941, the inactive American Palestine Committee was reconstituted upon the formal invitation of Democratic Senator Robert M. Wagner of New York and Republican Senator Charles F. McNary of Oregon. Its membership included three Cabinet members, sixty-eight senators, two hundred congressmen, twenty-two governors, and other prominent non-Jewish citizens, including clergymen, totaling over seven hundred names. The American Palestine Committee viewed itself as a "vehicle for the expression of the sympathy and good will of Christian America for the movement to re-establish the Jewish national home in Palestine." The *Christian Century* was not slow to castigate the American Palestine Committee's members for publishing their intentions "in a deliberate attempt to embarrass the British Government." It recognized the motive of the members as response to "a genuine humanitarian concern," but it criticized them for not making Great Britain's task "any easier."[31]

Following the entry of the United States into the war in December 1941, the Zionist movement felt it feasible to unleash a stepped-up public relations and political pressure campaign, which reached a crescendo with the establishment of the state of Israel in 1948. Since Britain was an ally of the United States, Zionists felt that the latter government was in a good position to influence British policy. The pressure campaign was launched at an "Extraordinary Zionist Conference" held at the Biltmore Hotel in New York City, from May 6 to May 11, 1942. With Dr. Chaim Weizmann, president of the World Zionist Organization, pleading for caution with regard to Zionist strategy in Palestine, and David Ben-Gurion of Palestine calling for greater militancy, the six hundred delegates, representing all factions of American Zionism, overwhelmingly followed Abba Hillel Silver's leadership and proclaimed Zionist policy to be the establishment of Palestine as a Jewish commonwealth. The former timidity of American Zionists was formally transformed into an enthusiastic Jewish nationalism.[32]

The Biltmore Program was a milestone in the campaign to rally both Jewish and Christian public opinion in the United States to the

Zionist cause.[33] In July 1942 a group of American Christian leaders declared Palestine to be the most practicable country available for Jewish immigration.[34] And on November 2, 1942, the twenty-fifth anniversary of the Balfour Declaration, the American Palestine Committee circulated a declaration entitled "The Common Purpose of Civilized Mankind," a reaffirmation of the "traditional American policy" in favor of a Jewish national home. The document bore the signatures of sixty-eight senators and 194 congressmen.[35]

Another meeting important for understanding the growth of pro-Zionist support was the American Jewish Conference held late in the summer of 1943 in New York City. The participants represented a broad spectrum of national Jewish organizations, including non-Zionist groups. The conference overwhelmingly adopted the militant Zionist position advocated by Abba Hillel Silver.[36]

Christian Council on Palestine

By the end of 1942, it became clear to the leaders of American Zionism that the purposes of their campaign would be better served if they would organize a distinct Christian clergy organization alongside the more political image of the American Palestine Committee. Wisely, they recognized that American public opinion at the grass-roots level is as much influenced by the views of local clergymen as by the opinions of national politicians—perhaps even more so. Such a separate organization would be particularly helpful in offsetting the vehement, anti-Zionist policies of the American Council for Judaism which not only alleged to speak for the Jewish religion, but sought to sow seeds of distrust regarding the "dual loyalties" of pro-Zionist American Jews.[37]

American Zionism did not have to search long for recognized Protestant personalities to head the proposed new organization. Reinhold Niebuhr had already expressed himself in favor of the Zionist solution to the Jewish problem. It was little wonder, therefore, that he helped organize and became active in the Christian Council on Palestine, an organization of Christian clergymen and religious educators formed to focus American religious public opinion on the role of Palestine in saving Jewish refugees. The chairman of the council was Henry A. Atkinson, general secretary of the Church Peace Union. Its executive committee included Niebuhr,

Holmes, Paul Tillich, the theologian, Daniel A. Poling, the editor of the *Christian Herald*, and William F. Albright, the archeologist.

This group developed in mid-1942 from an informal gathering of seventy clergymen who formed "the Committee of Christian Leaders, Clergymen and Laymen in Behalf of Jewish Immigration into Palestine," under the leadership of Atkinson and Niebuhr.[38] On December 14, 1942 the group was formally established as the Christian Council on Palestine, with the active support of the American Zionist movement. By March 1944 the organization had a membership of 1200 Christian ministers, the overwhelming majority of whom were Protestant. As defined by Carl Voss, the council's secretary: "It is the specific task of the Christian Council on Palestine to enlist the aid of ministers in their churches so that the lay constituency of the churches may be urged to action on these important problems affecting Palestine."[39] By and large, clergymen who had heretofore been members of the American Palestine Committee joined the newly organized Christian Council on Palestine. By the spring of 1946 (when the American Palestine Committee (APC) and the Christian Council on Palestine (CCP) merged into the American Christian Palestine Committee), some 3,000 American clergymen, primarily Protestants, had subscribed to the principles of this pro-Zionist group.[40]

More than one hundred local chapters of the American Palestine Committee—Christian Council on Palestine were organized across the United States. In addition to the $72,000 per year which the APC and the CCP received from the national American Zionist Emergency Council during the 1943-45 period (by 1947-48 their subsidies reached $150,000), local AZEC chapters were exhorted to provide additional funds and services to their Christian neighbors in order to help solicit their sympathy for the Zionist cause. As bluntly stated by the executive director of the Christian Council on Palestine: "We shall never be able to secure the widespread Christian support needed for the fulfillment of the Zionist aspirations unless we have the complete cooperation of Zionist groups in every community throughout the United States. . . ."[41] By mid-1946, the combined rosters of the APC and the CCP numbered 15,000 influential Christian supporters.[42] Clearly the local Zionist groups across the country had responded to the call. The Christian pro-Zionist partisans, in turn, reflected the statement of the council's executive director: "Socially sensitive Christians cannot but share a sense of com-

73

mon guilt for the tragedies and woes of the Jewish People. Now is the time for them to do something to cure an age old moral disease in our so called Christian civilization."[43]

In his statement at the founding meeting of the Christian Council on Palestine, Reinhold Niebuhr addressed himself to the clash of Arab and Jewish national rights in Palestine. He felt that there could be no simple "just" solution to such a conflict, but believed it possible to satisfy the Jewish claims "essentially under the compulsion of their great need," by compensating the Arabs in a total settlement of the Near Eastern situation. Though, in his opinion, the Arabs would not make any substantial contribution to the defeat of the Axis, it would be wise to allow the Arab world to be federated and "give it this higher unity in compensation for its loss of rights in Palestine." Such a quid pro quo, he insisted, would have to involve a genuine Arab disavowal of sovereignty over a sufficient part of Palestine to permit a Jewish state to be established. Niebuhr believed that American influence should be used to effectuate such a plan. "It would be ridiculous," he concluded, "to use our power merely to underwrite the past when we have a chance to underwrite the future; and to help in granting justice to a people who have been the first, and the most cruelly used, of Hitler's victims."

At the same founding conference of the Christian Council for Palestine, Methodist Bishop Francis J. McConnell of New York City called for continued Jewish immigration to Palestine so that "somewhere in the world there shall be a land in which the Jewish civilization is the primary civilization of a body of Jews." A professor of religion at Smith College, S. Ralph Harlow, felt that his three trips to the Near East convinced him that "awarding of Palestine to the Zionists . . . involves less of injustice . . . than any other solution" because Arab countries around Palestine "are crying for larger populations," the Arabs of Palestine have benefitted substantially from Jewish immigration, and "if there is any justice in humanity, it cries out on behalf of Israel's homeless children."[44]

It should be noted that none of the leading Protestant clergymen talked at the time of a Jewish state or a Jewish commonwealth. Such goals were expressed by the official American Zionist movement, not by pro-Zionist American Protestants. To the latter, Palestine loomed only as a haven of refuge or, at most, as a cultural homeland for the Jewish people. When Dr. Henry Atkinson, chairman of the Christian Council on Palestine, wrote the first full-fledged pro-

Zionist article in *Christianity and Crisis* in 1943, he argued for Palestine as "a haven of refuge for the millions of homeless Jews," and as "a homeland for the Jew."[45] The reason for supporting such a refuge or homeland was not to promote Jewish nationalism, but rather to provide an "answer to the Christian problem," anti-Semitism.[46]

By early 1944 the appalling facts of Hitler's "final solution" could no longer be ignored by American public opinion. Knowledge of these atrocities challenged the religious conscience of Protestant America. A decisive change became apparent in the statements of pro-Palestine American Protestant leaders, who came out in favor of the political Zionist position. Reinhold Niebuhr, in an introduction to the book *The Jew in Our Day*,[47] refused to go along with Waldo Frank, its Jewish author, who presented a religious concept of Jewish destiny as being that of Isaiah's "suffering servant." Collective Jewry must have a homeland, not only for cultural or spiritual fulfillment, Niebuhr maintained, but primarily for physical protection. "There must be a political solution to the problem of the Jews without reference to the final religious problem. . . . I do not see how it is possible to develop the prophetic overtone of high religion in the Jewish community fully if the nation does not have a greater degree of socio-political security."[48]

The Christian Council on Palestine began to pursue concrete political demands rather than ambiguous humanitarian goals regarding the future of Palestine. On March 9, 1944 a national conference in Washington, co-sponsored by the council, the American Palestine Committee, and national labor and civic groups, adopted a series of significant resolutions, one of which called for "the reconstitution of Palestine by the Jewish people as a free and democratic Jewish Commonwealth," language reminiscent of the 1942 Biltmore Program and of the 1943 American Jewish Conference.

The National Christian Conference was held in Washington at a time when congressional committees were considering Zionist-inspired resolutions subscribing to the Jewish commonwealth goal. The congressional resolutions undoubtedly would have passed the committees' hearings were it not for the pressures of the executive branch which opposed them in the name of "national security interests" in the Near East.[49] The influence of the Christian Council on Palestine, with its growing list of supporters and its local meetings attended by tens of thousands of Christians throughout the United

States, had made its mark on the Congress, if not on the executive branch.[50]

It would be erroneous to believe that all members of the pro-Zionist Christian groups accepted or even fully understood the Zionist goal of a Jewish commonwealth. One may assume, for example, that John Haynes Holmes did not agree with this aim, despite the fact that he remained on the executive committee of the Christian Council on Palestine. One might also say that other members of the council were interested in the Zionist cause for strictly humanitarian rather than political motivations. This became evident when the Christian Council on Palestine issued a statement in January 1946, signed by "spiritual" Christian Zionists like Holmes, and "political" Christian Zionists like Poling. This revealing statement accepted

> the essential validity of Zionism as a political and moral idea. We are not, however, officially committed to any particular formula of the Zionist purpose. Some of our leading members believe that the "Jewish commonwealth" conception alone offers the necessary directive; others, though agreeing on the substance of the Zionist aim, lay less emphasis on the significance of this formulation.[51]

The statement proceeded to list three major points of "basic agreement" among all signatories: a) that the gates of Palestine should be "forever" open to Jewish immigration; b) that the United Nations should extend "all possible aid" to encourage the Jews to develop the country's economic absorptive capacity; and c) that no political obstruction should be placed in the way of the Jews becoming a majority of the Palestinian population.

Even the binationalists could accept these points as long as they were understood to mean that, regardless of the majority group in the country, Palestine would be governed on an equal binational basis—Jew would not control Arab, or vice versa. However, the tragic fate of European Jewry and the frustrations of British policy in Palestine made it imperative that the main points of the statement be quickly realized and not ignored as merely a neat theory of binationalism, particularly by a guilt-ridden American public conscience. Abba Hillel Silver's militancy aroused American Jewry; American Jews influenced Christian public opinion. The subject was Palestine and Jewish refugees, not the respective rights of Zionists and Arabs to or in Palestine.

The voice of Christian anti-Zionism was not stilled by this upsurge in American Christian pro-Zionist sentiment. The *Christian Century* reluctantly acknowledged the "weighty" names associated with the Christian Council on Palestine, but refused to say that American sentiment had crystallized to the point where it believed in "making Palestine a Jewish state regardless of the Arab majority."[52] This comment undoubtedly was correct, because most Christian Americans were not manifestly concerned with the subject. However, the periodical was probably in error if it meant to assess the attitudes of those American Protestants who *were* interested in the subject. These seemed to reflect a pro-Zionist orientation, though, as the next chapter will reveal, they were challenged by less numerous anti-Zionist, pro-Arab American Protestant spokesmen who began to express themselves more forcefully on the subject as World War II neared its end.

To counter the new thrusts of leading American Protestants of anti-Zionist persuasion and to challenge the Defense Department's squelching of the pro-Zionist resolutions before congressional committees, the editorial notes of *Christianity and Crisis*, written by Reinhold Niebuhr, argued that

> Christians who do not believe that the "White Paper" restriction on immigration to Palestine should be abrogated, as advocated by a pending senatorial resolution, ought to feel obligated to state a workable alternative. The homeless Jews must find a home, and Christians owe their Jewish brethren something more than verbal sympathy. . . . The fact that General Marshall has intervened in the debate about immigration to Palestine, because in his belief, senatorial action might interfere with the strategy of oil pipe lines to Arabia, raises an issue. . . . To what degree shall problems of political justice be subordinated to necessities of military strategy?[53]

The war in Europe ended on May 7, 1945. President Harry S Truman had been in office less than a month and had already been briefed by the Department of State to be cautious about committing himself on the Palestine question.[54]

On June 22, 1945, the President sent Earl G. Harrison, dean of the University of Pennsylvania Law School and a former United States Commissioner of Immigration, on a fact-finding mission to Europe. Harrison was instructed to visit the displaced persons camps and to ascertain whether there really was an eagerness on the part of the camp inmates to go to Palestine. In late August, Harrison reported: "The desire to leave Germany is an urgent one. . . . They want to be evacuated to Palestine now. . . . To anyone who visited the concentration camps and who has talked with the despairing survivors, it is nothing short of calamitous to contemplate that the gates of Palestine should be soon closed."[55]

Some 250,000 Jews were in displaced persons camps at the end of the war. In June 1945 the Jewish Agency submitted a memorandum to the British government, calling for the immediate admission of 100,000 Jews to Palestine. President Truman, moved by Harrison's report, sent that report with a covering letter to Prime Minister Atlee, supporting the Zionists' request.

The British countered with a proposal to set up an Anglo-American Committee of Inquiry to examine the problem of Jewish refugees in Europe, with Palestine to be considered only peripherally as a possible haven of refuge. But Truman insisted that the main haven to be explored was Palestine. Four months after Harrison had submitted his report, the British yielded, and the formation of a joint committee of six British and six American members was announced on November 13, 1945.[56]

Anglo-American Committee of Inquiry

The year 1946 began with hearings of the Anglo-American Committee of Inquiry in Washington. In addition to Zionist and pro-Arab spokesmen, the committee heard several Protestant representatives who expressed the views of their respective groups regarding Palestine. Apparently, the American Protestant anti-Zionist groups had planned to have several distinguished witnesses testify before the committee, but they did not appear.[57]

Two pro-Arab Protestant spokesmen, however, did appear: one in a personal capacity; the other representing the Protestant missionary movement, the Foreign Missions Conference of North America, an affiliate of the International Missionary Council.[58]

The Christian Council on Palestine was represented by two spokesmen, Dr. Daniel A. Poling and Dr. Reinhold Niebuhr. Prior to their appearance in Washington, the Christian Council on Palestine sent a memorandum on January 3, 1946, to the Anglo-American Committee of Inquiry, in which it explained its pro-Zionist position on the Palestine question.[59]

Both Niebuhr and Poling were members of the executive committee of the Christian Council on Palestine, while the latter was also on the executive committee of the American Palestine Committee. When Dr. Poling appeared before the Anglo-American Inquiry Committee on January 12, the thrust of his remarks was essentially religious in nature. In fact, his views were close to the Dispensationalist attitude towards a restored Zion. He said: "Christians believe overwhelmingly . . . that Palestine was divinely selected as the site of the Jewish nation. . . . I am trying as the representative of the Christian groups to present what is, we believe, the Christian viewpoint. . . . I may say this viewpoint has been and is now being, with increasing fervor, expressed by representatives of the Evangelical Christian peoples of this country."[60]

Poling emphasized that the testimony of the Foreign Missions Conference representative before the committee[61] did not represent the policy of the Federal Council of Churches in the United States, which remained neutral on the subject.[62] When pressed by a committee member as to which Christian groups he spoke for, and would it not be more accurate to insert the word "some" or "many" before the phrase "Christians believe," Poling adamantly replied: "It would be more accurate to leave it as it is, but if you were to put in a qualifying adjective it would be 'overwhelming' in my judgment."[63]

When the inquiry committee member pressed further and asked: "Has any church voted on the question as to whether it is more preferable to have a Jewish or Arab majority in Palestine?" Poling replied unhesitatingly but not very convincingly: "I think that indirectly, practically every church has expressed itself on that. I would say again, overwhelmingly, in my opinion and in the opinion of my associate Christians in the United States, preferably Palestine should be a Jewish state."[64] Poling's views were not questioned further by committee members.

Dr. Niebuhr testified on January 14. Whereas Poling had suggested that the commitments made by the Allied Powers to the Arabs after World War I had "in substance been fulfilled," Niebuhr began his presentation by admitting that there was no perfectly just solution for the conflict of rights between the Arabs and the Jews in Palestine. He said:

> There is in fact no solution to any political problem. The fact however that the Arabs have a vast hinterland in the Middle East, and the fact that the Jews have nowhere to go, establishes the relative justice of their claims and of their cause . . . Arab sovereignty over

79

a portion of the debated territory must undoubtedly be sacrificed for
the sake of establishing a world [Jewish] homeland.[65]

Niebuhr ruled out a binational state in Palestine for, in his
opinion, such an entity would inevitably lead to conflict between
the Arabs and Jews. Said he: "To have a binational state with one of
the parties having its own hinterland makes it something less than a
bilateral state."[66]

Niebuhr was questioned closely on the need for a Jewish state
as against the more obvious need for Jewish immigration. He responded: "The Jews have survived as a people, so presumably they
will survive even if they don't have a Jewish state, but the . . . spiritual and physical price is terribly high. The physical price is very high
because they were almost liquidated. The price will continue to be
high because the group has to maintain itself in a minority position
wherever it is."[67]

The Anglo-American Committee of Inquiry heard testimony in
Europe, Egypt, and Palestine. On May 1, 1946, ten days after its
report had been submitted to the two sponsoring governments, it
was also released to the public.[68] The report recommended that the
1939 White Paper be rescinded, that 100,000 certificates for the admission of Jewish refugees to Palestine be authorized at once, that
proposals for partitioning the country be abandoned, and that Britain
continue governing Palestine under the terms of the mandate, pending a United Nations trusteeship agreement on a long-range settlement of the Palestine problem.[69]

President Truman expressed his approval of the recommendation to admit 100,000 Jews into Palestine immediately, but reserved
judgment on the long-range political questions. The British government, on the other hand, stated that there could be no admission of
Jews until the Jewish underground defense movement in Palestine
was disbanded.[70]

American Christian Palestine Committee

The American Christian Palestine Committee (ACPC), formed
shortly before by a merger of the American Palestine Committee and
the Christian Council on Palestine, felt the inquiry team's report to
be "woefully inadequate as a token of atonement" to the Jewish

people.[71] It called the report "unfair" in giving the impression that the contemplated Jewish commonwealth was of an extreme nationalist character bordering on the "exclusive" nationalism reflected in "the Arab definition of an Arab state."

The analysis proceeded with its own understanding of the Jewish commonwealth slogan: "As is well known, the Biltmore Program and the Jewish commonwealth conception are predicated on the idea of nondomination, explicitly provide for a democratic constitution with equality for all citizens, and make complete provision for the communal and cultural autonomy of the Arab section of the population."[72]

"As is well known" was not an accurate expression, for at the time, no official Zionist body had either accepted or rejected the notion that a Jewish state would be "dominated" by Jews. In fact, the term "Jewish commonwealth" was used in different ways after the Biltmore conference by the two recognized leaders of world Zionism. Dr. Weizmann, president of the World Zionist Organization, used it as a tactical political device for partition negotiations with Great Britain, whereas Ben-Gurion, the chairman of the Jewish Agency for Palestine, turned the Biltmore resolution into the new political Zionist postwar goal.[73] The Biltmore Program was made official Zionist policy by the World Zionist Congress only in December 1946. It drew 171 votes while a counter-resolution, sponsored by Dr. Weizmann and Rabbi Wise, asking for a resumption of partition negotiations with the British, received 154 votes. (The Congress also established an American section of the Jewish Agency, with Rabbi Silver as its chairman.) The militants were now in full control of the Zionist movement.

In analyzing the report of the Anglo-American Committee of Inquiry, the American Christian Palestine Committee advised the United States government to accept Great Britain's invitation, should it be offered, to share in the administration of the mandate on condition that the "trustee powers facilitate Jewish immigration into Palestine. . . ."[74] It was however particularly caustic about the report's recommendations ensuring Christian rights in Palestine:

> It is evasive and unwarranted to make an issue of "Christian rights and interests" in view of the complete freedom which the Christians in Palestine now enjoy. . . . The Christian conscience is outraged by such an attempt to put a brake on Jewish development of Palestine due to an inadequately defined "interest of the Christian world."

The Balfour Declaration and the League of Nations Mandate stipulated that the Holy Places be fully protected, a stipulation which has been meticulously observed by the Jews of Palestine. As Christians, we protest this effort to create an issue out of a situation which has never been a problem; and thus obscure the real issue at stake which is not only to create a haven for homeless Jews, but to build a national Home for a homeless people. To lump Jews with Moslems and Christians, and consider them solely as a religious group is historically and scientifically absurd, for the Jewish people is much more than a religious entity. The Jews as a people have an ethnic consciousness which makes their relationship to Palestine unique.[75]

The position taken by the American Christian Palestine Committee would make it appear that the Zionists had achieved their purpose of making the American public fully aware of the need to find a speedy solution both to the Palestine question and to the problem of Jewish refugees.[76]

The British government did not open Palestine as a homeland for Jewish refugees. Instead, on February 14, 1947, it referred the Palestine question to the United Nations.

Though the American Christian Palestine Committee continued its public relations work during the hectic period when the United Nations was considering the Palestine question and long after the state of Israel was established, its *primary* task, helping to arouse the Christian conscience of America with respect to a Zionist solution of the Jewish problem, had been successfully achieved.

6

Pro-Arab Strategies of American Protestants

WHILE REINHOLD NIEBUHR AND HIS PROTESTANT colleagues on the American Christian Palestine Committee were waging a systematic campaign to have American public opinion influence the Palestine policies of the United States government in favor of the Zionist position, other American Protestant leaders were trying to ensure an anti-Zionist United States government policy. With a few notable exceptions, the attitudes of the anti-Zionist Protestant groups were motivated largely by religious, nostalgic or economic connections with the Arab Near East. Many had served in the Middle East as members of missionary families, as participants or board members of Arab educational establishments, or as representatives of oil interests. Many had lived and worked among Arabs. They, or their fathers, or grandfathers, had tried to convert Arabs to Christianity. For them, concern for Arabs took priority over the Jewish refugee issue, and certainly over the prospects of a Jewish state. Although the pro-Zionist American Protestant groups were clearly not anti-Arab, but rather in favor of effectively saving Jewish refugees, the rival Protestant groups were blatantly anti-Zionist. To them, "Zionism" was a pejorative term connoting, at different times, anti-American, anti-democratic, and anti-Arab attitudes. Whether by design or inadvertently, the term "Zionism" was also used to express anti-Jewish attitudes. This stance emerged as a result of their strong opposition to the immigration of Jewish refugees to Palestine. The fact that these anti-Zionist American Protestant groups had a few anti-Zionist Jews on their boards did not lessen their anti-Jewish image.

Virginia Gildersleeve, dean of Barnard College, for example, described her anti-Zionist and pro-Arab feelings in her autobiography, while praising her association "with my Jewish friends in that excellent organization, the American Council for Judaism."[1] The fact that the latter organization's main purpose was to combat Jewish nationalism, under the guise of maintaining that Judaism was exclusively a religion, indicates the kind of Jews with whom Miss Gildersleeve found amity.[2]

Miss Gildersleeve was not alone among anti-Zionist American Protestants who praised the pro-Arab policies of the Council for Judaism or its key personnel. The *Christian Century* gave the council ample space for anti-Zionist articles[3] (though it also published replies of pro-Zionist supporters),[4] displayed its full-page ads, favorably reviewed its books and pamphlets,[5] and lauded the council's anti-Zionist positions in its editorials.[6] From the viewpoint of the Protestant weekly, the council represented the authentic voice of American Jewry. It continually reminded its readers that American Judaism was seriously divided on the subject of Zionism and that distinguished Jewish names—such as Lessing Rosenwald, board chairman of Sears Roebuck, and Arthur Hays Sulzberger, publisher of the *New York Times*—supported the council's position.

Committee for Justice and Peace in the Holy Land

One of the council's principal officers, Rabbi Morris S. Lazaron, was so obsessed by his anti-Zionist attitudes that he became a vice-chairman, and the only Jewish member, of the pro-Arab Committee for Justice and Peace in the Holy Land. Organized in February 1948 to induce the United Nations Assembly to reconsider its November 29, 1947 partition resolution,[7] the committee was headed by Miss Gildersleeve, whose anti-Zionist views have already been noted. Among its executive members were Dr. Henry Sloan Coffin; the Reverend Daniel Bliss; Bayard S. Dodge, president of the American University at Beirut; Dr. Harry Emerson Fosdick, minister of Riverside Church in New York City; Paul Hutchinson, editor of *Christian Century*; and Glora M. Wysner, a leader in foreign missions activities. Its secretary was the Reverend Garland Evans Hopkins, later a member of the *Christian Century*'s editorial board, and its executive director was Kermit Roosevelt, grandson of President Theodore Roosevelt.[8]

The committee, with headquarters in Washington, ostensibly sought to "further the best interests of all Jews, Christians and Moslems in the Near and Middle East, to foster friendly relations among the peoples of these three faiths throughout the world, and to strengthen the United Nations."[9] However, such respectable, even-handed goals were hardly detectable in the committee's statements or activities. As Miss Gildersleeve herself put it: "Almost all Americans with diplomatic, educational, missionary or business experience in the Middle East fervently believed that the Zionist plan was directly contrary to our national interests, military, strategic and commercial, as well as to common justice."[10] She herself in the 1920s had been influenced by Charles Crane of the King-Crane Commission and later by George Antonius, author of the *Arab Awakening* (which he dedicated to Crane). She also served as board member of several American educational institutions in the Near East.[11]

Miss Gildersleeve felt that the Zionist cause was unjust because the concept of a "national home" in Palestine conflicted with the cause of Arab nationalism. It was contrary to the principles of democracy and self-determination. She maintained that the Zionists "with ruthless efficiency" were pushing to get more and more immigrants into Palestine, and were supported by

a great many American Christians some few of whom, I an sorry to say, advocated the project because it would relieve us of doing anything ourselves to help the exiles. These unworthy Christians did not want to admit any more refugees into America. . . . Of the few who had any real knowledge of the circumstances, almost no one was willing to speak out publicly against a project of the Zionists. The politicians feared the Jewish vote; others feared the charge of anti-Semitism; and nearly all had a kind of "guilt complex" in their emotions towards the Jews because of the terrible tragedies inflicted upon them by Hitler.[12]

The Committee for Justice and Peace in the Holy Land began its lobbying work in Washington immediately after its organizing session.[13] Roosevelt secured an appointment for a small group to meet Secretary of State George Marshall. The delegation pointed out the "great peril to the interests of the United States" should "this precipitate action on partition" stand and urged a reversal of policy. "Though he could not commit himself definitely," reported Miss Gildersleeve, "I gathered that the Secretary of State was rather in sympathy with our views." When she called on Warren Austin, head of the United States delegation to the United Nations, in early March 1948, she learned that a new United States policy was being developed "much like that we had urged on Secretary Marshall." The State Department favored a reconsideration of the Palestine question by the General Assembly and a temporary trusteeship under the United Nations, as steps toward a democratic state that would retain the unity of the Holy Land.[14]

The committee's campaign against the establishment of a Jewish state failed. But it did not let up in its anti-Zionist public relations until it disbanded in February 1950.[15] For all intents and purposes, the Committee for Justice and Peace in the Holy Land was the first ad hoc pro-Arab American Christian (Protestant dominated) organization which lobbied systematically against a Jewish state. Had it been organized several years earlier, its chances for success might have been greater, though it would have been difficult to completely eradicate the pro-Zionist sentiment which had overtaken the country in the wake of the European holocaust. For indeed there were Christians—Protestants and Catholics alike—who, while expressing sympathy for the victims of Nazism, were not prepared to accept Palestine as the answer to the refugee problem. These American Christians never did organize for the specific purpose of opposing a Jewish state, either because they already belonged to religious groupings with ties to the Arab world, which spoke for them, or because they had no alternative haven to offer the Jewish refugees in place of Palestine. They merely vented their anti-Zionist sentiments in speeches or in American Christian journals of opinion like the *Christian Century*.

Most of these pro-Arab American Christians were members of religious or educational enterprises affiliated with the Near East. Whereas the great majority of supporters of the American Christian Palestine Committee had no personal contact with Palestine or the Arab world, but related to the Palestine question almost exclusively on the basis of humanitarian considerations, the American Protestant anti-Zionist adherents either shared the type of anti-Jewish nationalist bias expressed in the *Christian Century*, or had personal relations with Christian bodies or Christian-sponsored institutions in the Levant. They published opinions against the Zionist position which would invariably be answered by American Protestants favoring Zionism.[16]

Official Church Attitudes on the Palestine Question

A more concerted American Protestant anti-Zionist campaign appeared towards the end of 1944 and early 1945, when three study papers appeared on the subject of Palestine, two by missionary groups and one by the Department of Research and Education of the Federal Council of the Churches of Christ in America. The first paper appeared in the council's weekly *Information Service* of October 7, 1944. It presented what the *Christian Century* called "an impartial study of the Palestine problem."[17] Though the report presented the basic facts of the Palestine problem, the Christian Council on Palestine felt that "important omissions and doubtful interpretations make it an instrument easily used to support anti-Zionist viewpoints."[18] While, indeed, many statements in the Federal Council of Churches report seemed biased against Zionist interests, it is not possible to assess their impact on Protestant readers.[19]

In November 1944 the *Bulletin*, a publication issued by the Committee on Work among Moslems of the Foreign Missions Conference, carried a lengthy analysis of the Palestine problem. Written by the Committee's secretary, Glora M. Wysner, this second study paper did not pretend to be objective, for the sponsoring group was admittedly concerned with potential Arab converts to Christianity, not with a balanced evaluation of the Palestine question. It deliberately "made no attempt to elaborate on the Jewish situation [because] it is better known than that of the Arabs."[20] Inevitably, it identified the committee's interests with the pro-Arab position on Palestine.

The third major presentation of an anti-Zionist American Protestant viewpoint was a statement by the Foreign Missions Conference of North America. Reprinted in the October 17, 1945 issue of *Information Service* of the Federal Council of Churches, the statement reflected the work of a joint committee appointed by the Federal Council, the Foreign Missions Conference, and the Home Missions Council. Though the paper was approved by the two missionary groups, it never was adopted by the Council, and therefore it would seem that the statement could not be considered the official attitude of the Federal Council. The study paper was entitled "The Palestine Question: A Christian Approach." It did not pretend to speak authoritatively for organized Protestantism, but only for "a group of Christians." That it was published in full by an official organ of the Federal Council of Churches is significant, however.

The study was blatantly biased against Zionism. While it recognized the devotion of the Jewish people to the Holy Land—"to which a large majority of Jews subscribe"—it also stressed that there were "numbers of Jews to whom the Holy Land is dear who do not interpret the return to Zion in physical or geographical terms;

to them Zion is wholly of the spirit. . . . To many persons, both Jews and non-Jews, Jewish nationalism appears to be a philosophy of defeatism," concluded the study. The statement then proceeded to advise the Jews to make up their minds "whether they shall or shall not be a nation. . . . It seems to us that a clearcut decision is needed. . . . Jewish nationalists who themselves remain Americans, Britons, Frenchmen, compromise all Jews enfranchised abroad as well as those now resident in Palestine."

Perhaps the most unkind remark directed at Jewish feelings was the explanation that because the surviving Jews in Europe may prove to be "a pitifully small remnant," the Zionist leadership called for American Jews to settle in Palestine. "In these circumstances," concluded the statement, "there appears to be little likelihood that Jews can ever achieve a majority in Palestine, even if all restrictions upon entry should be abandoned." At the same time, however, the Protestant study paper insisted that one had to separate the problem of rescue from the problem of Palestine. The latter should be resolved by a new mandatory regime under the United Nations; the former by the United Nations' assigning quotas of refugees to different member states.

While one might have suspected the editors of the *Christian Century* of writing this statement—it closely paralleled their views —the sophisticated Protestant periodical dismissed the document as banal. Said the weekly: "One wonders why the declaration did not come boldly out for honesty as the best policy, the value of a stitch in time in saving nine, and the affirmation that a boy's best friend is his mother. . . . Unless . . . Christian bodies have more to say than the Foreign Missions Conference . . . they had better remain silent."[21]

The *Christian Century* was a far better teacher than it had reason to expect. Its readers mouthed its very words. But perhaps it would be more accurate to conclude that the periodical represented the views of those Protestant groups which had had ongoing relationships with the Arab world for many years.

The Christian Council on Palestine turned out to be first major American Protestant-dominated group concerned with the Near East which broke with the image of the *Christian Century* and the missionary organizations on the subject of Jewish nationalism. The council's scathing criticism of the three study papers revealed the vast difference emerging between the attitudes of the older American Protestant establishment on the one hand, and the newer, more critical, pro-Zionist group of Protestant leaders on the other. The council declared:

> The documents are replete with expressions of good will, and copious tears are shed for Jewish suffering. . . . But is it surprising . . . that these sweet words are regarded by the Jewish people as new examples of Christian hypocrisy since in final analysis the documents whitewash the British policy of the 1939 White Paper, and support without reservation the determination of the Arab League to keep the doors of Palestine closed to the Jews? Nowhere in these three memoranda is there any suggestion that Palestine should be opened for any Jewish immigration whatsoever. We submit that this is not the time for equivocal declarations of good will. It is time for definite action that will translate the oft-pledged Christian sympathy for the Jews into genuine, practical justice.[22]

Missionaries Project Protestant Anti-Zionist Image

American Protestant pro-Arab interests became increasingly vocal on the Palestine question as World War II neared its end and the pressures for a pro-Zionist solution were stepped up. Most pro-Arab Protestant spokesmen took a hard line against Zionism. Others, who were interested in Jewish converts to Christianity (along with Moslem converts), were more ambivalent on the subject.[23]

In the United States, the secretary emeritus of the International Missionary Council, the Reverend A. L. Warnshuis, utilized the pages of the *Christian Century* to rebuke those American Protestants who supported the Zionist cause.[24] He labeled their concern "hypocrisy" because they were not fighting for Jewish immigration to the United States. He raised the spectre of the Jews becoming a nation, with a geographic state of their own, warning that they "must either choose to be resident aliens or forswear their Jewish nationalism and become citizens in the lands where they live." At the same time, he reiterated the argument that the Zionists were having a difficult time "find[ing] enough Jews in Europe who are willing to go" to Palestine, and therefore were appealing for Jewish emigration from the United States.

At the 1946 hearings of the Anglo-American Committee of Inquiry in Washington, previously discussed in chapter five, the one official spokesman on behalf of Protestantism was the representative of the Foreign Missions Conference of North America, the Reverend Leland S. Albright of Canada.[25]

The committee already had before it the statement, "The Palestine Question: A Christian Position" mentioned above, which had been drawn up by a joint committee of Protestant groups, but which had not been endorsed by the Federal Council of Churches. Rather, it bore only the approval of the missionary movement. Albright explained to the committee members the organizational structure of the International Missionary Council, of which the Foreign Missions Conference of North America was a constituent member. He was the associate secretary of the International Missionary Council, but had never been to Palestine. When asked why a Canadian represented the council before the inquiry committee, rather than a United States citizen, he replied: "That is internationalism."[26]

Clearly, the International Missionary Council was interested in demonstrating its world-wide influence, rather than a United States "parochial" image which would have placed missionary activities in a far less dramatic light. Both the British and United States governments conceivably would be more sensitive and responsive to worldwide missionary pressures.

Albright's testimony to the committee followed the standard missionary line with respect to Palestine. That country, he said, "has already done its share and much more" in producing a refuge for over half a million Jews during the preceding twenty-five years. While indeed many "old" Jews remain in Europe, they should not be evacuated until relatives abroad were prepared to receive them, "a process which will take months and even years."[27] In the meantime, the surviving Jews should try to adjust themselves to the postwar situation in Europe. "For the first time," he insisted, "there is the possibility of better treatment under more democratic governments." At any rate, the problem of the relief of European Jews should be solved apart from further demands upon Palestine.

Albright urged the committee to view the Palestine problem not only in terms of injustice to the Arab population there, but also to face it "realistically." "It is significant," he said, "that the 126,500 Christians [in the Holy Land] tend to stand with the Arabs rather than the Jews, feeling that on the whole, their interests are safer with the former than with the latter in spite of all their assurances of just treatment."[28] He had no objection to a "purely religious and cultural Jewish home-center of limited proportions in Palestine, as long as it remained a purely religious and cultural center."

Apparently neither the Federal Council of Churches, nor any

Protestant denomination in the United States, had reached an official position on the Palestine question at the time of the hearings of the inquiry committee, for this would have been an opportune time for them to express their attitudes on the subject. It would appear that the executive committee of the Federal Council was split on the issue, and the pro-Zionist members (like Dr. Daniel A. Poling) were able to stave off a formal anti-Zionist resolution sought primarily by members associated with the missionary groups.

The only other Protestant spokesman at the Committee of Inquiry Hearings in Washington was a non-missionary representative, the Reverend Charles T. Bridgeman, who from 1924 to 1944 served with the Anglican bishop in Jerusalem as the representative of the American Episcopal Church. He appeared as a private person and admittedly did not represent any organization. His main thrust was to charge the United States government with "hypocrisy" for not opening the doors of America to more Jewish refugees, and "on the specious plea of 'humanitarianism' . . . urg[ing] Great Britain to bludgeon the peoples of Palestine . . . to accept more heavy Jewish immigration, making the absurdity greater by saying that it is the only country open to them."[29]

Bridgeman's successor in Palestine, the Reverend F. J. Bloodgood, was not as blunt as the aging Bridgeman when he testified before the committee in Jerusalem. Bloodgood was preceded in his appearance before the committee by the Right Reverend W. H. Stewart, bishop of the Church of England in Jerusalem. Stewart disapproved of the Zionist youth movements in Palestine and felt that "Christian sentiment would be profoundly shocked" if Galilee and Bethlehem "were sacrificed to any nationalist or imperialist scheme of industry or commerce."[30] Bloodgood merely expressed opposition to any change in the political status of the country. In his view, "recent history" had shown the Jews that "genuine Christians befriended them in every way during the dreadful years of Hitler." His statement implied that the Jews would continue to trust a Christian authority in Palestine, such as the existing mandatory regime. "Therefore as neither Jew nor Moslem has anything to fear from the Christians, it is reasonable to find in the future of Christianity in the Holy Land the best guarantee to Jew and Moslem against fear of each other."[31]

Seemingly, Protestant policy in Palestine preferred the preservation of the political status quo there. When the Reverend H. R. A.

Jones, representing the Church Mission to the Jews of Palestine, was repeatedly asked by committee members how many Christian Jews were in the country, after many years of missionary work there he was unable to provide "even roughly" a satisfactory answer, but concluded his evasive reply with, "are numbers important?"[32] Jones implied that numbers were unimportant as long as the country was ruled by a Protestant power which recognized and did not interfere with the principle of conversion to Christianity.

The Protestant missionary movement in the Levant had much more at stake than the small number of converted Jews in Palestine. It had a whole Arab world to contend with and hopefully to convert, a topic which became increasingly prominent in Protestant circles after the United Nations partition resolution was adopted. But the handwriting on the wall had been discernible long before. Following the approval by the United States Congress of a pro-Zionist resolution in December 1945, the Reverend Lewis Gaston Leary, an aging Presbyterian missionary who had taught at the American University in Beirut at the beginning of the century, expressed the frustrated feelings of most missionaries when he wrote: "Everyone zealous for Christian missions must feel a veritable heartbreak for the way in which the hasty and ill-advised endorsement of the Zionist program by Congress has nullified the sacrificial labors of generations of missionaries and educators."[33]

Counteracting the American Christian Palestine Committee

Meanwhile, the American Christian Palestine Committee was gaining the growing support of additional Protestant leaders. Several Protestant-establishment spokesmen, who were either sympathetic to, or pressured by, the organized anti-Zionist wing of American Protestantism, tried to mute its influence. Dr. Henry Smith Leiper, the executive secretary of the American Committee for the World Council of Churches, was prepared in June 1946 to sign a statement initiated by the American Christian Palestine Committee in favor of Jewish refugee immigration to Palestine, provided that the statement's sponsors would not be the American Palestine Committee or the Christian Council on Palestine. Dr. Leiper explicitly disapproved of both organizations because they were associated with political Zionism which he called "a boomerang" likely to cause more trouble than help to the Jewish refugees.[34] It is difficult to understand Dr. Leiper's agreeing to sign this statement, inasmuch as the American Christian Palestine Committee was the result of a merger of both organizations, but apparently he did so, despite his reservations, because of his personal friendship with the ACPC director, who assured him that there was no intention of relating the projected newspaper advertisement to "our so-called political organization."

A much more direct challenge to the ACPC came from the Reverend L. Humphrey Walz, who later headed the Americans for Middle East Understanding. This group was a citizens' organization whose stated aim was to better understand how Middle East affairs affected United States national interests. In February 1947 Walz, a minister of the Second Presbyterian Church in New York City, protested to the Reverend Carl Voss, the chairman of the executive council of the American Christian Palestine Committee, against the committee's publication of a pamphlet, "The Arab War Effort," which described the hostile or indifferent policies of the Arab states towards the Allied cause during World War II.[35]

Walz felt that the pamphlet contained half truths, because it did not convey an appreciation for Arab war collaboration expressed by Allied leaders. He wrote "personally" to Voss, in the hope that Voss would do something concrete "to repair the damage." Walz overlooked the fact, however, that the British government had been directing kind words to the Arab world because it was espousing a pro-Egyptian political policy which was to be the foundation of a pro-British Arab federation at the end of the war. He also ignored the many documents and statements reproduced in the pamphlet, which underscored its major thesis.

Walz accused the pamphlet of "inflammatory anti-Semitism (not forgetting that the Arabs are Semites)," and its sponsors of being "a small collection of American Christian individuals" who hide the fact of their "Zionist, non-Christian financial arrangements and staffing." He sent copies of his protesting letter to members of the executive council and the advisory council of the American Christian Palestine Committee.

Carl Voss replied to Walz in early March, after being requested to do so by members of the ACPC executive and advisory councils.[36] He upheld the "accuracy" of the document by referring the critic to the British intelligence papers reproduced at the back of the pamphlet. He also defended the "advisability" of the publication in order to remind the Arab leaders that "the world is catching up on them and is now aware of their duplicity."

Voss also enclosed a response from one of the ACPC executive council members, the Reverend Karl M. Chworosky, of the Universalist Church in Brooklyn.[37] Chworosky's letter asked Walz to explain "the sudden sentimental interest" of Christians in the cause of the Arabs. "Can it be that they hope thereby to 'win more Arabs for Christ'?" he asked. He reminded Walz of the debt Christianity owed to Judaism and suggested that Zionism offered an opportunity to the Christian world "to make a small down payment on this age-old debt."

Both Voss and Chworosky were particularly incensed at Walz's caustic assertion that the ACPC received its support from Zionist sources and that it was unrepresentative of American Christian opinion. With regard to the latter argument, Voss enclosed a pamphlet listing many prominent Christian sponsors, while at the same time recognizing that the Christian community was neither united nor unanimous in its support of the Zionist position. "You know well enough," he wrote, "that not all Christians agree even on such basic Christian imperatives as racial equality or the abolition of the poll tax." However, he was satisfied that a "sizeable and considerable portion of Christian sentiment favors a Jewish Palestine."

Walz's argument that the ACPC was supported by Zionist funds was countered by Chworosky:

> May I ask just what you expect us to do, since men like yourself seem quite willing to sit solidly and indifferently by while millions of Jews wait in vain for justice and succor? Since not enough so called "Christians" are willing to help us in our thoroughly Christian and humanitarian work, we are grateful indeed to accept Zionist financial support until that time when, by the grace of God, the cold hearts of a "Christian world" may have thawed and their callous indifference may have changed into a measure of mercy and goodwill. We are no more ashamed of this temporary and emergency arrangement than was the American Christian Refugee Committee ashamed a few years ago to accept the tidy sum of $250,000 from the Jewish Joint Distribution Committee.[38]

Partition Again

In 1947 as the United Nations prepared to debate the Palestine question, leading to its 29 November resolution to partition the country into Arab and Jewish states, American Protestant anti-Zionist forces began to express themselves more vociferously. On the one hand, they sensed the inevitable decision about a Jewish state; on the other, they tried in every way to delay the inevitable, if not to frustrate its realization. At the end of the hearings of the United Nations Special Committee on Palestine in the summer of 1947, even the *Christian Century* believed that partition was coming in Palestine, not because it was a correct solution, but because it was the only solution that could gain majority political assent and was "probably the best that can be hoped for now." But it was also a testimony "to man's littleness of spirit."[39] The journal had earlier agreed with British Foreign Secretary Ernest Bevin that President Truman's policies vis-à-vis Palestine were mainly dictated by the Jewish vote in New York,[40] and had conditioned its readers for the moment when the Zionists would insist that all of Palestine be given to the Jews.[41]

Dr. Henry Sloan Coffin, former president of Union Theological Seminary, also protested that American politicians jeopardized the peace of the world and the good name of the United States with three hundred million Moslems, "in order to fish for votes."[42] As a Protestant theologian, he denied that the Bible promised Palestine to the Jews, insisting that such promises appealed only to biblical literalists, "and to ignorant ones at that," for such promises were conditioned on obedience to divine law, and "Israel notoriously failed to fulfill the condition." Said Coffin: "The plea for the necessity of a Jewish national state is no more cogent than would be a similar plea for an Armenian national state."

American Protestantism was ill-prepared to absorb the shock of the United Nations partition resolution. Several weeks passed before it began to combat the establishment of a Jewish state. Commencing in early 1948, however, it pursued its anti-Jewish state campaign unabated.[43]

The first phase of the Protestant attack on the United Nations partition resolution was an effort to seek its nullification. The Committee for Justice and Peace in the Holy Land reflected this strategy. But the intellectual underpinning for the committee's public policies was provided by several leading American Protestant personalities.

Dr. Henry Van Dusen, president of the Union Theological Seminary, admitted that "honest men, including the editors" of *Christianity and Crisis* (of which he was one) could differ on the subject of Palestine. However, he was not prepared to "counsel Christians to make common cause for goals which they believe to be right with political forces which may espouse those goals for quite other reasons. . . ."[44] What were these "other reasons"? Catering to the voting strength of American Jews! The American political parties were not concerned with the humanitarian considerations of persecuted Jews, he maintained. They were concerned with the "shrewd calculation of the voting strength of their American kinsmen in key political districts." Perhaps Van Dusen was right, for if Congress was really sensitive to the problem of Jewish refugees, it could readily have opened the doors of America for them. But Van Dusen added a jarring note to his thesis: if the Palestine partition resolution would spawn conflict in the Near East, "American lives would be demanded." The frightening implications of this morbid prophecy were obvious. "The final outcome might be fuel for the always smouldering fires of anti-Semitism—which God may forfend!"[45] The intellectual rationale for aborting the Jewish state in Palestine was that such an abortion would stave off an increase in anti-Semitism in the United States.

Dr. Bayard Dodge, president of the American University in Beirut, who was in the United States on a fundraising drive in early 1948, agreed with Van Dusen's argument: "If the blood of American boys is shed, if American stockholders incur losses. . . . if the Hebrew people place their allegiance [in] an independent Jewish state ahead of their loyalty to the United States, it will increase anti-Semitism in America."[46] The partition plan would also "subject the Jews in the Near East to persecution and massacre." He urged that the United States use its influence in the United Nations Security Council to prevent sending troops to Palestine. Should the two parties to the conflict not reach a satisfactory arrangement, "then," according to Dodge, "fighting will be confined to Palestine as a local matter instead of being allowed to become a war of international proportions."

Dr. Dodge was not against establishing Jewish cantons in a federal state as long as they remained "spiritual" and "cultural" in nature and the number of immigrants to such cantons be designated by the Arab-dominated federal government. "Thus the Arabs are willing to compromise about almost anything except immigration," he concluded. His "compromise" design to halt Jewish immigration was the one issue which, to the Zionists, was the primary *raison d'etre* of their movement.

Although he also showed concern for United States business

interests, soldiers' lives, and American patriotism, Dr. Dodge's primary goal was clearly to continue the work of the Protestant missionary movement in the Near East without placing additional obstacles in its way. If the United States were to side with the partition resolution, the American Protestant–sponsored activities and institutions would be in jeopardy all over the Arab world. The way for America to ensure continued Protestant missionary influence among the Arabs was to back down on the partition resolution. "I am sure that it is the duty of Christian people to try to produce peace and progress in the Near East by sending technical experts, doctors, missionaries and teachers, instead of sending troops," he declared. "Arab progress depends more upon American industry and philanthropy than it does on Jewish example."

The partition resolution had not included any provision for sending foreign troops to ensure its execution, but in mid-February 1948 the five-nation United Nations Palestine Commission, responsible for supervising the resolution's implementation, advised the Security Council that it could not do so "unless military forces of adequate strength are made available" to it when the responsibility for administering the partition plan would be transferred to it.[47] The missionary interests in the United States were fearful lest American troops be included among these forces.

But even barring the need for troops, the missionary groups were not prepared to accept a Jewish state willingly. In the wider perspective of their overall interests, they had too much to lose in the Arab world. Whereas in January 1948, when Dodge arrived in the United States, he characterized as "erroneous" the impression that the day for Christian missions had passed—"the missionary enterprise is faced with its greatest opportunity in history"[48]—he was less certain of this position several weeks later. "If," he wrote in March, "American Christians insist upon sending large numbers of Jewish immigrants to Palestine, it will wreck much of the work which missionaries have carried on for a century among Oriental Christians and Moslems of the southern Near East."[49]

Commenting on Dodge's analysis of the Palestine situation in the same issue of *Christianity and Crisis*, Reinhold Niebuhr stated simply: "His position accurately reflects the prevailing opinion in the missionary movement in the Middle East."[50]

The Reverend Garland Hopkins, who had recently returned from a trip to Palestine as a representative of the Methodist Board of

97

Missions, was fearful lest the partition resolution not only hurt future mission activity in the Near East, but actually jeopardize the existing status of Arab Christians in Palestine. He reasoned that if partition were to be implemented, the Arab state would eventually federate with neighboring Arab countries, to the detriment of the Christian population. "At present," he wrote, "Christians are high in the councils of the dominant group in Palestine. Should Palestine become confederated with Syria, or more likely with Transjordan, they would become an insignificant minority."[51] The Muslim majority would overwhelm them.

In Palestine proper, as throughout the Near East, "a remarkable bias toward the Arab side" was detected on the part of American and British missionaries by a correspondent to the *Christian Century*.[52] The writer felt that the bias was so strong that it did "not even recognize merits of any kind in Zionism." Arab Christians in Palestine were solidly behind Arab nationalism, which was dominated by the Muslim Mufti. "Indeed," wrote the correspondent, "it is easy to become discouraged at the way Arab Christians subordinate their faith to their politics." If anything, he noted, the Arab Christians, in typical minority fashion, protest their nationalism more outspokenly than the Muslims. The Protestant establishments in Palestine, namely the British and Americans representing their respective churches in the Holy Land, were, in the opinion of the *Christian Century* correspondent, especially concerned about the fate of the Christian Holy Places. They felt that though the actual danger to such sites was remote, their incorporation in a Jewish state would convert them "to lifeless skeletons of stones with no special significance."[53]

After November 29, 1947 the dynamics of the Palestine situation were such that neither journalistic articles nor speeches could reverse the inevitability of Jewish statehood. Once the partition resolution was voted at the United Nations, the Jews of Palestine accelerated their preparations for statehood by strengthening themselves militarily and tightening the reins of self-government which they had enjoyed under the terms of the mandate.

The Aftermath of Partition

Naturally, the *Christian Century* was disappointed and bitter once the state of Israel was proclaimed on May 14, 1948. It blamed the "New York vote" for influencing President Truman to recognize the state and prophesied a bloody war which would favor the Zionists in its opening stages.[54] However, the Committee for Justice and Peace in the Holy Land published a letter dated May 26, 1948 from the Reverend Alford Carleton, president of the American College at Aleppo, Syria, in which he felt that "the events of the past ten days have given the Arabs a sense of power of coordinated effort which far more than offsets any weaknesses or failures that have come to light in the same period."[55] Carleton saw fit to draw a parallel between the current situation and the medieval Crusades—the Crusaders being analogous to the Jews in 1948. They will "be overcome by the implacable opposition of a much greater number of persons rooted in the land and supported by public opinion in every surrounding country," he wrote. It is difficult to ascertain from his letter whether this was meant to be a prophecy, a wish, or both.

Having failed in their first round of strategy to abort the establishment of a Jewish state in Palestine, the American Protestant anti-Zionist groups shifted to a lesser objective, one which remains their policy to this day. They attempted either to emasculate the state, or to project it in such a negative and often sinister light as to cultivate strong pro-Arab sympathies among American Protestants.

In July 1948, after President Truman nominated James G. McDonald as first United States ambassador to Israel, the *Christian Century* protested his nomination as "a shocking perversion of the very idea of a diplomatic service."[56] McDonald was widely regarded as a staunch friend of the Jewish people and the Zionist cause, and it was inconceivable to the periodical that his judgment on Israel would be reliable. Wrote the weekly: "A diplomat . . . is supposed to provide his nation with impartial, dependable counsel as to what course to pursue in its international relations." McDonald was obviously incapable of doing so, the editorial implied.

In September 1948, almost two months after the second Palestinian truce had been imposed on the combatants by the United Nations Security Council and after the state of Israel began receiving large numbers of Jewish immigrants, Dr. Daniel Bliss returned to the old argument of bringing the Palestine question to the International Court for an advisory opinion, in the hope of reverting to a federal state solution of the problem.[57] It was a futile attempt on his part. There was, however, an interesting concession in Bliss's proposal. If there would be no Jewish sovereign "state," he would allow the Jewish "cantons" to bring in as many immigrants as they wished. But Bliss was much too late. The Jewish state was growing stronger with every passing day.

In early February 1950 the *Christian Century* announced that on April 1 Garland Hopkins would join the journal's staff as associate editor. This notice augured well for the pro-Arab readers of the weekly. The journal's anti-Zionist ideology was due for a shot-in-the-arm. Hopkins, with close contacts in the missionary movement and the pro-Arab wing of the executive branch of the United States government in Washington, was just the man to accomplish this. In fact, in reporting Hopkins's new position on the *Christian Century's* editorial staff, *Newsweek* wrote, he "looks like a member of the State Department."[58]

The readers of the *Christian Century* were not disappointed. The first editorial dealing with the Near East that appeared after Hopkin's appointment was a virulent denunciation of American Protestants who visit Israel under the auspices of the American Christian Palestine Committee. Apparently, such clergymen, upon returning to the United States, had not been giving the Arab side of the story sufficient weight. "What Price a Free Ride?" asked the editorial.[59] Were such American Christians prepared to sell their souls for Zionist stipends? Furthermore, the editorial complained, Israel will soon be in line for United States grants and loans, and "the American taxpayer is not going to be given a free ride no matter who else receives one. . . . Christianity demands . . . that we encompass the whole situation and act in a really unbiased manner toward the two peoples."

Such was the *Christian Century's* updated line on the Israel-Arab conflict when Hopkins joined its editorial board. It was not "fair" for Christian visitors to Israel to report about the ingathering of Jewish exiles without at the same time noting the tragedy which had befallen the Arab refugees. The fact that such refugees were located outside Israel's borders and that their Arab host governments, in most cases, refused to provide visas to Christian visitors under American Christian Palestine Committee auspices, was not cited in the editorial. Equally absent was any attempt to present a balanced discussion on the causes of the refugees' plight. Only a blanket condemnation of the Israeli position was published, in the hope of reversing American public opinion about Israel.

Hopkin's tirade against "free riders" was provocative enough to call forth a spate of angry rebuttals in the "Letters to the Editor" pages of the *Christian Century*. The Reverend David R. Hunter of Boston, later deputy executive secretary of the National Council of Churches, accused the paper of demonstrating a consistent "myopic partisanship" on the problem of Palestine. Hunter had recently visited Israel under American Christian Palestine Committee auspices, and felt that, indeed, a compromise plan such as envisaged by "the competence and impartiality of the United Nations Special Committee on Palestine" was eminently fair to both Arabs and Jews. Hunter said: "When I remember that . . . the editors of the *Christian Century* looked with scorn on the United Nations plan and contributed to its collapse, I wonder if . . . [it] should not apply the plea for impartiality to [itself]." The writer also took issue with the "impartial scrutiny of political facts" by American missionaries in the Middle East, who continue to meet with "Arab bigwigs but had never had an interview with a Jewish leader or visited a Jewish settlement."[60]

A subsequent issue of the *Christian Century* carried a large number of letters pro and con the "What Price a Free Ride?" editorial.[61] Those who supported the editorial position were interested in ascertaining the financial support given the American Christian Palestine Committee by Christian sources, a matter alluded to previously. Those who condemned the editorial called it "irresponsible" and "a new low in Christian journalism in line with Senator [Joseph] McCarthy's efforts." One clergyman asked: "Do not mission boards, government agencies, scientific and all sorts of societies send people all over the earth as a recognized procedure? . . . Is not the *Century* all the time paying people to gather information and write articles?" He concluded that what miffed the Protestant weekly was not how Protestant clergymen get to the Holy Land, but that they do not report differently than they do.

Garland Hopkins served on the *Christian Century*'s editorial board for less than two years. His distinctive anti-Israel approach was solicited in early 1952 by the American Friends of the Middle East (AFME), a new, subtly pro-Arab organization begun by Dorothy Thompson in June 1951. In announcing his indefinite leave of absence from the periodical, the editors wrote: "One of the great assets which Garland Evans Hopkins brought to the *Christian Century* when he joined its editorial staff was his unusual knowledge of the Middle East and the affairs of the Muslim world. Now, the same asset has caused the recently formed American Friends of the Middle East to ask him to become its Executive Vice President."[62]

American Friends of the Middle East

The American Friends of the Middle East (AFME) has been the most important American pro-Arab group organized since the founding of the state of Israel.[63]

On May 15, 1951 twenty-four persons met at the home of Dorothy Thompson in New York City to launch the AFME. In early November, the founders invited Garland Hopkins to plan and direct the operations of the new organization. In December the AFME was formally constituted with a five-member board of trustees, three of whom served on the executive committee: Dorothy Thompson, president; Garland Hopkins, vice-president; and Cornelius Van H. Engert, former United States minister to Afghanistan, secretary-treasurer. A fourth board member was the Reverend Edward L. R. Elson, minister of the National Presbyterian Church in Washington, D.C., and the fifth was Harold Lamb, an author from California. The organization also had a national council of sixty-three members, eighteen of whom were recognized leading Protestant clergymen. By its fourth year of operation (1954/55), its board of directors also included Rabbi Elmer Berger, executive director of the anti-Zionist American Council for Judaism, and Harold B. Minor, formerly in the State Department, later United States ambassador to Lebanon, and at the time an official of Aramco. Its national council numbered seventy-two members, including six vice chairmen, three of whom were Protestant clergymen: Edward Elson; Daniel Bliss, a Congregationalist from Greenwich, Connecticut; and Robert Anders, a Presbyterian from Lake Forest, Illinois.[64]

The AFME council was a carefully selected group of people, clerical and lay, who had one characteristic in common: they were anti-Zionist and hostile to the state of Israel. In reporting on the contribution of the AFME members to American society, Garland Hopkins stated, in the organization's third annual report: "They have helped create the climate in American public opinion which once again allows newspapers and radios to present the Middle East in its proper perspective. They have given the lie to half truths and unfactual propaganda spread by special interest groups. They have had a real part in restoring the American way in America."[65]

In the same report Hopkins came to grips with the attitude of his organization to the state of Israel. "What is the Middle East?" he asked, and replied:

> AFME believes . . . that the Middle East can best be defined as comprising those countries between the pillars of Hercules and the Straits of Macassar in which, if any injustice is perpetrated in one, a protest will be raised in the others—plus Israel. We say "plus Israel" because Israel does not today conform to the pattern sug-

gested. However, Israel is with the Middle East, and of the Middle East, and must eventually conform to the pattern, or it has no other alternative but to cease to exist.[66]

These definitive words were loud and clear. They revealed the primary purposes of AFME: to protest any political injustices in the Middle East and to compel Israel to conform to the cultural and social pattern of the Middle East. The "injustice" referred to, of course, was the establishment of the state of Israel. That state had the option of eventually becoming a predominantly Arab state, thereby conforming to the Middle Eastern pattern of states, or ceasing to exist.

But such a formula for survival or extinction would not sit well with the American public without a long-range educational strategy. Conscionable Americans were in no mood to accept unquestioningly the destruction of more Jews, having but recently been exposed to the holocaust period. Nor would over five million American Jews let them forget the holocaust so soon. A long-range plan was required to begin to soften up American opinion, to teach Americans the truth about the Near East, and eventually to bring them to the point of pressuring their government to reverse its position on the Jewish state issue. Nowhere is such a strategy outlined in AFME literature, but after studying the organization's annual reports, pamphlets, personnel, and activities, one may reasonably conclude that this was AFME's intent.[67]

AFME's range of activities was broad and impressive. In the United States the organization had departments of intercultural affairs which subsidized and promoted Arab speakers in the United States and pro-Arab American speakers in the Arab countries, of public relations, of research and publications, of student affairs, of academic placement, etc. The AFME tourist program promised "excellent liaison" with Middle East consulates, and offered a special card to visitors applying for visas to any Middle Eastern country—except Israel, of course—inviting the traveler to contact the AFME office in that country.[68] AFME's fifth annual report indicates that the organization had six full-time overseas staff members, and "representatives" in fifteen Middle East countries, but none in Israel.[69] It also reported on AFME regional offices in the United States, and local committee representatives in seventeen states and forty-three cities.[70]

When Hopkins returned from a Near Eastern trip in October

1955, that is, after the Russian arms deal with Egypt had been announced, he told the American press:

> It is high time the American public began to demand why this had happened; to discover how so few people have been able to block the best interests of the United States in that strategic area. . . . [This] requires a reappraisal of American policy in the area—a reappraisal based on America's best interests rather than one formulated as a result of pressure from any special interest groups or any foreign power. It is not enough to announce a policy of "sympathetic impartiality," as great a step forward as that was. We must now proceed to implement that policy in such a way that no question of our love of fair play, or our devotion to justice, can properly be raised.[71]

The only "special interest groups" Hopkins had in mind were the Americans, Jews and non-Jews, favorably disposed to Israel. The only "foreign power" he was talking about was the government of Israel.

Yet the AFME had to go through the motions of not being blatantly anti-Israel. It would have been difficult for the organization to pursue its ultimate objective, to persuade the United States government to reverse its position on Israel's right to exist as an independent, sovereign state, if its strategy were too aggressive. A low-key approach was more likely to succeed. In planning its first annual conference, the AFME solicited the views of twelve organizations interested in the Middle East, but only "informally contacted several Jewish agencies."[72] According to AFME, the spokesmen of these Jewish groups, "cognizant of Arab-Israeli tensions . . . requested that no invitations be extended to them."[73] While twenty-nine voluntary organizations and agencies are listed as participating in the conference, no single Jewish agency is cited by name as having been invited.[74] To remove the stigma of being anti-Israel, the AFME invited an Israeli professor of philosophy at the Hebrew University, Dr. Samuel Hugo Bergman, to be one of its six Middle Eastern visitors in the United States during 1954, and he accepted. That same year it sent the editors of the *Christian Century* and the *Commonweal* to the Middle East, as well as Rabbi Morris Lazaron, who represented the anti-Zionist *Jewish Newsletter.*

The latter two sponsorships led to embarrassing moments. Rabbi Lazaron, a rabid anti-Zionist, was not allowed to enter Jordan because he was Jewish. Later, when John Cogley, executive editor of the Catholic *Commonweal*, stated that he had returned from his trip neither as a partisan of the Arabs nor of Israel, he was sharply criticized for his remarks at the luncheon session of AFME's second conference. Said Cogley: "The role of an American should be that of a peacemaker. . . . I think [we] should bury the past as much as possible and begin with the present situation as it actually exists. . . . We have to make it clear that in our minds and in the minds of the United Nations, Israel is here to stay, and the sooner the Arabs accept that fact, the better for everybody."[75]

Cogley's remarks brought forth the protests of several delegates who approached the dais in rebuke.[76] A statement by the chairman that Mr. Cogley was free to express his opinions did not mollify the Arab participants. Representatives from Egypt, Iran, Saudi Arabia, Syria, Iraq, Jordan, and Afghanistan conferred on the floor, after which a Syrian delegate to the United Nations advised Garland Hopkins that they were withdrawing from the convention. Said Rafik Asha: "How can you invite such a man? We thought you were our friends." Embarrassed, Hopkins replied that AFME did not necessarily endorse Cogley's views. On the other hand, another member of the AFME board of directors, Harold B. Minor, while praising the "humanitarian" aspects of Cogley's speech, proclaimed that the United States was responsible for creating Israel at the expense of the Arabs.[77]

At the evening session of the conference, Hopkins prefaced his address by referring to the earlier episode. "At lunch today," he said, "some of our good friends from the Middle East were somewhat offended by certain remarks of our final speaker. Since then I have conferred with both the speaker and with these friends from the Middle East. . . . It is never our intention to give offense." He then continued:

> I am happy to say that the speaker of the occasion has instructed me to state that he had no intention at all of offending and that he offers his regrets and apologies if any offense was taken. It is my opinion that the old bugaboo of semantics caused our speaker to be misunderstood. . . . I want to reiterate that the AFME has taken no stand on the political questions he touched on. We are a non-profit and non-political organization. . . . I reiterate our deep debt of gratitude to a number of our friends from the Middle East, particularly His Excellency, the Ambassador of Jordan, for his kind helpfulness in helping us work out an otherwise difficult situation.[78]

What were the sources of AFME funds? Its fourth annual report (1954-55) indicates receipts of over $497,000, with over $433,000 coming from foundations, while the following year's report lists "foundations" as contributing eighty percent of its income. What were these "foundations"? Apparently Hopkins had sent an appeal to many foundations, but only a few responded.[79] Among the latter was the Dearborn Foundation which came into existence on February 28, 1952, shortly after AFME was founded. On June 21, 1963 Bushrod Howard, a former employee of Socony Mobil Oil told the Senate Foreign Relations Committee that the United States government had put several millions of dollars "into an anti-Israeli organization." In secret testimony before a House subcommittee, he related that in 1954 oil men were told by one of their top executives that the Dearborn Foundation was a channel for CIA funds.[80] After 1956 the annual reports of AFME omitted any reference to the Dearborn Foundation.[81]

Hopkins and other leaders of AFME probably would have preferred to plunge the organization into systematic political action. In his 1955-56 report, he raised the question of reappraising the strategy of the group: "Should we scrap our basic program and expend our energies in a frontal attack on those who were subverting America's interests in the Middle East?"[82] But apparently the bulk of AFME leadership, or the group's financial backers, cautioned against this radical approach.[83] Hopkins left AFME in 1956, and established the Continuing Committee on Muslim-Christian Cooperation, in which he emphasized his belief in cooperating with Muslims rather than in converting them to Christianity.

The activities of AFME remained essentially intact, and the organization continued to consider Israel's existence in a hostile vein.[84] Little has changed since Hopkins's time; the goals of AFME, aimed at emasculating the state of Israel, have remained the same —renegotiate the United Nations partition resolution with the Arabs; divorce Israel from the world Jewish people; stop Jewish immigration; allow the Arab refugees to return and swamp the country by their massive numbers and irreconcilable disloyalty to its Jewish government. Whatever kind of Israel would result from such operations would be wholly acceptable to AFME, and hopefully to the Arab world.

The AFME has been the most potent of American anti-Israel organizations. While its admittedly small but undisclosed membership has not been exclusively Protestant, its leadership has been predominantly so.[85] Its clergy and lay members served as a pro-Arab counterpart to the pro-Israel American Christian Palestine Committee. The latter organization, however, was far larger in recorded supporters and was tied to, and supported by, an indigenous American Jewish citizenry deeply concerned with Israel's security and future. The AFME has had no grass-roots American support, has relied almost exclusively on contributions from vague sources; and above all it began its operations too late, after the state of Israel had begun to consolidate itself as a sovereign entity. AFME has continued to remain a thorn in the public relations image of Israel, but thorns alone cannot destroy sovereignty.

7

The Internationalization of
Jerusalem

FOLLOWING THE ESTABLISHMENT OF THE STATE OF
Israel, two principal subjects occupied the interest of American Protestantism: the internationalization of Jerusalem and the Arab refugee problem. This chapter will deal with attempts to internationalize Jerusalem after the partition of Palestine in 1947. In the following chapter the problem of Arab refugees will be discussed.

Attempts by the United Nations to Reach a Solution

The partition resolution adopted by the United Nations General Assembly on November 29, 1947 called for an international regime for Jerusalem. It read:

> The city of Jerusalem shall be established as a *corpus separatum* under a special international regime and shall be administered by the United Nations. The Trusteeship Council shall be designated to discharge the responsibilities of the Administering Authority on behalf of the United Nations.[1]

The Trusteeship Council prepared a draft statute for the government of the city during its second session, January to March 1948, but because of lack of agreement among council members, and the continued Arab opposition to the basic partition resolution, the council decided, on March 10, 1948 to postpone a formal vote.[2] On April 21, the council voted to refer the question of the statute to the second special session of the General Assembly which, at the request of the Security Council, had convened on April 16 to "consider further the question of the future government of Palestine."[3]

No new instructions were issued to the Trusteeship Council by the General Assembly during its second special session in April and May 1948. Instead, the assembly appointed a neutral special municipal commissioner, acceptable to both Arabs and Jews, to coordinate the municipal functions hitherto performed by Jerusalem's civil authorities after the British evacuation of the city.[4] On May 22, Harold Evans of the Society of Friends left New York on his way to Jerusalem, but because of the chaotic military and political situation there, he did not reach the city nor assume his office. The Secretary General of the United Nations subsequently reported to the third session of the General Assembly: "The Arab authorities were unwilling to cooperate under existing conditions with any Jerusalem Commissioner appointed by the United Nations, while the Jewish authorities had declared their readiness to cooperate with him."[5]

The General Assembly's second special session did not reach agreement on the more permanent provisions for the administration of Jerusalem. A joint United States-French proposal for placing the city under a United Nations Commissioner responsible to the Trusteeship Council failed to receive the necessary two-thirds majority vote.[6] The General Assembly's main achievement at its second special session was the creation of the position of a United Nations mediator, who was empowered, among other things, to "assure the protection of the Holy Places, religious buildings and sites in Palestine."[7]

The resolution on the Palestine question with respect to Jerusalem, which was adopted by the General Assembly on December 11, 1948 during its third session, neither referred to the November 1947 resolution nor to the Jerusalem statute considered by the Trusteeship Council during 1948. It merely stated that Jerusalem was to be accorded "special and separate treatment from the rest of Palestine," and placed under "effective United Nations control."[8] A United Nations Palestine Conciliation Commission, created by this resolution to take over many of the mediator's responsibilities,[9] was instructed to present to the fourth regular session of the General Assembly detailed proposals for a permanent international regime for the Jerusalem area, which would provide for "the maximum local autonomy for distinctive groups consistent with the special international status of the Jerusalem area." Accordingly, the Palestine Conciliation Commission[10] submitted to the Fourth General Assembly (1949) a plan whereby the Jerusalem area would consist of the old and new sections of the city, and certain surrounding towns, the most southerly being Bethlehem.[11]

When the General Assembly reconvened in the winter of 1949, and considered the recommendations of the Palestine Conciliation Commission, both Jordan and Israel opposed them. Jordan was in full control of the area encompassing the old city of Jerusalem and Bethlehem, which contained the major Holy Places, and resented a United Nations desire to infringe upon its sovereignty. Israel was in full control of the new city of Jerusalem which had no major Holy Places, but which did contain a population of 100,000 Jews. It had already begun moving its central government offices there, after Israel's Parliament had recognized Jerusalem as the capital of the state of Israel. The General Assembly rejected the specific recommendations of the conciliation commission, but reiterated its support on December 9, 1949 of an internationalized territory of Jerusalem. (The vote was 38 to 14, with 7 abstentions.) It relieved the conciliation commission of further consideration of this subject. Then the General Assembly again asked the Trusteeship Council to return a statute for the projected internationalized city.[12]

The Trusteeship Council met during December 1949 and January 1950. It asked Israel to revoke the measures taken to move its government offices to Jerusalem.[13] At its sixth session, on January 19, 1950, the Trusteeship Council heard a report from its president, the French representative, Roger Garreau, who had been asked to prepare a draft statute for its consideration.[14] The report again upheld the concept of a *corpus separatum* for Jerusalem, but added that the area be declared an economic free zone, and that it be divided into three sectors—Arab, Israeli, and an international city. The international sector would incorporate the Holy Places and be administered by a United Nations governor, but would also include a section of the new city to balance that part of the old city incorporated therein.

The Trusteeship Council invited reactions to Garreau's recommendations from interested parties, including Israel, Jordan, and various church groups. Jordan reacted bluntly: it would not participate in any discussions relating to the internationalization of Jerusalem. Israel advised the council that it too was against the territorial internationalization of the city, but instead favored the administration of the Holy Places in Jerusalem by the United Nations.

The American Christian Palestine Committee sided with the

Israeli viewpoint, while the Commission of Churches on International-
al Affairs, jointly established by the World Council of Churches and
the International Missionary Council, sent the Trusteeship Council
a copy of the memorandum it had submitted the previous May to
the Palestine Conciliation Commission. In this memo, the Commission of Churches on International Affairs had stressed the need to
protect human rights and freedoms, the right of access to the Holy
Places, and the obligation of Israel and Jordan to return church and
mission properties to their owners.[15]

It became clear that the proposed internationalization of Jerusalem was not going to take place because the two states controlling sections of the city were not prepared to cooperate in implementing such a design. Still, the pressure of the governments of the
Catholic states at the United Nations, in addition to the urging of
the Arab states (excluding Jordan) and the Soviet bloc, was strong
enough for the Trusteeship Council to approve a *corpus separatum*
statute for Jerusalem on April 4, 1950.[16] In June, however, the council's president reported that Jordan did not even reply to his invitation to discuss the statute, and he felt it would be inappropriate to
discuss it only with Israel. On June 14, 1950, the Trusteeship Council dispatched a special report to the General Assembly, advising it of
the frustrations encountered.[17]

The General Assembly debated the matter in December 1950.
At its Ad Hoc Political Committee, all states seemed to recognize
the need to reconsider the subject, but the Catholic bloc and its supporters were still intent on trying to salvage the principle of territorial internationalization. A Belgian resolution calling for further
study of the Jerusalem question was passed at the Ad Hoc Political
Committee by a simple majority, but when it was voted on at the
General Assembly plenum, it did not receive the required two-
thirds majority.[18] For all intents and purposes, the status of Jerusalem
remained frozen, with Israel and Jordan controlling their respective
sectors, until it was changed as a result of the 1967 Six Day War.

The Vatican Bogey

What were the attitudes of American Protestants with regard
to the internationalization of Jerusalem?

One can detect several elements in Protestant policy. One element reflected a fear of undue Catholic and specifically Vatican influence in Jerusalem. This apprehension was expressed by the *Christian Century*, a periodical as vehemently anti-Papal as it was anti-Zionist. Even in September 1947, before the United Nations voted to partition Palestine into Arab and Jewish states, the journal reacted sharply to a rumor that the Vatican hoped to receive a mandate over Jerusalem and the Holy Places. It termed the rumor "a trial balloon that had better be pulled down."[19] It called the Palestine situation "forbidding enough without making it still worse by injecting this proposal to turn Jerusalem and Bethlehem over to the Pope." It expressed amazement that the "opportunists in the Vatican . . . should have had the nerve to hint at such a proposal."

A month after the state of Israel was proclaimed, the *Christian Century* reacted sharply to an article in the Vatican paper, *L'Osservatore Romano*, which had minimized the Jewish and Muslim claims to the Holy Land and Holy Places, while stressing the pre-eminent significance of the sites to Christians. The Protestant weekly reasoned:

> If Palestine's Holy Places are such for Christians only, and if the Roman church, as it asserts, is the only true Christian body, can this mean that the Vatican is starting to lay the groundwork for a claim to administer the United Nations reserved portion [Jerusalem and Bethlehem] which are to be in neither Arab nor Jewish territory?[20]

The potent political influence of the Vatican on the deliberations of the United Nations was described by the Protestant periodical when, with some discernible pleasure, it informed its readers of Israel's failure to be accepted to the United Nations on its first application, despite the support of the Soviet Union and the United States. The paper correctly attributed Israel's inability to muster a two-thirds majority of United Nations members to Vatican pressures on predominantly Catholic states. Such Vatican power, declared the periodical, further illustrating its usual anti-Catholic bias, demonstrated beyond doubt the degree to which the Roman church was to be regarded as a political force "even more than a religious force."[21] In a single editorial, the paper was able to attack both the Israelis and the Vatican.[22]

The *Christian Century*'s antagonism toward the Catholic church was so strong that it stated categorically that "most of the Christian religious shrines in the Holy Land were of doubtful histori-

city."[23] The periodical deliberately sought to link the alleged deceptive historicity of the shrines with their being controlled by Catholic
interests. In 1950 when first the Franciscans[24] and later the Vatican[25]
proposed that a new basilica of the Holy Sepulchre be built in Jerusalem, with seven separate churches having access to the "traditional
but unauthenticated Tomb of Jesus," the Protestant periodical fought
such a proposal. Ostensibly, the plan aimed to replace the twenty-
two over-crowded chapels inside the Holy Sepulchre by having the
Catholic, Greek Orthodox, Armenian, Copt, Syrian and Abyssinian
denominations, along with a Protestant denomination—the Vatican
invitation went to the Lutherans and Anglicans—build a new compound of churches surrounding the Church of the Holy Sepulchre
and share in its control.

The *Christian Century* objected to the proposal for two main
reasons. First, it would reaffirm the Roman Catholic claim to "a pre-
eminent position in the sanctuary."[26] Second, it would give credence
to the historicity of the shrine.[27] The periodical expressed the hope
that the Lutherans and Anglicans would reject the proposal because, of all the doubtful historical sites in the Holy Land, "none is
more probably spurious than the Church of the Holy Sepulchre. Protestants and Anglicans should have no part in palming off dubious
historical monuments on credulous pilgrims."[28]

The Quest for Protestant Status

The problem which Jerusalem posed for Protestantism after the
partition of Palestine was not only religious—whether the shrines were
authentic and were thereby deserving of a modern religious mystique
—but political as well. Without spelling out their fundamental griev-
ance in detail, Protestants were both resentful and envious of the
status of other branches of Christendom in the Holy Land, while they
were at best tolerated by them and at worst ignored. The division of
ecclesiastical political power over the Christian Holy Places in Palestine, which established a base both for prestige and for profit, had
been determined by the Sultan's firman of 1757, and had been reaffirmed in 1852.[29]

Protestants were excluded from the long and fierce struggle
between the Catholics and the Greek Orthodox over control of the
Holy Places. All they could do in relation to the shrines was to visit

them as individuals, but they could not worship in them as a Christian denomination. Their own worship was conducted in newly established churches built by their respective denominations.

Though American Presbyterians and Congregationalists were among the first Protestant missionaries in the Near East, they did not become a significant presence in Jerusalem proper. The British Anglicans and German Lutherans preempted them there.[30] In fact, the Anglicans began to concern themselves with the conversion of Jerusalem's Jews to Christianity shortly after the American missionaries began their work in Turkey and Syria.

Protestant mission work among the Jews of Palestine first began in the 1820s by the Anglican-affiliated London Society for Promotion of Christianity among the Jews. This British group, founded in 1809, and originally concerned only with proselytizing London Jews, soon became an advocate of Protestant Zionism.[31] Affected by the millennarian spirit of the time, it wished to accelerate the Second Coming by helping to fulfill the Adventist prerequisite of having Jews not only restored to the Holy Land, but of being converted to Christianity therein. The London Society first dispatched a medical missionary and subsequently a Danish minister, who laid the foundations of a Protestant church in Jerusalem. Meanwhile, German and Swiss missionaries were also taking an interest in evangelism among the Jews and Muslims of Palestine.

The principal aim of American Protestant missions was far less dramatic. It had no bearing upon millennial doctrines. Their purpose was to convert masses of Muslims to Christianity. The Jews were merely a by-product of this strategy. The American missions, therefore, concentrated their efforts in Turkey and Syria, rather than in sparsely populated Palestine. As expressed by a leading American missionary of the time: "Taken as a whole, the Palestinian Jews hardly concern our present work, for they form no organic part of the native inhabitants of Turkey."[32]

The various activities conducted by European Protestant church groups in the Holy Land had nothing to do specifically with the Holy Places. This fact may have led the European Protestants to play down the importance of the Holy Places when the subject of Jerusalem's internationalization was under discussion in 1948. It was primarily the Catholic countries that favored internationalization of the city of Jerusalem in order to give the Holy Places a viable economic and political hinterland.

When American Protestant missionary groups joined the Catholics in pursuing this strategy, it was not because they were pro-Catholic, but because they opposed Jewish nationalism. A Jewish Jerusalem would represent yet another manifestation of viable Jewish peoplehood as well as another setback for the Protestant policy of converting Arab Muslims to Protestantism. The American missionaries clearly resented placing any part of Jerusalem under Israeli jurisdiction, but hardly protested against Jordan's occupation of the old city and its Christian shrines. (When the city was reunited under Israeli rule in 1967, the Protestants once again protested Israel's role, as we shall see later.)

From this perspective, one can more readily appreciate the 1948/49 debate within American Protestantism surrounding the subject of Jerusalem's internationalization. The question was whether to side with those who wished internationalization of the Holy Places only or of the whole city of Jerusalem including both the old Jordanian sector and the new Jewish sector. That is, some American Protestants were interested only in the Holy Places themselves, all of which were in the old city and controlled by Jordan. Others wished to internationalize the one-hundred square-mile *corpus separatum* territory which also included the new city of Jerusalem, although the new city contained no major Holy Places at all but had an overwhelmingly Jewish population. According to the latter design, if American Protestantism could not share in the control over the Holy Places, it might be able to compensate for its previous weakness by acquiring a new voice in the affairs of a larger area which also incorporated the Holy Places. By internationalizing the whole city of Jerusalem American Protestantism could make up for losing the partition fight against Israel, by denying Israel control over new Jerusalem.

For the Catholics, the *corpus separatum* status for Jerusalem was ideal. First, it strengthened the Vatican's influence in the area. Secondly, it offset the pre-eminence of the Greek Orthodox who could, at best, count on the support of Greece and possibly of Russia, while the many Catholic states at the United Nations would have backed the policies of Rome. During the United Nations debate it became clear that these Catholic states were indeed attuned to the Vatican's signals and fought diligently for territorial internationalization of the area.

The debate on the internationalization of Jerusalem in American Protestant circles, on the other hand, did not stir European Protestantism. Many American Protestant denominations and the Federal Council of Churches supported some form of "internationalization" without, however, understanding the nature of Jerusalem's inner problems. European Protestant groups were far more sophisticated about the problems of the Holy Land and Jerusalem, having had many more years of experience in the country than did the Americans. They were not prepared to lend active support to the political goals of the Vatican. Nor did their guilt-ridden conscience towards the Jewish survivors of the European holocaust allow them to deny Israel its claim over the overwhelmingly Jewish new city of Jerusalem. Moreover as a result of having been excluded from even a shared control of the Holy Places themselves, European Protestantism developed a sentimental reverence for the Holy Land, rather than for any particular holy shrines or even cities. As long as Protestants could worship in the country in freedom, European Protestant denominations were not overly concerned about achieving political control over any portions of the Holy Land.

These reasons motivated the European Protestant states at the United Nations to accept the reality of Jerusalem's political division, rather than to impose internationalization of the city on Jordan and Israel. It is a matter of speculation whether this attitude would have prevailed had Jordan not adamantly rejected any form of internationalization. Great Britain, which at the time enjoyed political influence over Jordan, had to soften its general anti-Israel policy in order not to jeopardize Jordan's position. The British reasoned that if the new city of Jerusalem were not internationalized, the old city would be spared a similar fate. The Protestant Scandinavian countries were, from the start, not unsympathetic to Israel's policy of internationalization of the Holy Places rather than internationalization of the city.

The United States government was influenced in its policy by several factors. On the one hand it successfully withstood the pressures of official American Protestant groups which, because of the missionary influences, would have preferred a *corpus separatum* for the entire Jerusalem area. The United States government was equally pressured by both the Zionist movement in the United States, which supported Israel's policy on the question of Jerusalem, and non-official American Christian groups supportive of the Zionist position, like the American Christian Palestine Committee. Finally, the

United States was undoubtedly ambivalent about the whole subject of internationalization, for its implementation, unquestionably, would have brought greater Soviet influence to bear on the Near East.

Protestants for Internationalization of the City of Jerusalem

The *Christian Century*, of course, sided with the American Protestant establishment's policy of internationalization of the city of Jerusalem. In November 1949, while admitting that "good men" are divided on the subject, it noted the weight of opinion among "Christians in Palestine, missionaries there, teachers in mission institutions throughout the Near and Middle East, and the mission boards" to be predominantly in favor of territorial internationalization.[33] For that reason, "our own partisanship" favored that policy, the periodical admitted.

American Protestant policy followed the recommendations of the United Nations Palestine Conciliation Commission. It was pleased that all of Jerusalem, including the new sector of the city, would come under international political control. Protestants took this position despite the fact that not a single religious Holy Place defined in the 1757 Ottoman *firman* was located in the new city. In April 1948 before the state of Israel was proclaimed, the president of the Federal Council of Churches, Charles P. Taft, wrote to the United States representative on the United Nations Security Council, Warren Austin, urging that measures be taken to insure the protection of Jerusalem as "a holy city sacred around the world to those of all three faiths and containing places whose destruction we cannot accept as permissible."[34] Taft urged further that the city be put under a "trust" status and that its character be declared an "open city." He also asked that the United Nations provide necessary police forces to carry out this action. The executive committee of the Federal Council of Churches subsequently approved this communication.

In September 1949 the Foreign Missions Conference of North America, through its Committee of Reference and Counsel, heartily endorsed the plan of the United Nations Palestine Conciliation Commission.[35] In October 1949 the House of Bishops of the Protestant Episcopal Church at its convention at San Francisco advocated the internationalization of Jerusalem and its environs "as the nearest approach to a just recognition of the claims of Moslem, Jew and Christian." The Episcopalian House of Deputies concurred in the resolution.[36] Similarly, in April 1949 the Near East Christian Council, a constituent member of the International Missionary Council, a body uniting Protestant missions in the Near East, called for placing "the greater Jerusalem area" under United Nations administration.[37] In a subsequent supplementary statement to the International Missionary Council, the Near East Christian Council said: "Christians should be encouraged not to yield to the natural and widespread desire to emigrate to more prosperous and peaceable lands. We do not wish to see the Holy Land abandoned to Jews and Muslims."[38]

Finally, in May 1949 the Commission of the Churches on International Affairs (CCIA), jointly established by the World Council of Churches and the International Missionary Council, submitted a memorandum to the Palestine Conciliation Commission meeting at Lausanne.[39] In the first part of the document the CCIA, clearly repeating the missionary line, insisted that explicit safeguards be incorporated to ensure the "freedom to extend one's faith by processes of persuasion and the appeal to reason and conscience."[40] The second part of the memorandum stated that "our primary concern is with people, not places. . . . Nevertheless we cannot ignore buildings and sites which are monuments of sacred events in the past."[41] The document proceeded to express the "strong conviction" that "artificial separation of historic religious sites from the community in which they are located . . . would be an inadequate method of exercising international responsibility."

The last point was the most telling of the Protestant arguments. It claimed that the holy shrines required an internationalized hinterland large enough to make them economically "viable" rather than subjecting them to the jurisdiction of any one state. In effect, the logic of the argument was subtly anti-Israel. The geographical area around the Holy Places in the old city of Jerusalem was largely populated by Arabs, whether under the control of Jordan or of an international body. But the old city of Jerusalem, picturesque and reverential as it may be, could surely benefit from the modern supportive facilities of the new city. In the latter part of the twentieth century, one could reasonably doubt whether the old city could stand by itself without the economic assistance and social influence of the large, modern community nearby. Even during the British mandate, it was the new city which was the dynamic hub of central governmental operations. To rely only on the immediate environment of the holy shines in the old city for the latter's viability was not at all a certain prospect.

An even more important reason impelled American Protestants to favor a territorially internationalized Jerusalem including the new city. While not expressed in any explicit statement, it seems obvious that the religious notion of "Jerusalem" implies an integrated whole which cannot be broken down into separate geographic sectors. Protestants in particular did not welcome the prevailing divisive practice of Christian denominational rights and restrictions in the Holy Places, and were disenchanted with the pettiness and bickering which surrounded the prevailing governance of the shrines. As described by one observer:

> Arguments as to which portion of which door was assigned to each sect, who should clean which steps and which door, and the like, have at times led to pitched battles between clerics. As recently as Easter 1967, there was a near riot at the Church of the Holy Sepulchre. Several people were injured by flying stones, some thrown by the Patriarchs themselves. It was because the quarreling between the sects in this church was so fierce that the Turks always stationed a Muslim doorkeeper there to preserve order.[42]

Since American Protestants did not benefit from the singular religious status quo affecting Jerusalem, they had little appreciation for the several religious and ethnic quarters—Armenian, Jewish, Muslim, Christian—which divided the old city. They were unhappy with its hygienic standards and the growing commercialization of its religious sites. If Jerusalem was to remain a significant concept in modern Protestant thought, it had to incorporate the modern city as well. Only such an integrated, internationalized Jerusalem could enjoy the religious support of modern-day Protestants.

Protestants for Internationalization of the Holy Places

Not all American Protestant groups accepted a policy of territorial internationalization of Jerusalem. Even the members of the Commission of Churches on International Affairs (CCIA) were not in unanimous accord. When pressured heavily by its missionary component at its July 1949 meeting in England, the CCIA withstood a drive to send its own fact-finding commission to Palestine "to clarify our duty and responsibility as Christians" with respect to the protection of the Holy Places (as well as the Arab refugee problem and the safeguarding of human rights). Reporting to the International Missionary Council meeting of September 30, 1949, the executive secretary of the council told the group that the CCIA felt that such a fact-finding committee "would not add substantially" to the information already available to church leaders.[43] It would also seem evident from the oblique references to territorial internationalization in the CCIA's memo to the United Nations Conciliation Commission (rather than a forthright advocacy of such a policy), that official Protestantism had not clearly defined its position on the question.

The American Christian Palestine Committee labored under no such uncertainties. Initially it advocated that the new city of Jerusalem be annexed to Israel, while the old city and Bethlehem "which occupy a particularly revered place in the hearts of millions all over the world" should be placed under the direct supervision of the same international body entrusted with safeguarding the Holy Places.[44] Thus, the ACPC supported the notion of a *corpus separatum* for Jerusalem. But it differed from most spokesmen for American Protestantism on whether this new internationalized area should contain new Jerusalem as well. Subsequently, after the armistice was signed between Jordan and Israel in April 1949, it became an advocate of internationalization of the Holy Places alone.

Following publication in October 1949 of the United Nations Palestine Conciliation Commission's proposals to internationalize the entire Jerusalem area, ninety leading members of the American Christian Palestine Committee, mostly Protestants, appealed to President Truman not to support such a plan.[45] The letter stated that "the peace of Zion, a concept so sacred to Christian tradition, cannot be erected upon the discontent and resentment of civilian populations who are averse to being governed by an international regime, and are desirous of union with the national entities to which they, as Israelis and Arabs, rightfully belong." The statement advocated a special United Nations commission to guarantee free access to the Holy Places in the Jerusalem area, but recommended that the political administration of the two sectors of the area, Arab and Israeli, should rest with the national states of which they are a part. The letter specifically recognized the new city of Jerusalem as the "natural and historic capital" of the state of Israel and stressed that "the universal interest in Jerusalem, and the fulfillment of the national aspirations of the people of Israel are in no way incompatible."

In November 1949, as the General Assembly was about to debate the recommendations of the Palestine Conciliation Commission, fifteen distinguished Americans, most of them Protestant churchmen, submitted to the General Assembly of the United Nations a proposal for an international "curatorship" for the Holy Places in Palestine.[46] Of the fifteen signatories, only five names, including that of Reinhold Niebuhr, had appeared on the earlier October letter to President Truman.

The curatorship proposal criticized the Palestine Conciliation Commission's plan because it would create a new class of 130,000 "displaced persons" living in the Jerusalem area, 100,000 Jews in new Jerusalem, 30,000 Arabs in old Jerusalem and environs. The criticism hovered on ridicule, stressing that the commission's scheme was to protect and assure free access to ten Holy Places (seven Christian, one. Muslim, and two Jewish) "all in territory held by the Arabs." The conciliation commission's plan would rob both local Arabs and Jews of citizenship in their respective states, and would require a sizeable United Nations military and administrative presence. Instead, the curatorship proposal for the Holy Places throughout Palestine, including those in the state of Israel, would be implemented by a United Nations commission composed of representatives of the Catholic, Protestant, Jewish, Greek Orthodox, and Moslem faiths. This commission would have the power to employ guards and would be responsible to the Security Council.

It is difficult to assess the impact of this forty-six page analysis of the Palestine Conciliation Commission's recommendations. As has already been noted, the General Assembly rejected the commission's recommendations, but under heavy Vatican pressure requested the Trusteeship Council to come up with a new plan for the territorial internationalization of Jerusalem.

The Catholic states, the Arab states (except Jordan), the Soviet bloc, and the American Protestant missionary forces were making a last ditch effort to establish the hundred square-mile internationalized Jerusalem plan. The missionaries were pressing the CCIA for a more forthright stand on territorial internationalization, but counter pressures in official Protestant circles largely neutralized the CCIA on this question. On December 16, 1949 Reinhold Niebuhr wrote to the Reverend Frederick Nolde, director of the Commission of Churches on International Affairs: "If the Protestant Church is disposed in any way to support anything like the Vatican plan, I will feel bound to break ranks and try to organize a group to oppose it."[47] Niebuhr objected to the plan on two grounds: the inequity to the populace of Jerusalem, both Jews and Arabs, who opposed it; and the hazard of Russian involvement in an international regime controlling Jerusalem.[48]

On Janury 19, 1950 a group of six Protestant leaders who occupied leading positions in several American denominations, reported on a fact-finding trip to Jerusalem which was held under the auspices of the American Christian Palestine Committee.[49] The report supported internationalization of the Holy Places with no international territorial sovereignty over the area as a whole. It recommended that a supervising international commission be given guarantees by both Jordan and Israel assuring the freedom and sanctity of the Holy Places within their territories. "This is all that the Christian world has a right to require of two sovereign states." The statement was particularly critical of all United Nations plans calling for the internationalization of Jerusalem, because they were drafted without regard to the wishes of its citizens, "but rather from the political considerations of the various member governments of the United Nations and by outside interests." The obvious "outside interests" were the Vatican and the Protestant missionaries.

The Protestant missionaries were actively involved in trying to influence American Protestant policy through the Federal Council of Churches, and international Protestant policy through the CCIA. One member of the fact-finding group, Samuel Guy Inman, who was also a member of the Federal Council of Churches Commission of Justice and Goodwill, was therefore specifically requested by the commission's secretary, the Reverend Walter Van Kirk, to state publicly that his views as reflected in the fact-finding group's report were strictly his own.[50] Van Kirk stressed that the Federal Council of Churches had no connection with the investigating group and did not support any specific plan for the internationalization of Jerusalem.[51]

Though not having any specific plan to offer, the National Council of Churches of Christ, which succeeded the Federal Council of Churches, reminded the United States delegation to the United Nations on September 17, 1953 that it was still in favor of internationalization. The National Council of Churches intimated that "the great majority of the people of our churches would like to see this recommendation put into effect."[52] It was clear that the missionary elements represented on the council were exerting persistent pressure to keep the issue of internationalization alive, even after the United Nations itself had abandoned it at the end of 1952.[53]

The Jerusalem question did not appear on the United Nations agenda for the next fifteen years. No government expressed concern about the internationalization of the city, nor for the status of its Holy Places. After 1953, except in pro forma allusions, neither did representatives of any of the major American Protestant groups seriously attempt to raise this question.

Status of Jerusalem: Post–1967

This passive acceptance of the political status quo in Jerusalem was upset in 1967 by the Six-Day War between Israel and her Arab neighbors. The Israelis scored a major victory over the Egyptians who were menacing their country from Gaza, the Sinai Peninsula, and the Straits of Tiran at the mouth of the Red Sea. When Jordan joined its Egyptian ally, Israel felt no compunction about eliminating Jordanian control of the old city of Jerusalem, and indeed over the entire west bank of the Jordan River.

Israel's opponents in the United Nations reacted to these events in two ways. First, they sought to secure the condemnation of Israel as an aggressor. In this they failed to win the necessary United Nations General Assembly approval.[54] Secondly, they sought to invalidate Israeli measures affecting the control of the entire city of Jerusalem. In this, they were successful, at least by resolution.

On July 4, 1967, the General Assembly adopted a Pakistan proposal which considered Israeli measures vis-à-vis Jerusalem to be invalid and called on Israel to rescind them.[55] Ten days later the General Assembly adopted another resolution on the same subject, in which it deplored Israel's failure to implement the resolution of July 4.

What did Israel do to the old city of Jerusalem when her forces drove out the Jordanians? It deliberately avoided the term "annexation" and instead applied the term "reunification." On July 27, 1967 the Israeli Parliament adopted three specific measures, which extended the operation of Israeli law, jurisdiction, and administration to the eastern part of Jerusalem (the old city), empowered the Minister of the Interior to enlarge the boundaries of any municipality (i.e., new Jerusalem) by the inclusion of an area designated under the first measure, and enacted severe penalties for anyone desecrating a Holy Place or violating the freedom of access thereto.[56]

It is unlikely that the status of Jerusalem will be permanently determined and universally approved until a peace agreement has been reached between Israel and her Arab neighbors. But the actions of the United Nations following the 1967 war do not seem to indicate that even Israel's opponents are apt to press for internationalization of the entire city. The resolution of July 4 was directed solely against Israeli administrative measures aimed at reunifying the city. In effect, it sought either to restore the status quo ante, with Jordan continuing to rule old Jerusalem, or to pave the way for the internationalization of the Holy Places previously controlled by Jordan. Both alternatives fell short of suggesting territorial internationalization of the whole city of Jerusalem, including new Jerusalem.

While the United Nations had impliedly given up on the subject of territorial internationalization, American Protestantism, apparently under the persistent goading of its missionary components, was still holding out for some sort of "international presence" in Jerusalem. At the executive committee meeting of the National Council of Churches of Christ on July 7, 1967 an attempt to adopt an "even-handed" resolution affecting both Israelis and Arabs was manifestly unsuccessful. The statement insidiously blamed Israel for the Arab refugee problem and took Israel to task for its alleged expansionist policies, including its conquest of old Jerusalem.[57] While stating that Israel's existence as a state was no longer subject to debate—twenty years and three wars after it was established—and that it should be recognized as a state by its opponents, the resolution refused to approve "Israel's unilateral annexation of the Jordanian portions of Jerusalem. This historic city is sacred not only to Judaism but also to Christianity and Islam." As a substitute for Israeli control of the city the statement supported "an international presence in the heretofore divided city of Jerusalem which will preserve the peace and integrity of the city, foster the welfare of its inhabitants, and protect its holy shrines with full rights of access to all." Apparently, the National Council of Churches of Christ was still in quest of an unspecified international aegis for all of Jerusalem, including the new city.[58]

This unrealistic policy was not enthusiastically subscribed to by all Protestant groups. On July 12 a small group of notable American Protestant theologians issued a statement which said, among other things: "For Christians to acknowledge the necessity of Judaism is to acknowledge that Judaism pre-supposes inextricable ties with the Land of Israel and the City of David, without which Judaism cannot be truly itself. Theologically, it is this dimension to the religion of Judaism which leads us to support the reunification of the city of Jerusalem."[59]

Among the signers of this statement was Kirster Stendahl, professor of biblical studies at Harvard Divinity School, who subsequently elaborated his position at a scholarly colloquium.[60] There, he asserted that Jerusalem was viewed differently in Judaism, in Islam, and in Christianity. To the latter two religions, the city was one of holy sites, and their concern, rightfully, was to assure access to these shrines. To Judaism, however, with the exception of the Wailing Wall—which, according to Stendahl, "came to take on much of the . . . character [of a holy site] partly under influence of the Christian example"—the focal points of reverence were not sites but the city itself, "not what happened *in* Jerusalem, but *to* Jerusalem." Stendahl felt that for Christians to overlook this basic difference was tantamount to practicing "another form of a patronizing *interpretatio christina.*" He concluded his argument by suggesting that it "would be more than natural," even "preferable," for Christians to worship in a united Jerusalem, de facto controlled by Jews, "since that it is how it was when it all happened." The drama of Jesus was enacted under similar circumstances, though the country and the city were de jure under Roman rule.

Opposition to resurrecting the territorial internationalization solution to the Jerusalem question was not confined to leading American Protestants. Immediately after hostilities had subsided in June 1967, leaders of the World Council of Churches expressed a decided coolness to such a scheme.[61] It is difficult to assess the full motivation for this attitude, but it would appear that a primary reason was to blunt the Vatican's aggressive campaign to achieve such a result. A survey of Protestant and Greek Orthodox clerical leaders by correspondents of the *New York Times* in different parts of the world disclosed no opposition to the internationalization idea in principle, but conveyed a general belief that it was inappropriate for religious groups to back any specific political plan. The *Times* reported: "Most agreed with Reverend Eugene Carson Blake, general secretary of the World Council of Churches. He said in Geneva that the status of the city [of Jerusalem] and its Holy Places was primarily a political matter, and that religious interests could only be raised once there is a political agreement."[62] The newspaper quoted Blake as favoring a supervisory committee of all the religious groups with the purpose of "enhancing the spiritual value of the Holy Places." It later reported him as saying that the World Council of Churches assigned the question of Jerusalem's future status "a lower priority" than the basic problem of "a long range peace."[63]

It seemed clear from the attitude of those Protestants who were prepared to adjust themselves to the new status quo that freedom of access to the Holy Places and their protection under Israeli aegis was at least as tolerable as having them incorporated in a *corpus separatum* largely influenced by the Vatican, if not by the Kremlin.

Conversely, those Christian bodies, Protestant or Catholic, who continued to pursue a plan of territorial internationalization, had much more in mind than merely the sanctity of the Holy Places. They were clearly concerned with a base of political influence, whether for purposes of prestige, economic gain, or missionary activity. They shared one purpose: to blunt Israel's sovereignty over the Holy City.

8

The Refugee Problem

AS MUCH AS AMERICAN PROTESTANTISM HAS BEEN
exercised by the topic of the fate of Jerusalem since the establishment of the state of Israel, it has been more seized by the problem of
the Arab refugees. Two principal motifs are discernible in Protestant
concern for the refugees: the injustice involved in prohibiting the
Arabs to return to present-day Israel and the human misery which the
refugees suffer. It has been assumed that American Protestants have
been united in genuine sympathy for the refugees' plight and that
they have been split only on the question of whether justice meant
that the refugees should be returned to Israel or integrated into the
adjacent countries to which they had fled. The record of the Protestant establishment, however, does not even support the assumption
that it was primarily concerned with the refugees' suffering.

The Arabs' Flight from Palestine

Pro-Israeli American Protestants insisted that the great bulk
of the Arab refugees had left their homes in 1948 at the insistence of
Arab leaders. The Reverend Karl Baehr, representing the American
Christian Palestine Committee, listed the reasons for the refugees'
flight given to him by Msgr. George Hakim, archbishop of the Greek
Catholic Church in Palestine.[1] The Melkite clergyman—"an Arab
and a former supporter of the Mufti . . . [who] cannot be accused of
being 'pro-Jewish' "—reportedly cited to Baehr four factors which
precipitated the flight of the Arabs:
1. Palestine had been abandoned by the more moderate local
Arab leaders during the early stages of the conflict. They feared,
Msgr. Hakim suggested, that if they stayed, they would be sub-

jected to the same kind of harassment and intimidation perpetrated during the 1936-39 riots by extremist Arab groups. They decided instead to lock their homes and to go to Lebanon or to other countries.

2. The pending withdrawal of the British from the Haifa area caused panic among the Arabs. Over 80,000 Arabs fled the city while the British were still in control, despite the fact that representatives of the Jewish community guaranteed their safety and civic rights. Many Arabs fled by sea to Lebanon after their local leaders abandoned them, and the British authorities could no longer assure protection to those who remained.

3. The Arab radio stations in the neighboring countries urged repeatedly that Arabs leave the battle areas. The broadcasts promised that after the Arab armies had overwhelmed the Jews, the refugees would return to retrieve their property and absorb captured Jewish property as well.

4. Genuine fear had been created by Jewish extremists, who in April 1948 inflicted heavy casualties on the Arab village of Dir Yassin.[2]

"The Arab refugees cannot go back to Israel," declared J. Henry Carpenter, executive secretary of the Brooklyn Division of the Protestant Council of New York City in 1951.[3] He wrote: "Many of us were pro-Arab and some of us were anti-Israel. I personally was in this group. . . . But I want a solution . . . based on all the facts. . . . There is nothing left for them to come back to." Carpenter was referring to the fact that while several hundred thousand Palestinian Arabs were refugees outside of Israel, an approximately equal number of Jews had left their homes and property in Arab countries and had come to Israel. Former Arab property in Israel was occupied. J. Coert Rylaarsdam, an assistant professor of Old Testament theology at the University of Chicago, explained:

> The Jews of Yemen and of Iraq, the Jews of North Africa and of other Arab centers, were uprooted by the same Arab war on Israel that uprooted the Arabs of Palestine. . . . They, too, left their property behind them, they too suffered indignity, abuse and death. Their rehabilitation, in contrast to their Arab counterparts is due to the fact their own cared for them. Isn't it ironical that this act of responsibility and compassion should have deprived Israel of a propaganda weapon so cleverly used by its neighbors?[4]

There was, of course, another basic reason why Israel refused to take back a large number of Arab refugeees: her security was at stake. Karl Baehr quotes the Reverend Garland Hopkins, "long a sympathizer with the Arab point of view,"[5] who, upon returning from the Near East, was reported to have said: "Arab liberals and intelligentsia are organizing to take over the leadership which has often been left to incapable and venal rulers. The end view is to strengthen the Arab nations to the point that they will be able to expel the Jews from Palestine."[6] Baehr added: "One cannot complain that Mr. Hopkins and his Arab friends lack candor. Nor do they hide their intentions." Even the *International Review of Missions* editorialized: "Realistic comment on the situation allows for the suspicions entertained by Israel lest a 'fifth column' inspired by the doctrine of revenge still being preached by certain elements among the Arabs should find its way."[7]

The anti-Israel American Protestants continually reminded their audiences of the injustice perpetrated on the Arab refugees by Israel. These American Protestants found it difficult to distinguish between what they viewed as the immoral basis for the creation of the state of Israel and the unjust stance taken by Israel towards the refugees in not allowing for their return. They would quote two U.N. Assembly resolutions. The first, of December 11, 1948, stated that refugees "wishing to return to their homes and live at peace with their neighbors should be permitted to do so at the earliest practicable date."[8] The second, of December 7, 1950, directed the U.N. Conciliation Commission to work out arrangements for implementing the first resolution.[9] The commission did not succeed in doing so.

A group of pro-Arab American Protestant leaders, who sharply disagreed with Carpenter's aforementioned article in the *Christian Century*, asked bluntly in a letter to that publication: "Is it to be continued injustice and suffering for one group of people, while we try to compensate for past suffering of another group of people? . . . [Is] there any valid reason why the present resolutions of the U.N. should not be implemented?"[10]

This rhetoric continued throughout the period following Israel's establishment. The rival groups in American Protestantism were simply talking past one another, with neither group answering the other's viewpoint convincingly. The position of the pro-Israel faction who argued for Israel's security needs, was ignored by the pro-Arab group. The latter's claim for justice for the refugees was all but brushed aside by the former group.

The *Christian Century* offered a "compromise" solution. By mid-1951 it conceded that "the right of the Jews to Israel is no longer the question. Whatever the rights or wrongs that accompanied its birth, Israel exists. It must continue to exist."[11] It added, however, that Israel's territory should be decreased substantially to enable Arab refugees to return at least to the areas relinquished by Israel. A senior editor of the weekly, Harold Fey, writing from Israel in early 1954, suggested that at least 150,000 Arab refugees could return to the lands which would be given up by Israel, though he acknowledged that in terms of security, "such actions might make Israel's situation more precarious."[12] In 1956 the Near East representative of the American Friends of the Middle East called for a flat twenty percent reduction of Israel's territory in addition to allowing 300,000 refugees to return to their previous homes.[13] The same year, Theodore A. Gill, another senior editor of the *Christian Century*, writing from Israel, asserted that the notion that Jewish suffering had to be assuaged by the creation of a Jewish state "lost force . . . [because] Israeli policy produced not incomparable Arabian suffering, and no Arab will ever admit—and who will say that he should—that *fait accompli* outweighs justice in any scales."[14]

Abstract Justice

After the state of Israel was created, the question of justice in the Palestine situation was expressed by Protestants, both pro- and anti-Israel, not in legal but in philosophical terms. Pro-Israelis no longer relied on the Balfour Declaration nor even exclusively on the United Nations partition resolution. Instead, they spoke in terms of an "atonement to which all Christians can give support . . . an atonement for the persecution of Jews by Christians throughout centuries, and the perpetuation until recent times, of Jewish national homelessness."[15] A member of the American Christian Palestine Committee claimed: "Concern for the Arab refugees is commendable. . . . [But] the wide and insistent demand for return of the refugees, even in the midst of Israel's fight for life, seemed motivated by something besides humanitarian sentiment."[16] Indeed, even pro-Arab sympathizers occasionally admitted that the Arab leaders were using the refugees for their own political ends, "both by shaping the opinions of the refugees and in seeking to affect the opinion of the world."[17] This point was reiterated in an editorial by the *International Review of Missions*.[18]

The pro-Arab American Protestants expressed their viewpoint of the problem of justice in terms of moral rectification. The American representative of the Jerusalem YMCA was quoted as stating bluntly, "The Jews had no right to take over Arab property. They should be expected to return it to the owners."[19] The field representative for the Near East of the Presbyterian Board for Missions rationalized the reluctance of the Arab states to help solve the refugee problem by explaining that the Arab governments felt that the United Nations should bring pressure upon Israel to have the refugees returned to their original homes. He said: "For the neighboring countries to intervene and undertake on their own part the acknowledged responsibility belonging to the United Nations would be to connive in the injustice done to these exiled people."[20] Theodore Gill of the *Christian Century,* after admitting that political motivations of the Arab leaders kept the refugee problem brewing, nonetheless asked: "But who gave those leaders the chance and the material in the first place?"[21] Israel was clearly morally liable.

And so the interpretations of morality and justice in international affairs seesawed back and forth. Beginning in the 1950s, largely in response to the Korean crisis, a distinctive attempt was made by several Protestant clergy and laymen to deal with these elusive concepts, including their application to the Palestine question.[22] It became apparent that these spokesmen represented the pragmatic morality espoused by Reinhold Niebuhr. On the occasion of the twentieth anniversary of *Christianity and Crisis,* Professor Robert T. Handy of Union Theological Seminary recalled that the genesis of the publication was due to the editors' challenging "perfectionist and utopian ideas widely held by American churchmen."[23] The editors of the publication were motivated by the conviction that it was the duty of Christians to make their decisions "in terms of actual alternatives before them," rather than by dwelling on "ideal possibilities of a brotherly world."[24]

Kenneth W. Thompson, professor of international relations at Northwestern University, criticized the testimony of the Reverend Walter Van Kirk of the National Council of Churches before a subcommittee of the United States Senate on technical assistance programs in 1955, because the clergyman allegedly held that "the issue of right and wrong is unequivocal and unmistakable."[25] Thompson said: "If there is an absolute in the realm of political ethics, it is that no single proximate moral standard, whether self-determination or the United Nations, can be held up as an absolute. . . . In politics, interest or power or morality can rarely be conceived of in isolation, and ethical judgments must be made not in the abstract but in relation to the contingent realities of the particular situation."[26]

Earlier, another of Niebuhr's students, A. Roy Eckardt, wrote: "Some kind of workable decision, at least regarding Palestine, must be made partly on the basis of the relatively greater need of one party over another, recognizing that it is impossible to find a completely just solution for one or the other party. In the present case, the Jews clearly have a greater need than the Arabs. . . . While Arab nationalism is strong, it does not reflect a collective will to survive flowing from a complete lack of a homeland."[27] The Jews, as a people, had no place to go to but Israel. The Arabs, on the other hand, had sovereign states other than Palestine which offered them similar language, mores, culture, and even religion. Considering the historic relationship between the Jews and Palestine and their desperate need for a modern, sovereign, national homeland, Eckardt believed the Jews commanded a relatively more just claim on the territory called Israel than did the Arabs.

The Refugees' Plight

The portrayal of the pathetic human state of the Arab refugees by Protestant reporters from the Middle East was also subjected to critical analysis. While most reports conveyed the sense of frustration felt by the refugees, several depicted minor achievements among the refugees and tended to present their plight in a less unfavorable perspective.[28] The overall picture of the refugee problem, however, remained dismal, primarily because of their "organized intransigence" and the "calculated indifference of the Arab states."[29]

The latter phrase represented the assessment of the refugee problem by Dr. Elfan Rees, an English clergyman, who was the acknowledged expert on refugee problems for the Commission of the Churches on International Affairs (CCIA) and the World Council of Churches. Most American Protestant churches were affiliated with these bodies.

The reportage of Dr. Rees was distinguished from that of other Protestant clergymen by its pragmatic expertise in the field. It was void of pious rhetoric. Dr. Rees's principal concern was the living conditions of the refugees, regardless of political considerations. He sought to deal with them as people—as they were wherever they were to be found. He was analytical in appraising the refugee situation and steered away from emotionally charged descriptions. Based at the Geneva headquarters of the World Council of Churches, Rees visited the refugee camps numerous times and participated in several Arab refugee conferences held in the Near East.

In his first report—privately circulated in late 1949—to the Department of Interchurch Aid and Service to Refugees of the World Council of Churches, Rees had the following to say:

> I found refugees who had fled from Haifa not because they were afraid to live in Israel, but because they had been misled into expecting an Arab victory, and were more afraid of [Jordanian King] Abdullah's vengeance on "collaborators" than of "Jewish terror." I found many who had been evacuated by well-meaning British troops during the Mandate, and who remained convinced that one day British troops would return to repatriate them. . . .[30]

> I am regretfully persuaded not only that the Arab states are doing nothing to help the refugees, but that their attitude towards them is positively uncharitable and unhelpful, and that the only concern they have for them lies in their political value as a bargaining point at Lake Success, and before the bar of public opinion.[31]

Rees went on to explain that while most of the refugees were Moslem, ninety-five percent of the voluntary relief work among them "was Christian in origin." He sharply criticized the work of the Protestant missionary societies which preferred to view their relief activities as an ancillary effort of their principal task of conversion rather than channel such services through the local Arab churches. Rees said: "A great opportunity of strengthening native churches is being allowed to slip by."[32] However, he criticized the local Arab clergymen for failing to distinguish between Protestant aid given to them for their churches and aid given to them for the refugees. They tended "to appeal for the former in the name of the latter."[33] Finally, Rees reported that while he understood the pro-Arab sympathy of the American and European Protestant clergy in the Middle East, because they identified themselves with the sufferings of the refugees, "it came as a rude shock to a visitor . . . to discover to how great a degree these sympathies find expression in forms of a very positive anti-Semitism."[34]

In a subsequent address to a meeting of the Syracuse, New York, Ministers Association, Elfan Rees was reported to have complained about the "grievously partisan" pro-Arab stance of many American Protestant leaders, accusing them in effect of playing the political game of the Arab states by preferring to have the refugees remain a bartering factor.[35]

In 1957 while speaking before a conference in Geneva of nongovernmental organizations concerned with refugees, Rees bluntly came out in favor of integrating the Arab refugees into their host countries instead of holding up to them the deceptive promise of repatriation to Israel.[36] The speaker reminded his audience that given the fact of Israel's existence and its population density, the repatriation of a million Arab refugees was physically and politically impossible. Rees therefore came to the solution of integrating the refugees into the host states. Political issues aside, he maintained that

> the Arab refugee problem is by far the easiest postwar refugee problem to solve by integration. By faith, by language, by race and by social organization, they are indistinguishable from their fellows of their host countries. There is room for them, and land for them, in Syria and in Iraq. There is a development demand for the kind of manpower they represent. More unusually still, there is money to make this integration possible. The United Nations General Assembly, five years ago [1952], voted a sum of $200 million to provide, and here I quote the phrase, "homes and jobs" for the Arab refugees. That money remains unspent . . . simply for political reasons which . . . it is not my business to discuss.[37]

The British clergyman recognized "the unfinished business of moral restitution for the wrongs suffered by the refugees" and felt this debt should be shared by Israel, the international community, and the Arab governments. He believed that on grounds of compassion Israel should allow for the reunion of families; that the international community through the United Nations was paying its debt by concentrating large sums on the Arab refugees; that the funds which the world's Christian agencies paid to the Arab refugees amounted to one-third of the United Nations contributions, but that the churches, despite a request from the United Nations, could not cover the latter's portion as well; and that the debt of the Arab states would simply involve "regarding these people as human beings and not as political footballs."[38] Rees called the work of UNRWA[39] "a clinical study in frustration."[40] While praising its staff of professionals, he laid the blame for the agency's meagre accomplishments directly on the Arab governments and the refugees themselves:

> By chicanery, [UNRWA] is feeding the dead [through the misuse of identity cards of deceased persons]; by political pressure, it is feeding non-refugees; its relief supplies have been subjected in some instances to import duty; its personnel policies are grossly interfered with; and its "constructive measures," necessarily requiring the concurrence of governments, have been pigeon holed. The net result is that relief is being provided in 1959 to refugees who could have been rehabilitated in 1951 with "homes and jobs" without prejudice to their just claims.[41]

Rees recommended less emphasis on relief and more stress on rehabilitation—on vocational training that leads to work, and on work that leads to integration. "The essential new factor," he maintained, "is that relief should become ancillary to works and not the only acceptable service" to the refugees.[42]

Rees's Viewpoint Ignored

How did American Protestant spokesmen react to the views of world Protestantism's foremost authority on the Arab refugee problem? During the initial years of the problem, they were understandably concerned with relieving the refugees' suffering, and concentrated their attention on relief shipments of clothing and drugs under the auspices of Church World Service, an overseas relief agency of the National Council of Churches.[43] Nonetheless, the *Christian Century* rarely divorced the humanitarian aspects of the problem from their political implications. Its first editorial on the Arab refugees could not resist contrasting the Arabs' plight with that of Jewish refugees who were still displaced in Europe. In the fall of 1948 the periodical opined that in comparison with the Arab refugees' misery, the displaced persons in Europe were living in luxury, and that Arab rights will not be assured "until they are able to return to their homes and live there in security."[44]

From the start the *Christian Century* and other pro-Arab American Protestant spokesmen linked the solution of the Arab refugee problem to the restoration of the refugees to their homes and property in Israel.[45] The Protestant weekly was primarily concerned with a political solution, *not* a humanitarian resolution to their plight. Despite its expressed sympathy for the refugees' suffering the paper directed its editorials to radical political alternatives—all at Israel's expense. Its attitude was political repatriation or nothing and remained completely oblivious to the fact that "nothing" meant continued human suffering. To add an emotional dimension to its anti-Israel position, the paper invariably advised its readers that the refugee problem was caused by Jewish atrocities.

When, for example, in early 1952 the Protestant weekly reported that a group of American churchmen advocated a large-scale development and resettlement plan in the Near East, which would alleviate the refugee problem, the *Christian Century* played down the plan with obvious skepticism. It also volunteered its opinion that the refugee problem was caused by the Dir Yassin incident.[46] The editor of the *Nation* retorted in a letter to the *Christian Century:* "Do these proposals [representing two years of research] really merit the scorn you have heaped on them? . . . I do not see what useful purpose is being served by your injection of the massacre at Dir Yassin. War breeds atrocities . . . on both sides. But constant revival of the atrocity stories is precisely what has prevented a settlement from being reached."[47]

Though the American-controlled Church World Service was the principal coordinator in the United States of funds and materials for the Arab refugees, the disposal of such charitable contributions was increasingly left to the Near Eastern Christian Council. This body of Protestant-affiliated churches in the Near East was for many years controlled by United States missionaries residing in the region. By the mid-1960s, however, leadership of the council was taken over by local Arab clergy.[48] Protestant establishment spokesmen in the United States had argued the Arab refugee plight primarily in humanitarian terms, while concealing any political intent. The growing indigenous Arab influence on the Near East Christian Council, however, more openly advocated a political solution to the refugee problem.

The Refugee Conferences

In May 1951 the Near East Christian Council, then largely dominated by American and European Protestant missionaries, initiated a conference in Beirut on the Arab refugee problem.[49] The Beirut Conference was jointly sponsored by the World Council of Churches and the International Missionary Council, the latter primarily responsible for Protestant ecumenical activities outside Europe. Of the 73 participants at the Beirut meeting, only 19 were indigenous to the Near East.[50] All but two of the others were either American or British, the bulk of them residing in the Near East as missionaries or employees of branches of international Protestant organizations such as the YMCA, the YWCA, and the Lutheran World Federation. The principal speakers and chairmen of all planning sessions were Anglo-Saxon, as were the chairmen of the four working committees.

The Beirut Conference was primarily concerned with the coordination of Protestant relief work which was being performed by local church committees in the Near East. Henceforth, coordination would be carried out through the Near East Christian Council's Committee for Refugee Work (NECCCRW). As a result of the conference, the administrative costs of this committee were met by the World Council of Churches, while its operational budget through the early 1960s was largely provided by American churches entering direct negotiations with the Church World Service in New York City.[51]

In 1964 the Near East Christian Council became the Near East Council of Churches, with the area's Arab clergy officially taking over the council's leadership from the American missionaries. As a result of this historic shift in institutional power and because American churches became increasingly involved in funding projects to alleviate poverty and racial problems in the United States, American contributions to NECCCRW were reduced. The slack was taken up by Protestant churches outside the United States.[52] In 1967, as part of a constitutional revision of the Near East Council of Churches, the NECCCRW became one of its autonomous divisions.[53]

The policy of American and world Protestant bodies towards the Arab refugee problem was already discernible at the first Beirut Conference. With the Americans controlling the NECCCRW during its early years the resolutions of the Beirut Conference reflected a decided ambivalence between stressing human compassion—Elfan Rees' position—and political action. The result was a carefully worded compromise. The conference's principal resolution stated:

> Along with millions of refugees in other parts of the world—Europe, India, Pakistan, Korea and elsewhere—the greater proportion of the Palestinian refugees are the victims of a catastrophe for which they

themselves are not responsible. A deep injustice has been inflicted upon them, a measure of suffering they never deserved. To them is owed a debt of restitution by their fellow men, especially by those who in any way shared in the responsibility for their present plight. Yet we realize that nowhere in the world today can the claims of absolute justice be enforced, and that only the healing hand of time, and the exercise of a spirit of forgiveness can release those forces which will make for peace, mutual understanding and reconciliation. We are convinced that there can be no permanent solution of the problem of the Palestinian refugees until there is a settlement of the outstanding political differences between the Arab states and Israel. Churches are not competent to lay down the lines of a political solution. . . . A careful appraisal of the total situation has compelled us to conclude . . . that many Palestinian refugees will have to settle in new homes.[54]

Rees's viewpoint is clearly detected in this resolution, though he later acknowledged that he was blamed for not emphasizing sufficiently the "element of injustice" to the refugees.[55]

In 1956 the World Council of Churches, under the growing Arab influence in the Near East Christian Council, convened a second refugee conference in Beirut. The terms of reference of this meeting—as compared to those of the first conference[56]—included a distinctive political component. It was stated that the conference, "without propounding political solutions," was "to seek greater contemporary understanding both in the Near East and the West of the political issues that must be faced."[57] Nonetheless, the second Beirut Conference continued the ambivalence between emphasizing the humanitarian needs of the refugees (integration into their host countries), and their politically "just" rights (restoration to Israel). It continued to speak in generalities. However, as one observer noted: "In none of the Conference statements was the spiritual need of the situation separated from the political."[58] The conference moved a bit closer to making the long-range political dimension of the refugee problem its principal concern, while sacrificing the immediate human needs of the refugees. Still, it did not overthrow the general humanitarian thrust of the first conference.[59]

In May 1959 a letter seeking to crystallize the official policy of the World Council of Churches and the International Missionary Council towards the Arab refugee problem was dispatched through the Commission of the Churches on International Affairs to the Secretary General of the United Nations.[60] Over the signatures of O. Frederick Nolde, director, Elfan Rees, European representative, and

Kenneth G. Grubb, chairman, the memorandum made the following four points, among others:

1. Relief, though possibly on a diminishing scale, was essential and inevitable.

2. In any new UNRWA program, "relief should become ancillary to works, and should indeed become conditional on works being made financially and, above all, politically possible."

3. Israel was obligated to take the initiative in thawing the political iceberg. However, "we have no illusion as to the practicability, on political and economic grounds, of unrestricted repatriation [of Arab refugees], but we feel that the possibility of repatriation— under international control and possibly on an annual quota basis— must be one element in an overall settlement."

4. "We are not sanguine that the present political climate is propitious for large scale resettlement programs in the host countries, but we do believe that given adequate resources, a family 'self help' and 'homes and jobs' movement would soon acquire momentum."

The policy enunciated in the letter seemed to veer from Elfan Rees's earlier emphasis on the refugee question. While some aspects of his thinking are still discernible, one may conclude that pressure from pro-Arab American missionary circles and Arab representatives on the World Council of Churches compelled him to tone down his insistence that the most humane solution to the problem was immediate integration of the refugees into their host Arab countries. Instead Rees joined Nolde in forcing Israel's hand in this matter.[61] Urgent humanitarian aspects of the problem were henceforth of secondary concern. The primary strategy became one of political pressure on Israel to accept the principle of repatriation.

The combination of American missionary interests and the growing role of the Arab-dominated Near East Council of Churches in the affairs of the World Council of Churches outweighed the forthright advocacy of integrating the refugees into their host countries. The refugee problem ceased to be a question of how human suffering could be most expeditiously alleviated and became a question of politics, the not illogical outcome of American Protestantism's anti-Israel position.[62]

9

Adjusting to the Political
Reality of Israel

ANTI-ISRAEL SPOKESMEN FOR AMERICAN PROTES-
tantism found it difficult to accept the establishment of a Jewish state
after 1948. Their adverse response to the restoration of Jewish sovereignty over part of Palestine, however, differed from the policy of
the Arab governments in one notable way: albeit grudgingly, they
acknowledged the factual existence of the state of Israel.

While statesmen and Protestant spokesmen wrestled with the
problems of Jerusalem's governance and of the Arab refugees, the
very reality of Israel brought into play new concerns for American
Protestantism. A viable, vibrant and victorious Jewish sovereign entity was a novel phenomenon in modern history. Even loyal Jews
could not easily adjust to its reality.[1] It is doubtful even to this day
whether a satisfactory ideological position has been established by
the Jews of the Diaspora toward the state of Israel. It is not surpris-
ing, therefore, that American Protestants are still struggling with the
concept of a "resurrected" Israel, both practically and theologically.

Detractors of the New State

It is a fact, however, that some elements within American Protestantism found this struggle more tedious than others. Those Protestants who were most active in opposing a Jewish state during the
decade before its establishment did not suddenly disappear. Some
of them continued to harbor and express strong sentiments of anti-
Jewish statehood, though their extreme viewpoint gradually became
a minority opinion even among the pro-Arab American Protestants.

A typical spokesman for this intransigent anti-Israel attitude
was Dr. Henry Sloan Coffin, a former president of Union Theologi-

cal Seminary and an officer of the International Missionary Council. What made his views even more important was his status as an editor of *Christianity and Crisis*. His anti-Zionist statements contrasted sharply with those of another editor, Reinhold Niebuhr. Niebuhr upheld the Zionist solution to the Jewish problem, as we have noted earlier.

In February 1949, during the period in which the armistice agreement between Israel and Egypt was being concluded, Coffin contributed an article to *Christianity and Crisis* entitled "Perils to America in the New Jewish State."[2] In this article he bitterly assailed the "resurgence of fanatical Jewish nationalism," the "precariousness of its [Israel's] parasitic economic basis," "the aggressiveness of this new state" and its "covetous eyes" on Arab lands, and above all, its "stimulation of anti-Semitism" in the United States. Coffin wrote:

> Many of our Jewish fellow citizens will gain for themselves the sus-
> picion of being hyphenates . . . half Israeli and only half American.
> This undoubtedly will prove a source of prejudice and be an added
> difficulty for all Christians eager to end the hideously anti-Christian
> feeling against Jews in many of our communities. No greater blunder
> could have been made by American Jewry than to espouse Zionism
> if it wished to do away with anti-Semitism in this country. . . . For
> the present we can do nothing but accept the fact of this [new]
> nation. We can give our sane Jewish fellow citizens our hearty sup-
> port in their effort to be members of our nation alone and to repudi-
> ate Jewish nationalism.

Dr. Coffin, who was echoing the line espoused by the American Council for Judaism, was criticized as well as praised for his views in the pages of *Christianity and Crisis*.[3] The author and news analyst Edgar Ansel Mowrer wrote: "As a Christian I felt ashamed of, and as a Protestant I wish to protest against the article. . . . It seemed to me outrageous in tone and factually untenable." Former United States Secretary of the Interior Harold Ickes suggested that "Christianity would make more progress in the world if so many crimes were not committed in its name." A. Roy Eckardt, a former student of Coffin, challenged his teacher's equating "fanatical Jewish nationalism" with the birth of Israel.[4] He advised Coffin that the Jew could have little influence in alleviating Jewish hatred, for "the race problem in this country is one for gentiles . . . to solve." Eckardt concluded: "The fact seems to me to be that the rebirth of Israel is simply one more occasion for proclaiming the anti-Semitic gospel."

141

Another leader in American Protestantism who did not find it possible to come to terms with the reality of Israel's existence was William E. Hocking, professor emeritus of philosophy at Harvard University, a long-time antagonist of political Zionism, and proponent of missionary interests.[5] Three years after the state of Israel was established, Hocking asserted that "anti-Arab policies are un-American policies," and resented that his taxes contributed to United States grants-in-aid to Israel.[6] America's "natural ally" was the Arab world, not the Israelis, Hocking insisted. While the Arabs were a "historical community," the Israelis were a heterogeneous group of individuals drawn from different parts of the world and "forced . . . to begin community life *de novo* with an artificial constitution in which parliamentary forms can be exhibited as if they were outgrowths of deep-rooted democratic convictions."[7]

Most American Protestants holding an anti-Israel position appeared not to be as extreme as Coffin and Hocking in their traumatic encounter with the reality of a Jewish sovereign state. While Coffin "for the present time" could "do nothing but accept the fact" of Israel's existence—clearly implying that such passivity on his part was not permanent—most American anti-Israel Protestants seemed to practice a policy of painful adjustment to the new circumstances. The first stage in this adjustment process was to transfer their hostility from attacking the concept of a Jewish state to trying to damage the state's image by pointing up, from their viewpoint, its imperfections and shortcomings.

Following the signing of most of the armistice agreements between Israel and her Arab neighbors in early 1949, the *Christian Century* admitted how "frankly surprised" it was "by the speed and ease of the Zionist victory."[8] It attributed the victory to Israel's "fanatical confidence in the ability of science and techniques" and began to concern itself about the spiritual quality of the Israeli society. It questioned whether the new state would "smother" the ethical heritage of the Hebrew prophets "under an arrogant nationalism which despises spiritual values." Apparently, the value of a people's collective survival was not spiritual enough to warrant approval.[9]

When in May 1948 Israel's provisional parliament proclaimed the establishment of the Jewish state and did not use the term "Almighty God" in the document, but rather the more poetic expression "Rock of Israel"—a perfectly valid biblical term to designate the Divinity[10]—the *Christian Century* at first sharply criticized Israel's Declaration of Independence in an editorial entitled "Israel Knows no

God";[11] later apologized with an editorial "Zionist Censor Cuts Out God,"[12] and finally determined that its apology was "premature."[13] It was obviously interested in conveying to its Protestant readers an image of an atheistic Jewish state rather than analyzing for them the nuances of religious belief and behavior on the part of the Israeli population, as well as the admittedly atheistic beliefs of a small minority thereof. Even the more conservative publication the *International Review of Missions* acknowledged that the majority of Israel's Jews viewed their religion as integral to their "national inheritance," though it felt that superficially they made "no clear difference between the Torah and the Balfour Declaration."[14]

When the *Christian Century* was not accusing Israel of promoting atheism, it was charging it with excessive clericalism. Without explaining its position, the journal asserted that the "reactionary religious bloc" in Israeli politics would become "a serious obstacle to Western, and especially to American policy in the Middle East."[15] It therefore felt free to call on "the rabbinate of the West" to set before the population of the new state an interpretation of the Jewish religion "which is compatible with modern thought, and a challenge to higher ethical levels of living by men in the modern world."[16] Were the *Christian Century* sincere in its felicitous concern about the state of religion in Israel, its purported hope of incorporating into Israel's East European and Levant Orthodoxy a strong component of Western Jewish religious thought and practice would probably have been welcomed by its pro-Israel readers. But the carping tenor of the publication's editorials, at least throughout Israel's first decade, was so blatantly and consistently prejudicial to Israel's public image and national interests, that the journal's infrequent favorable observations about the Jewish state could not offset the impression that the *Christian Century*'s policy was geared to downgrading the quality of the Israeli society. It is doubtful whether the *Christian Century*'s own example of objectivity and fair play with regard to Israel could ever have served as a desirable model for Israelis in achieving "higher ethical levels of living."

Stressing the Negative about Israel

During a visit to Israel in 1954, one of the senior editors of the *Christian Century*, Harold Fey, published a series of articles in that journal which underscored the deficiencies of the country as he saw them. He doubted whether one of his travelling companions, the Reform Rabbi Morris Lazaron of the anti-Zionist American Council for Judaism, would be permitted by the Israeli rabbinate to hold a religious service there, because of his liberalism and his opposition to the formation of the state.[17] Fey opined that the Israeli talk about the "spiritual significance" of the ingathering of hundreds of thousands of Jews from all over the world was due to the "continuing threat of extinction which hangs over them." Though the secularists succeeded in defeating the efforts of the religious "obscurantists" to incorporate the latter's views in the country's constitution, according to Fey they did so "only at the price of leaving the country without a written constitution." The article continued to raise doubts about the stability of Israeli life. The author quoted a German-born Jew in Tel Aviv who had arrived in Palestine in 1936, as saying that it was impossible for him to become friends with Levantine Jews in Israel, but that perhaps his son and their children would learn to understand one another.

Fey was appalled by his visit to a collective settlement, a kibbutz, which had no building for worship, and he wrote approvingly of a Muslim religious judge in Nazareth who attacked "materialistic communism." The Protestant editor asked: "Could it [the Muslim judge's speech] have been occasioned by the growth of communist danger in Nazareth . . . or could it have been aimed at the continued despoilation of the 170,000 persons in the Arab community of Israel?" While admitting that the Israeli Supreme Court had "often" ruled in favor of Arabs, Fey asserted that the Israeli military authorities did not always heed the court's appeals, and that the military's "general purpose," in addition to defense functions, "seem[ed] to be to create a Jewish majority in every area where the Arabs are now in the majority."[18]

The author devoted the major part of his second article in the *Christian Century* to describing the Arabs of Israel as Class B citizens.[19] In addition to presenting the Israeli replies to his questions about the status of Israeli Arabs—"the survival of Israel must take priority"—the author proceeded to offer the Israelis a series of friendly suggestions on how they could improve their public image. The essence of Fey's proposals was that Israel should rectify its "fantastically unrealistic boundaries" by offering whole areas of land, including western Galilee and that part of new Jerusalem contiguous to the old city, to the Jordanians. Fey admitted, however, that his suggestions could be risky for Israeli security, "but the present policy is not without elements of danger either."

Having put up a straw man—without effectively answering either Israel's claim for security or the Israeli Arabs' grievances of being treated as Class B citizens—and then knocking it down, Fey then proceeded in a third article to offer what he considered a "moral" solution to the Israeli-Arab conflict. If Israel would only abandon her "imperialistic dreams" and identify herself with her Arab neighbors by lowering her standard of living, it would be easier for her to rectify her borders, take back some refugees, and compensate others. "In the course of time, a country which has shared its neighbors' poverty might slowly rise with them to share their plenty as the region developed."[20]

Fey's articles were met with a series of protesting letters in which both Jews and Christians expressed outrage at his factual presentations. A Reform rabbi, Charles Shulman of Chicago, advised him that Rabbi Lazaron could have readily held a religious service in Israel without the consent of any Israeli rabbis. Only the laws of personal status, marriage and divorce, were in the hands of the Israeli rabbinate.[21] Leaders of the American Christian Palestine Committee questioned the veracity of Israel's "imperialistic dreams." After all the Israeli government had agreed to grant Jordan port privileges on the Mediterranean and to compensate Arabs for land abandoned by them, and it had expressed willingness to participate in the regional development of water resources.[22] Finally, the executive secretary of the Tulsa Council of Churches reminded Fey that the plight of Arabs living in Israel should be understandable to anyone who knows about war.[23] "Having served as an Army Chaplain during the two World Wars, I know that individual rights quite frequently must be made subservient to larger ones." Quoting the new King of Saudi Arabia, who pledged the sacrifice of ten million Arabs to wipe out Israel, the writer concluded: "Let's not have any more chatter about Class B citizens in Israel as long as Arab leaders hold such attitudes."

Israel's Moral Image Impugned

During the early years of Israel's existence, the *Christian Century*, while acknowledging Israel's physical right to exist, persistently sought to impugn the moral basis of her existence. It quoted the executive secretary of the Southern Baptist Conference who shared the view of most conservative Christians that the Jewish people were chosen by God. "The new nation Israel is a miracle. In honesty, I must add that it is an 'immoral miracle.' "[24] These two words, claimed the *Christian Century*, "sum up all that we have been saying in these columns over the past years about the advent of the new nation." It went on to opine, as it did repeatedly, how the attack of a Jewish terrorist group against an Arab village Dir Yassin in April 1948 frightened the Arab population of Palestine, many of whom subsequently abandoned their homes during the Israeli-Arab war, thereby helping to create the Arab refugee problem. It neglected to mention how roundly this act was condemned by the official Jewish community in Palestine. The paper's main purpose was to depict the immoral behavior of the Israelis and their responsibility in creating the refugee problem. The *Christian Century* overlooked the attacks of Arabs on Jewish settlements and civilians while the British were still in control of Palestine, it ignored the incursions into Palestine by organized Arab armies from neighboring states once the British abandoned the mandate, and it seemed to forget that the Arabs, not the Jews, sought to frustrate by violence the implementation of the United Nations partition resolution.

During the first dozen years of Israel's existence, her alleged immorality was a favorite topic in the *Christian Century*. At times the paper would even associate Israel's policies with the "harsh morality" of the Old Testament. Such a journalistic device was certain to arouse latent religious prejudices in some of the publication's readers. On the eve of the Suez War, in the fall of 1956 when Arab fedayeen had stepped up their attacks on Jewish settlements from Jordan, Egypt, and Gaza, Israeli policy was to search and destroy fedayeen bases on Arab territory. The Protestant weekly was critical of this policy, stating: "The old law of an eye for an eye has apparently been supplanted in Israel's ideology by a more savage rule: a head for an eye. . . . Israel may well believe that . . . she could crush Egypt, blight the growing Arab unity, and push her own borders east to the Jordan River. If such ideas indeed lie behind her recent large scale military actions, the world must pray to be delivered from so mad a reversion to Old Testament thinking."[25] To the liberal Protestant periodical "Old Testament thinking" was apparently pejorative enough a term to arouse the anger and contempt of its readers.[26]

Harold Fey's recommendations on how Israel could improve

her moral image were not the only suggestions offered by the *Christian Century*. Earlier it had maintained that a possibility of peace in the Middle East could come about if Israel were to give up her policy of unlimited Jewish immigration.[27] While the *International Review of Missions* admired Israel's immigration policy, calling it "an idealism of purpose of an almost mystic kind,"[28] the *Christian Century* felt it merely justified Arab fears of Israeli territorial expansionism. When after the 1956 Suez War the *Christian Century* published the speech of an assistant to the publisher of *Time*, advocating an Arab recognition of Israel's existence on condition that Israel modify her borders, agree to Jerusalem's internationalization, restrict her immigration policy, and assume greater responsibility for the Arab refugees, the *Christian Century* approved the plan in principle, but felt that Israel's territory should be even further reduced.[29] The periodical's frustration with its own ambivalence toward Israel's existence presents a fascinating study of the vacillation of American Protestantism in general with regard to the reality of the Jewish state. As late as September 1958—ten years after the state's establishment —the *Christian Century*, while recognizing again Israel's right to exist, had to qualify this recognition in the following manner: "This is not to say that Israel should have been established in the first place, at least in the way it was established, or that all the problems created by its rise may be swept under the rug and forgotten. It is to say that 1958 is not 1948, that new realities must be accepted for what they are."[30]

But the *Christian Century* did not find it easy to come to grips with the "new realities." During the late 1950s it attempted to cover up its anti-Israel bias by calling on the major powers to end all arms sales to both sides in the Middle East conflict, knowing full well that the Russians were inaugurating a massive buildup of weapons to Egypt and that Jordan was receiving arms from both the United States and Great Britain. "Russia is obviously doing all it can to produce chaos by selling arms to Egypt," the *Christian Century* conceded, "but it is hypocrisy to put all the blame on the Russians and say nothing about the French sale of jet fighter planes to Israel."[31]

Though the *Christian Century* held Egypt responsible in September 1955 for breaking off negotiations with the United Nations secretary general for a return to peace on its borders with Israel, the journal qualified its accusation in this manner: "Yet it should not be forgotten that the recent Israeli elections were interpreted as a mandate for a more 'activist' policy along the frontier."[32] In the same editorial the periodical invoked the power of the United Nations for a "dependable appraisal of responsibility for the continued fighting," and if it found "both sides equally to blame, then the United Nations could begin to bring into play the peaceful sanctions of its Charter."

The *Christian Century's* faith in the United Nations, though undoubtedly sincere, was politically naive. When in 1957 President Eisenhower asked Congress to approve the Eisenhower Doctrine, promising United States aid to any Middle East state which asked for assistance against Communist aggression, he stated that the United Nations could not dependably protect the freedom of other nations when the interests of the Soviet Union were involved. The *Christian Century* protested this slur against the United Nations by referring to recent events in Hungary: "We do not believe this downgrading of what happened in Hungary, where the returns are not all in."[33] However, as Russian influence in the Near East, through the attempted intervention of Egypt and Syria in the internal affairs of Lebanon and Jordan, became a distinct possibility towards the end of 1957, the *Christian Century* suddenly reversed its position, abandoned its espousal of the United Nations, and dramatically advocated a strong policy against Russia. "It is better to run the risk of war involved in resisting the Russian advance," proclaimed the journal, "than it would be to compound that risk by giving Russia the means of further aggression."[34]

"Christianity and Crisis'" Editors Differ on Political Morality

It would appear that *Christianity and Crisis* was far more realistic than its rival publication in appraising the place of national power in international affairs. Its principal editors, Reinhold Niebuhr and John C. Bennett, however, disagreed as to the moral implications of the use of power, especially its use in the Near East. Niebuhr maintained a consistent pro-Israel stance. Bennett's position was more critical of the Jewish state.

In April 1956 Niebuhr raised the possibility that war in the Near East could result from the Russian arms buildup in Egypt. He warned that "the very life of the new nation of Israel" was at stake.[35] In the following month he advised the publication's readers that the

148

United States had "a special interest" in the preservation of Israel, both because the Jewish state was an outpost of western democracy and because of "humane considerations."[36] Regardless of its shortcomings the state of Israel was "a heartening adventure in nationhood," asserted the writer. "Whatever our policy or religious positions may be, it is not possible to withhold admiration, sympathy and respect for such an achievement." Politically, Niebuhr felt it futile for the United States to appease the Arabs at the expense of Israel, because "the Communists have found a way to Nasser's heart through the gift of modern arms."

Once the Suez War broke out, Niebuhr criticized the moral complacency of America. He explained the policy of the British, French and Israelis, as the result of their "lost confidence in our capacity and inclination to protect them against the threat of the new Egyptian dictatorship supported by Russia."[37] He did not go so far as to applaud this policy, recognizing that "they may have been quite wrong in their military venture." But he took American public opinion to task for developing a pacifistic outlook on the grounds that the Near East problem might lead to a nuclear war. Niebuhr continued:

> If we come to the conclusion . . . that force is under all circumstances ruled out, the Russians will only have to threaten force to persuade us to yield. It is this general pacifism which prompts Europe to lose confidence in us. . . . It is . . . possible that . . . [Russia] took the risk [in Hungary] only after we had proved in the Suez crisis that we had ruled out force as an instrument of policy. . . . [We] must risk war to protect people from tyranny or the Russians will take advantage of us at every turn.[38]

A more equivocal attitude toward both morality and power was expressed by Niebuhr's co-editor of *Christianity and Crisis*, Union Theological Seminary professor John C. Bennett. Immediately after the shooting had died down at Suez, Bennett discussed the rights and wrongs of the situation in specific Israel-Arab terms.[39]

He analyzed the Arab-Israel conflict as consisting of "four wrongs": the organized extermination of Jews by the Nazis; the establishment of the state of Israel, "a wrong done to Arabs who called Palestine their home"; the expansion of Israel, or its "self defense policies"; and the provocations of the Arabs, or their "self defense policies."

The latter two points were issues "on which men who agree on most other issues are in complete deadlock," Bennett asserted.

He held that the first two "wrongs" could not be undone, but regarding the latter two, Israel must admit that "the Arabs have a real case," and the Arabs must "accept the fact that Israel has been given a right to exist, and has lived by that right long enough to have a real case." Finally, Bennett admitted that there must be a recognition that the final settlement will not be fully just "in relation to past wrongs."[40]

While Niebuhr was concerned with a political approach to morality, Bennett was more interested in assessing political situations in moral terms. To Niebuhr, politics was the means to achieve moral ends. To Bennett, it would seem that both the means and the ends had to be unidimensionally "moral."

Though Bennett acknowledged Israel's right to exist, he believed that the Arab case was not fully appreciated. In his view Niebuhr was not sensitive enough to the need for finding "substantial compensation" for the Arabs. "Israel's aggression [against Egypt] was provoked," Bennett admitted, "but the existence of Israel has been a continuous source of provocation."[41] Bennett was delighted that Israel escaped the penalty of United Nations sanctions, not because she was right in her stubbornness not to yield captured Egyptian territory without an international guarantee ensuring her borders from attack, but because Russia was not punished for her actions in Hungary.[42] "The contrast in the treatment of Israel and Russia would have made the application of sanctions in this case an occasion for cynicism. . . . [However], if we had been put in the position of backing Israel when she was technically in the wrong . . . we would have greatly increased the vulnerability of the Middle East to Russian influence."[43]

It appears that Bennett philosophized about morality. Niebuhr, on the other hand, sought to apply it to concrete situations. To Bennett, public morality seemed to connote absolute standards; to Niebuhr, a nation's morality seemed to be justified on grounds of situational ethics.[44]

10

Adjusting to the Religious
Reality of Israel

THERE CAN BY NOW BE LITTLE DOUBT THAT PROTES-
tant thought was seriously challenged by the establishment of the
state of Israel. The very dynamics of a Jewish sovereign state in the
Holy Land and its implications for Jews and Christians inevitably
called into play new patterns of Protestant religious thinking affecting the Jewish people. Even the *Christian Century* reflected a drastic
change in attitude towards the subject of Israel.[1] Such a policy shift
climaxed almost two decades of that periodical's tortuous adjustment to the new Jewish reality.

The principal question facing the Christian world since the
advent of the Jewish state has been: "What is 'Israel'?" As the *Christian Century* admitted in 1967, it had consistently questioned the
wisdom of interpreting the terms "a faith and a folk," used throughout the centuries, to mean a political state.[2] But having made the
"necessary journalistic adjustments," the periodical believed that as
the word "Israel" became increasingly identified with a particular
political entity, it would forfeit some of its theological mystique.
"As the word moves from general, abstract meanings to a specific,
concrete focus, it inevitably loses its broad and deep spiritual significance" for both Jews, and especially non-Jews. Jews might gradually
tend to give up the use of the term as a literary symbol for "a heritage, a folk, a community, a faith"; Christians might slowly become
deprived of the figurative meanings of the word which has been used
"as a synecdoche for the Christian church, the whole Christian community."

The Protestant weekly concluded that the right of Zionists to insist that Israel be granted diplomatic recognition by her Arab neighbors was valid. On the other hand, it warned Jews that Israel would
henceforth be judged by the same standards applicable to all other

states "without appeals for special consideration based on . . . spiritual and non-political values." Christians, it asserted, will continue to "owe to Israel—the faith, the heritage, the community—a debt they can never fully discharge, but history has not made the state of Israel the collector of that debt."[3]

Protestant Theologians' Reactions to the New State

Not all Protestant thinkers were prepared at last to adjust their thinking to a valid dichotomy between Israel the state and Israel the faith. To the Protestant adherents of the millennial hope, the Jewish state was merely an extension of the Jewish faith. These millennarians applauded the creation of the state as a fulfillment of prophecy. William M. Smith, professor of Bible at the Fuller Theological School, told his readers in the mid-1950s: "The promise to Israel of Palestine as a permanent possession is *at no time cancelled.* Not only has the idea of Israel's permanent occupation remained unfulfilled, but . . . when has Israel ever enjoyed the permanent, uninterrupted peace and prosperity here promised? . . . If we take the unauthorized liberty of cancelling these prophecies, why may we not with equal liberty cancel any other prophecy with which a particular theory would lead us to disagree? The promises regarding Canaan were made to one nation, Israel, and to no other."[4]

The executive editor of *Christianity Today*, L. Nelson Bell, rejoiced in 1967 when East Jerusalem fell to the Jews, claiming that this event "gives a student of the Bible a thrill and a renewed faith in the accuracy and validity of the Bible. . . . If we say, as the Arabs do, that Israel has no right to exist, we may prove blind to her peculiar destiny under the providence of God."[5] And William Culvertson, president of the Moody Bible Institute, reminded his readers that though the Jews have returned to their land "in unbelief," it is only when "the Redeemer comes to Zion that all Israel will be saved" (Rom. 11:26).[6]

Less fundamentalist Protestant leaders also viewed the emergence of the Jewish state as an act of God. Edwin T. Dahlberg, president of the National Council of Churches, wrote in 1957: "If we did not believe in an omnipotent God, we might well fall into despair concerning the situation in the Middle East. . . . But of one thing we can be sure: in the land of Israel a work of God is going on that will affect the future history of the human race as truly as in the days when Moses led the children of Israel through the wilderness from the land of Pharaoh to the land of Canaan."[7]

Kyle Haseldon, maverick editor of the *Christian Century* from 1964 to 1967, upon visiting Israel in 1965 wrote: "Any one travelling through the land, looking and listening, is soon convinced that some agent—which cannot be defined as anything less than spiritual —has transformed the sea of diversity which swept into this little country into a people, a nation, and has done so in much less time than the forty years required by Moses for a similar project. This story cannot be told dispassionately. . . . As a Christian, I want to believe that the people who produced the prophets and from whom came Jesus of Nazareth are still chosen to witness to all nations."[8]

A. Roy Eckardt, professor of religion at Lehigh University, found the state of Israel playing a crucial theological role in that the Jews refused "to subordinate the 'natural' domain to the 'spiritual' domain (always, though, at the risk of secularization)." He lauded the Jews' return to their land "as living refutation" of the Christian contention that Israel must be barred from its land until it fulfilled the "conditions upon which the church fancied it had a monopoly. But Israel *has* returned. It is almost as though God has deliberately said 'no' to Christian pretensions."[9]

Needless to say, not all Protestant spokesmen were equally approving of the positive theological role of the state of Israel. Some of them, especially Europeans, while not fully convinced of this role, nonetheless were prepared to have an open mind on the subject.[10]

European Protestants were far more theologically oriented than were the Americans. When their respective representatives met together, the Europeans would invariably influence the Americans' thinking: the Europeans were the teachers, the Americans the students. This pattern was demonstrated at sessions of the World Council of Churches and at other international church conferences. Robert C. Dodd, director of the Committee on Ecumenical Affairs of the National Council of Churches, placed several agonizing questions before the readers of *Christian Century* when he reported on an international conference of Christians and Jews held in England in 1966.[11] It would seem clear that the formulation of these questions was primarily due to the influence of European Protestant and Jewish participants, for prior to Dodd's report, similar penetrating queries were absent in the American Protestant press. Dodd wrote:

If the continuing existence of the people of Israel has been an embarrassment to Christianity, then the existence of a political entity known as the state of Israel may be an even more acute embarrassment. . . . Is it possible in biblical terms to comprehend the plan of God for the children of Israel apart from the land which He promised through Moses? . . . Are there any official church actions which recognize, either in support or in condemnation, of this new state? If not, why are the churches and such of their agencies as the World Council of Churches silent about its existence? . . . Is it legitimate for Christians to hope and to pray for changes in the state of Israel that might make it a light unto the nations and a faithful—yes, and suffering—servant of the Most High? Can Christians say that the existence of Israel is either outside or in opposition to the divine plan?

If there were Protestants who remained uncertain about the state of Israel's role in the drama of divine salvation, and were prepared to study it, there were others who were quite certain that the Jewish state and its nationalistic ideology was anything but part of a theological design. Immediately after the state was established, Millar Burrows, professor of biblical theology at Yale, and president of the American Schools for Oriental Research in the Near East, suggested that "the present resurgence of Jewish nationalism is a repetition of the same fatal error that caused Israel's rejection of Jesus. It is the focal point at which Christian opinion, in all brotherly love, should make clear and emphatic its disagreement with the dominant trend in contemporary Judaism."[12]

During the same period, the *Christian Century* expressed fear lest Jewish nationalism "further emasculate the *religious* contribution of the universal religion of Judaism to the spiritual purification and strengthening of Western society."[13] It direly predicted that the extent to which Jewish congregations "now become absorbed in the support of a national state which is neutral toward, and largely indifferent to, the fate of Judaism as a faith, to that extent the remarkable triumph now culminating in the emergence on history's stage of the new Israel may turn out to be one of the darkest tragedies in the record of Judaism." On the eve of Israel's tenth anniversary, the periodical still was of the opinion that the "most difficult of all" problems facing that society was "how to rescue Judaism, the religious faith, from Zionism, a nationalistic creed."[14]

Even Protestant fundamentalists were not of one mind on the theological significance of the state of Israel. O. T. Ellis, formerly professor of Old Testament at Princeton Theological Seminary, raised this question: "What other people in the world would venture to demand that the clock of history be put back two millennia for their benefit?"[15] The author maintained that God's promise to Abraham's seed to give them title over Palestine "was conditioned on obedience to the will of God," and that for the Christian, Palestine had only sentimental interest. Only "racial pride and nationalistic aspirations" make it important for a Jew "who still lives more or less in the Old Testament Dispensation" to possess Palestine. "There are many open spaces in the world, many friendly nations, in which oppressed Israelites can find a refuge and a home without imperiling the peace of the world," Ellis contended. He did not specify any such places, but instead concluded his article as follows: "Does the Israeli cause deserve to succeed? . . . We believe the verdict of history will be, No!"

The Evanston Assembly

This adamant opposition to the Jewish state was understandably shared by representatives of Arab churches who participated in the international meetings of the World Council of Churches. Perhaps the most notable of such meetings was the Second Assembly of the World Council of Churches held in 1954 in Evanston, Illinois. This gathering is especially pertinent to our investigation because, for completely different reasons, a coalition of Arab and Asian representatives at the Assembly and a majority of the American Protestant delegation succeeded in eliminating any reference to "Israel" from a key resolution.

Six years earlier, at the First Assembly of the World Council of Churches, held in Amsterdam, the meeting refused to express a judgment on the "rights" and "wrongs" of the Palestine problem. Instead it appealed to "the nations" to deal with the problem not as one of expediency, "but as a moral and spiritual question that touches a nerve center of the world's religions." It called on the churches to pray and work for an order in Palestine "as just as may be in the midst of our human disorder."[16]

At the time of the first World Council of Churches assembly in September 1948 the representatives from the Arab countries had not been as numerous or outspoken as they were in 1954. Instead the delegates representing American missionary interests were the principal antagonists of Israel, while those representing the Western

European lands of the holocaust expressed sympathy for Jewish concerns.

The theme of the World Council of Churches' second assembly was "Christ—the Hope of the World." The Advisory Commission of the World Council of Churches which prepared a list of recommendations for the assembly had included several references to Israel— not to Israel the state, but to Israel the mystical people.[17] In addition to the recommendations of the Advisory Commission, another resolution was forwarded to Evanston by a pre-assembly caucus which met at Lake Geneva, Wisconsin. Convened by the American Committee of the International Committee on the Christian Approach to the Jews, the caucus resolved:

> The Christian hope cannot be fully comprehended without relation to the hope of Israel, manifested not only in the Old Testament, but also in God's continuous dealings with the Jewish people. The existence of the synagogue and of the Jewish witness to the God of Abraham after 2000 years of church history is a challenge to the church. The church cannot rest until the title of Christ to the Kingdom is recognized by His own people according to the flesh.[18]

As reported by an officer of the International Committee on the Christian Approach to the Jews, Robert Smith, it was clear from the outset of the debate at the assembly that the Arab delegates were determined to object to any reference made to the term "Israel."[19] The first sentence which aroused opposition seemed to be "innocuous." It called for "a statement of the New Testament concept of the ultimate fulfillment of God's promise to the people of ancient Israel, and the consequent special responsibility of the Church of Christ for the proclamation of the hope in Christ to the Jews." Delegates representing the Orthodox Patriarchate of Antioch, the Coptic Church of Egypt, and the Evangelical Churches of Syria and Lebanon, as well as non-Arab Protestants residing in the Near East, objected. The Anglican bishop in Jerusalem, W. H. Stewart, said that he lived in an area where every statement about Israel was apt to become bitterly controversial and stressed that many hopes other than that of Israel were fulfilled by Christ's coming. He was against placing special stress on Israel.

An Arab representative, Mr. Audeh, hoped that the assembly would not make the task of the churches in the Near East more difficult. Another Arab representative, Mr. Atiya, called it a disservice to the World Council of Churches in the Near East to mention

Israel.[20] It mattered little that other delegates at the meeting emphasized that the references in the proposed statment were to ancient Israel, not to Israel as a political state.

The Arab representatives found support for deleting the statement from American Protestant delegates who did not object to its first part, "the people of ancient Israel," but rather to its second part, which spoke of "the hope in Christ to the Jews." Led by Charles Taft, a Protestant lay leader of the National Council of Churches, this group of American Protestants objected to the entire notion of missionizing to the Jews. In Taft's opinion such a statement would tend to jeopardize Christian relations with Jewish friends.[21]

An ironical situation was thus created at the assembly where the missionary point of view was opposed by the Arab delegates in the name of anti-Zionism and by philo-Semitic Americans who were motivated by sensitive consideration for Jewish opinion in the United States. This coalition defeated the proposed statement by a vote of 195 to 150.

The greatest support for the statement came from the Western European church representatives who came from countries which had experienced Nazi persecution. According to Robert Smith, the continental delegates were astounded by the debate; "they were bewildered by what they thought was anti-Semitism in a new guise." They were especially upset with the position taken by the Anglican bishop in Jerusalem "whose very title should have made him a champion of Israel."[22]

Two subsequent assembly decisions somewhat softened this rejection of the missionary-sponsored resolution. A minority declaration was read which had been signed by twenty-four delegates, a fourth of them from the United States.[23] It stated:

> Our concern in this issue is wholly Biblical and is not to be confused with any political attitude towards the state of Israel. . . . We . . . believe that God elected Israel for the carrying out of His saving purpose. . . . Whether we are scandalized or not, that means that we are grafted into the old tree of Israel (Rom. 11:24), so that the people of the New Covenant cannot be separated from the people of the Old Covenant. . . . To expect Jesus Christ means to hope for the conversion of the Jewish people, and to love the people of God's promise.

The second action at the assembly to ameliorate the anticonversion impact caused by defeating the missionary's resolution was to ask the Central Committee of the World Council of Churches to conduct further study and consultation on the Hope of Israel.[24]

The debate at the World Council of Churches assembly seemed to shed added light on the Protestant attitude to Jewish nationalism.[25] It is apparent that the Protestant world was not prepared to deal with the theological consequences of a modern Jewish state. It shunned the topic lest its relationship with Arab Protestant bodies represented in the National Council of Churches be upset. While it vigorously insisted on its neutrality with regard to the political subject of the Israel state, it was, in effect, siding with the Arab point of view. It would appear that politics and a power base in the Middle East, not theology, were uppermost in the minds of most Protestant representatives.

Even more serious was the tendency on the part of most delegates to distort both the Old and New Testaments with respect to the subject of Israel. By expunging all reference to the people or faith of Israel—lest such reference be construed as Protestant interest in the state of Israel—their action represented a serious break with the historic Protestant tradition. This "recrudescence of Marcionism" was vividly described two years later by the president of Aleppo College, in Syria, who attended the second Beirut Conference of Churches on the Arab refugee problem. Said Dr. Horace McMullen: "The word 'Israel' gags the present church because of its contemporary associations. . . . The painful significance of the term 'Israel' has led in many churches to carefully expurgated readings of the Old Testament, and in some to an almost complete rejection. . . . Thus the whole historical basis of the Christian faith is at stake, and there is danger of its becoming a moralistic or mystical religion."[26]

At Evanston the split within the missionary movement on the subject of Israel flared into the open. It became clear that those missionary groups involved in pursuing the conversion of Jews to Christianity were far more sympathetic to Jewish ethnic sensibilities than those working among the Arabs in the Near East. The latter became obsessively anti-Israel. On the other hand, nonmissionary American Protestant elements who pragmatically had begun to accept their American Jewish friends as they were, without any intention of converting them to Christianity, were so sensitive to Jewish feelings that they rejected outright the notion of organized missionary conversions.

Finally the Second Assembly of the World Council of Churches at Evanston in 1954 highlighted the nationalistic components of world Protestantism. Shattering the notion that Christianity was a universal religion devoid of nationalistic nuances, the debates revealed that the power of nationalism was still very potent. The Western European delegates approached the subject of the Jews from their national experience and perspective. The Arab representatives reflected their nationalistic interests. It was simply a fiction to pretend that Protestantism was not strongly influenced by the pressures of various nationalist experiences. As Robert Smith reported: "At Evanston we were reminded again of the nationalist features in the churches."[27] Interestingly, compared to the chauvinism of other national groups, he held up the Jew as "a living witness against the idolatry of nationalism." To which the Anglican bishop in Jerusalem responded: "I wish that my experience enabled me to echo that sentiment. If he would amend it to 'every Christian Jew,' I would gladly do so."[28] Bishop Stewart did not spell out how a Christian Jew in Israel was any less nationalistic than a Hebrew Jew.

Protestant Evangelism in Israel

It seemed clear from the deliberations at Evanston that the European Protestants had greater conviction about the conversion of Jews to Christianity than did their American counterparts.[29] American missionary efforts were largely geared to Asia, Africa and the Near East, and in the Near East they concentrated on converting Arabs, not Jews. Missionary work in Palestine was left largely to Europeans, with the Anglicans and German Lutherans filling the largest missionary role. American Protestant literature is, therefore, largely silent on the subject of Christian Jews in Palestine. The *Christian Century*, for example, was less concerned with the position of the relatively few Protestants in Israel than it was with the overall Israeli-Arab problem. The American missionaries who influenced or shared the paper's views on the latter question were more immediately motivated by political than by theological factors. They were committed to the Arab cause and could find little virtue in Israel's development. Their concern for the internal problems of the country was minimal. When interest was expressed, it was biased against Israeli interests. It is little wonder, then, that the *Christian Century's* editorials about Israel's religious life were largely negative in outlook, stressing the weaknesses in Israeli Judaism without, however, analyzing the historic and sociological background of the Jewish religious milieu there.[30] Neither did the editorials present any inkling of the positive components permeating the country's Jewish religious ethos.[31]

By contrast, conservative spokesmen of American Protestantism were more concerned with the religious life of Protestants in Israel than with the overall Arab-Israeli political conflict. These American Protestants appeared genuinely interested in coming to terms with Jewish sovereignty in the Holy Land. Gradually they learned to adjust themselves to its reality. Most of their spokesmen were not hampered by the struggle within Protestantism for and against recognizing Jewish peoplehood and Jewish nationalism. They were interested in having ethnic Jews in Israel become Christian Hebrews, not in exorcizing their Jewish ethnicity. They repeatedly stressed that in becoming religious Christians, Jews would not have to break with Jewish peoplehood.[32] Said the editor of *Christianity Today*: "The Jew is not being pressured to become a Gentile; when a Jew comes to the Messiah, he does not cease to be a Jew, but a Jewish believer. And there is surely no need, on this basis, for him to separate himself from his people."[33]

What concerned the evangelical Protestant leaders, therefore, was whether the Israeli government would tolerate Christian missionary work among the Jews of the Holy Land. This was clearly a delicate issue.

The Protestant evangelical leadership initially professed to justify its proselytizing strategies on the grounds that Israeli religious life lacked "spirituality" and did not embrace most of the population.[34] For this assumption they found support among other Protestant groups. The *Christian Century*, in accordance with its consistent policy of embarrassing Israeli society, insisted that Judaism's contemporary "despiritualization" was due to the influence of both modern Zionism and "medieval" Israeli orthodoxy.[35] The evangelical spokesmen, on the other hand, recognized positive manifestations in Israeli religious life,[36] but felt that Judaism lacked theological substance. Some of their leaders resented Zionism, not because it was a nationalistic movement, but because its success might provide modern Judaism with a substantive religious component which would make their missionary task all the more difficult.[37] As the *International Review of Missions* admitted in 1950, the response of Jewish immigrants to Israel's open-door immigration policy "creates an element of spiritual fulfillment which missionaries recognize may well become a further bulwark against acceptance of the Christian faith."[38] Though these Protestant leaders may have been unhappy with the Zionist dynamism for their own special reasons, they did not begrudge the establishment of a Jewish state, as did other leading American Protestants.

The primary objective of Protestant evangelical leadership was to relate to Jews in Israel in a way which would facilitate their conversion to Christianity. This purpose, interestingly enough, was tolerated by the Israel government, but the success of the missionary efforts has been poor.[39] The missionaries were not stopped in their work by the Israeli authorities as long as their strategy was not blatantly offensive to the Jewish population. When such insensitivity prevailed, the missionaries were invariably subjected to hostile Jewish protests.[40]

In July 1961 the *Christian Century* reported on one such confrontation resulting in the cancellation of Protestant religious services in a Jerusalem church.[41] Said the editorial: "The civic morality and durability of a Jewish nation are being tried by what it does to its Christian minority." William L. Hull, American director of Zion Christian Mission in Jerusalem, reacted to the editorial as follows:

> Myself a Christian worker in Jerusalem for twenty-five years, I have been disturbed by the unfortunate publicity given this incident. . . . Anyone who has had any reasonable length of service in Israel knows that the way the Church of Christ missionaries attempted to establish a mission here was bound to fail. . . . The Church of Christ missionaries were asking for trouble when they brazenly opened their doors in an Orthodox Jewish district, and offered inducements for Jewish children to attend their meetings. . . . In Israel today there is more actual religious freedom to propagate the gospel than there was under the Protestant Christian mandatory government.[42]

Since 1950 a Christian religious service arranged by different church groups has been broadcast each Sunday afternoon as a public service on the government radio station. But perhaps the most celebrated manifestation of religious toleration expressed by the Israeli government to the missionaries was reflected in the rejection by Israel's Parliament of a private member's bill aimed at preventing Jewish children from attending missionary schools. The Minister of Education opposed the bill on the grounds that it would deprive parents of the right to choose the schools their children attend.[43] At the same time, the apparent policy of the government was to preserve an immigration quota for missionaries based on their number in Palestine in 1948.[44] The government was not prepared to encourage Christian missionary work, nor to open its doors to an excessive number of missionaries. From conversations with Israeli officials, it appears to the author that the Israeli government was more prone to issue visas to missionaries involved in health and education projects with Israeli Arabs, than to those interested primarily in the religious conversion of Jews.

The Israeli government's ambivalent policy towards Protestant missionary work was appreciated by the evangelical leadership. A missionary representing the United States Southern Baptist Convention in Israel declared, after residing in Israel for six years, "Israel is struggling today for her very survival . . . [and] can little afford to favor any factor which may bring dissension among her people."[45] *Christianity Today* reported at length the views of "a Christian source in Jerusalem" who explained the general hostility of the Israeli society towards the missionary as follows: "He is an intruder, with no objective but to eliminate Judaism. . . . The long run work of evangelism in Israel must be done by young, intelligent Hebrew Christians who are trained in a secular profession. They must love Israel and their brothers enough to . . . work there, raise and educate their children and prove their undivided loyalty to the people and nation."[46] The editor of *Christianity Today*, after visiting Israel in 1961, complained that few missionaries there became permanent residents of the country: "They seem but tenuously related to this new land of intense nationalism."[47] He criticized them for being "timid." "That may be one reason the modern Israeli does not take the Christian missionary too seriously," he concluded.[48]

Israeli Christian Hebrews echoed these sentiments. Said the pastor of the Messianic Assembly of Israel in Jerusalem: "We . . . view our work as an . . . Israeli church, rooted in the country . . . since almost all our members, including our pastor, are Jews."[49] Wrote a Christian Hebrew from Haifa: "The missionaries . . . place Judaism on the same level as paganism and are not satisfied or content with a believing Jew until he eats pork or does some other thing in contravention of the Law of Moses. . . . The state and rabbinic leaders of Israel are not the only ones wishing the missionaries to 'leave us alone.' Many of us messianic Jews fervently pray that God may send them back home."[50]

To offset the fears expressed by Israelis regarding Christian missionary intentions, a joint statement was issued in 1963 by representatives of all Christian groups in Israel—Roman Catholic, Greek Catholic, Orthodox, Anglican and Protestant. It read:

> We do not exploit the economic situation of an Israeli citizen—his poverty, unemployment, inadequate housing or desire to emigrate—in order to induce conversion. . . . Nor do we take advantage, with a view to conversion, of a negative psychological attitude some Jews may feel towards Israel, whether evidenced by bitterness, or the desire to escape from their Jewishness; for we are convinced that a Jew who becomes a Christian still remains a member of his people. . . . [We] welcome as members of our churches those who ask to be admitted of their own free will and from strictly religious motives, and who have been under probation long enough to prove their sincerity, disinterestedness and ability to share the difficulties which are the lot of every religious minority.[51]

Israel's Christian Hebrews received a setback when the Israel Supreme Court ruled in 1963 that a Christian Hebrew was not covered by the country's Law of Return, under which any Jew the world over could migrate to Israel and automatically acquire Israeli citizenship solely on the grounds that he was Jewish.[52]

If the state did not consider Christian Hebrews to be Jews, how was the law of personal status, affecting marriage, divorce, conversion, and inheritance, to be applied to them? Following the precedents established during the mandate period, personal status was determined by the religious groups recognized by the mandatory government. Nine such groups were recognized, but none of them were Protestant.[53] There are only 2,000 Anglicans, Protestants, and Copts in Israel, a small percentage of the country's 56,000 Christians.[54] What makes the status of Protestants different from that of the other Christian groups is not their relatively small numbers but the fact that they are latecomers to the Holy Land. The American Protestants were practically the last Protestant group to arrive in the country. "Small as it is," observed a writer, "the Protestant community is broken into numerous sects, some of them consisting of only one or two self-ordained individuals. Which groups should be given 'official status'?"[55]

In practice, Israel's Protestant clergymen have been accorded de facto the right to perform marriage ceremonies for the members of the same denomination, and to register each marriage with the Israel Ministry of Religious Affairs. However, they remain subject to

Israeli civil courts in matters of divorce and the legal admission of converts.[56]

Besides pursuing their missionary and ecclesiastical interests, Protestant groups in Israel have established new forums.[57] Though these innovative patterns have affected some Protestants in the United States, it appears that thus far their impact on official American Protestant policy vis-à-vis Israel has been minimal.

In 1959 the Israel American Institute of Biblical Studies, an American Protestant evangelical foundation, opened in Jerusalem with fourteen American students and two American teachers.[58] Its course of studies stresses Judaica, and gives particular attention to contemporary Israeli problems. Its founder, the Reverend G. Douglas Young, dean of the Trinity Seminary of the Evangelical Free Church of America in Chicago, Illinois, asserted that the need for the Institute became apparent to him when he led a group of tourists to the Near East three years earlier and became alarmed at their ignorance about Israel.[59] He became especially aware of their bias against Israel after they had spent a large amount of time touring the Arab lands. On the other hand, Young and his millennarian colleagues reached the conclusion that "current events in the Middle East seem to fulfill the prophecies of the Bible."[60] After negotiating with the Israeli field representative of the Christian and Missionary Alliance, the institute began to function in the building of the Christian and Missionary Alliance, with students drawn from ten different theological schools in the United States. A new group of students is in residence every six months, and the institute is open to non-Americans as well. Though the institute has a director in Jerusalem, Young continues to direct and promote its activities from Chicago.

In May 1961 some 3,000 members of twenty-four millennium-oriented Pentecostal organizations, about half of them Americans, attended the Sixth Pentecostal World Conference in Jerusalem.[61] The combined membership of these Protestant groups is estimated at ten million. In 1964 an all-Protestant agricultural settlement, *Nes Amim*, was established in Israel "to heal the breach which has existed between Jews and Christians for two thousand years."[62] This village is settled mostly by European Protestants.

Since the establishment of the state of Israel, the Holy Land has taken on an additional significance in the lives of Israeli Protestants, while not yet affecting the standard theology or policies of American Protestantism. As expressed by the Reverend Peter Schneider, advisor to the Anglican bishop in Jerusalem:

The stress on community, and the Israeli attempt to integrate the various Jewish communities from the Diaspora into one homogeneous community in Israel, has had its ecumenical effect upon the Christian churches. By a strange coincidence, one of the most forceful Jewish factors toward integration, i.e. the use of modern Hebrew, is also an ecumenical factor for the churches. Liturgies that have for centuries been used in different ecclesiastical languages have for the first time in Israel been used in the one common language of Hebrew. Sometimes the only common language between various Christian leaders and groups is that of modern Hebrew. The modern state of Israel . . . continuously reminds the Church of its historic sources. Some of these are admittedly shared with the Jewish people, but even those associated directly with the New Testament cannot, in Israel, be viewed out of their Jewish setting.[63]

11

The Six-Day War

THE PERIOD SURROUNDING THE SIX-DAY WAR IN
June 1967, between Israel and three of her Arab neighbors—Egypt,
Jordan and Syria—served as a notable watershed in the attitudes of
Protestantism towards the state of Israel and the Jewish people. Not
since the establishment of the Jewish state nineteen years earlier had
there been such a dramatic opportunity to assess the nature and test
the quality of these attitudes.

On May 16, 1967, President Gamal Abdul Nasser of Egypt requested that the buffer United Nations Emergency Force positioned
by the United Nations after the 1956 war between Israel and Egypt
be withdrawn from Sinai and Sharm El Sheikh at the entrance to the
Gulf of Aqaba. United Nations Secretary General U Thant con-
sented on May 18. Five days later Nasser announced a blockade of
the Straits of Tiran, sealing off access to Israel's key southern port,
Eilat, and on May 30 he concluded a military agreement with his
erstwhile enemy, King Hussein of Jordan.

The Israelis were understandably alarmed, and Jewish organizations throughout the world closed ranks in support of the Jewish
state. Since its establishment Israel had become to Jewish communities throughout the world a symbol of collective pride. Its development and achievements had blunted to some extent the pain and the
shame felt by Jews at the close of the holocaust period. It was little
wonder, therefore, that Jews outside of Israel were most apprehensive about the events unfolding on Israel's borders.

American Protestantism Remains Silent

During the tense weeks before the outbreak of hostilities, daily
newspapers and communications media in the United States gave

prominence to Israel's plight, but official Christian organizations were strangely silent. When it appeared that Israel might become the victim of Arab aggression, a number of individual Catholic, Protestant, and Orthodox Christian leaders as well as a few Christian journals of opinion publicly supported Israel's political integrity and navigation rights.[1] The official publications of Protestant (and Catholic) bodies, however, scarcely referred to the subject. American Protestant churches expressed no support for Israel's right to exist as an independent state, nor was there any indication that they were disquieted by the explicit Arab radio broadcasts threatening Israel's destruction. Whether judged from a moral or a humanitarian standpoint Israel's continued existence seemed to be irrelevant to American Protestantism. To many American Jews this indifferent attitude of American Christendom was reminiscent of the churches' stance towards the plight of European Jewry during the holocaust period.[2]

The silence of the churches was all the more disturbing to American Jews because there had been for years interfaith dialogues between representatives of organized Jewish bodies and Protestant church groups. American Jews had expected an official expression of Christian concern for Israel's plight, but no such reaction was forthcoming. It was clear that the interfaith dialogue had failed to make clear to American Christendom the centrality of the land of Israel in Judaism. While one Jewish spokesman active in the interfaith movement admitted that he "did not expect Christian institutions to accept the Jewish understanding of the religious and cultural significance of Israel and Jerusalem to Judaism," he did hope for a Christian response to the threatened destruction of Israel's citizens. Rabbi Marc Tannenbaum, national director of the Interreligious Affairs Department of the American Jewish Committee, declared: "It was the moral and human issue of the potential massacre of 2,500,000 Jews that demanded a spontaneous outcry from those authorized to speak for the Christian conscience in this nation."[3]

Typical of official Protestant reactions to the threat facing Israel was the "Background and Guideline Memorandum" issued on May 31, 1967 by the Division of Christian Social Concern of the American Baptist Church. The document ascribed the tense Near Eastern situation to Israel's Declaration of Independence "before the United Nations had completed its deliberations" on the future of Palestine, the Arab refugees, and unsettled boundaries. The memorandum did not in the least refer to the military threat to Israel's very existence.

American Protestantism's insistence on linking the rights of Arab refugees to any formula supporting Israel's right to exist as a state was evident in the telegram sent by the president of the National Council of Churches, Dr. Arthur S. Fleming, to President Johnson on June 6, 1967, three days before the cease-fire took effect. In pressing for a cease fire through the United Nations, the telegram clearly spelled out this relationship.[4]

Other Protestant officials did not even bother to mention Israel's dilemma but were content merely to offer "prayers." On June 5 the Reverend Frederick Nolde, director of the International Affairs Commission of the World Council of Churches, assured U Thant of his "prayers that action by the United Nations may yet avert catastrophe."[5] On June 7, four officers of the World Council of Churches—two of them Americans—urged the member churches "to make the strongest representations to their governments" to bring about a cessation of hostilities, and to "especially remember in their prayers churches in the area of conflict and all those who are suffering as a result of hostilities."[6]

In none of these statements was there any suggestion that Protestantism supported Israel's right to exist. As expressed by an American Jewish spokesman, "In the face of what appeared to most Jews as the imminent prospect of another Auschwitz for the corporate Jewish body in Israel, this rhetoric, with its echo of the earlier flight into pietism by Christian leaders in Nazi Germany, contributed to a pervading sense of gloom in American Jewry."[7]

Jewish religious leaders across the country found it difficult to arouse the concern and compassion of their Christian colleagues when asking them to adopt declarations supporting Israel's survival. As one rabbi revealed, "Clergymen and theologians were begged to sign a statement of conscience in behalf of Israel, and in large numbers they refused. . . . The pity is . . . that when at last voices were raised, they were in the main voices evoked by the pleas of Jews."[8] One such public statement issued on May 29, 1967 on behalf of eleven nationally prominent American clergymen was initiated by several of their Jewish friends.[9] The statement read:

> Men of conscience must not remain silent at this time. We call on our fellow Americans of all persuasions and groupings, and on the administration, to support the independence, integrity, and freedom of Israel. Men of conscience all over the world bear a moral responsibility to support Israel's right of passage through the Straits of

Tiran. The people of Israel have a right to live and develop in tranquility and without fear.

The statement's endorsers, prominent as they were, did not speak for organized American Christendom.[10] As characterized by Judith Banki of the American Jewish Committee, "The reluctance of the two powerful 'umbrella' organizations—the National Council of Churches and the National Conference of Catholic Bishops—with whom Jews had been carrying on a continuous dialogue for some years, to commit themselves unequivocally on the basic question of Israel's survival, especially in the face of Arab threats to annihilate the whole population, came as a surprise to many Jewish leaders. Neither of these two groups issued any clear cut statement to this effect during the saber-rattling days in May."[11] Mrs. Banki continued: "Jews did not expect unanimous Christian support for every policy decision of the state of Israel. What they did expect was an outpouring of protest at the threats to annihilate human beings—the Jews of Israel—and an affirmation of the right to defend themselves and their nation."[12]

During and after the hostilities several Christian religious spokesmen echoed Mrs. Banki's remarks, but they were clearly in the minority. A. Roy Eckardt, editor of the *Journal of the American Academy of Religion* and professor of religion at Lehigh University, and his wife Alice disputed the thesis that it was wrong for the churches to take sides in view of the murky morality inherent in the Palestine question. Such an allegation, they held, was not creditable because "a fundamental of ethics is the necessity to distinguish among the facts of a case where there can be no absolute right or wrong, and the responsibility to act in behalf of the side more nearly in the right."[13] The Eckardts asserted "the Arabs are wrong in their would-be politicide against the Jewish nation. That policy is not just 'partly' wrong and hence to be only 'partly' opposed; it is altogether wrong and ought to be fought unqualifiedly."

Theological Bias Against Israel

The Eckardts explained the callousness of the churches toward Israel on theological grounds. First, the Christian mind was conditioned by Greek dualism to differentiate between "matter" and "spir-

169

it," against the Hebraic insistence on life's unity. Israel, being a secular state, was defective in its spirituality and undeserving of Christian support.[14] Secondly, and perhaps more significantly, there were many millions of Arabs in "great spiritual need" who represented a huge reservoir for converts to Christianity. It was essential to avoid alienating them and also to ensure the safety of Christian missionaries hard at work among them.[15] Third, and even more revealing,

> The entire movement to re-establish the Jewish people in their ancient homeland . . . has been a traumatic experience from which the collective Christian psyche has never entirely recovered. . . . How presumptuous for Israel to be "reborn" in clear violation of Christian eschatology! Just as in 1933-45 unnumbered people in the churches were quite convinced that the Nazis were the unwitting allies of God—since the Jews were "no longer" His people—so in 1967 a powerful ideological affinity is manifest between Christian predispositions and the annihilationist designs of the Arabs. . . . The pathological collective unconscious of Christendom has at last come to the surface. . . . The Jews are *the* enemy; the more they *appear* to be helpless victims, the more they are *in actuality* conspiring as the devil's own agents of destruction.[16]

The Eckardts' analysis explained the continued silence of the churches, "revolting though this explanation is."[17]

This attack on the churches did not go unanswered. Paul E. Hoffman of the Lutheran World Federation challenged the Eckardts to "at least adapt the formal courtesy of not impugning the motives of one's opponents."[18] Henry P. Van Dusen, former president of the Union Theological Seminary and an active leader in the Protestant missionary movement, labeled their views "distorted and . . . disordered imagination. Such an imagination appears incapable [of assuming] that a mind, especially a Christian mind, can be authentically objective and unbiased toward the Israeli-Arab confrontation in the Middle East."[19]

It is doubtful whether Dr. Van Dusen himself portrayed an "objective and unbiased" attitude toward the conflict when, in a letter to the *New York Times*, he declared:

> All persons who seek to view the Middle East problem with honesty and objectivity stand aghast at Israel's onslaught, the most violent, ruthless (and successful) aggression since Hitler's blitzkrieg across Western Europe in the summer of 1940, aiming not at victory but annihilation. . . . anyone who voices such judgments knows that he risks alienation from honored and beloved Jewish friends and as-

sociates. It is perhaps better that it be declared by one who no longer holds Christian office than by those, many of whom are expressing similar views privately, whose responsibilities in the "Christian Establishment" stop them from forthright public speech.[20]

Eckardt, a former student of Van Dusen at Union Theological Seminary, replied to this letter:

> I find it hard to believe that Dr. Van Dusen is really the source of this unspeakable distortion of the facts. . . . The pathological collective unconsciousness of Christendom, nurtured by centuries of the churches' "teaching of contempt" (Jules Isaac) for Jews has at last risen to the surface. . . . The only eventuality that would mutually satisfy Communist, Arab and Christion detractors of Jews for the latter's "aggression" would be for Jews to consent to lie down and be slaughtered. At least this would fulfill one side of the traditional yearning of Christendom, as described (and opposed) by J. Coert Rylaarsdam: "The only good Jews are dead Jews."[21]

Eckardt's viewpoint was not widely shared by Protestant religious leaders. A notable exception was Reinhold Niebuhr who compared the Six-Day War to the story of David and Goliath. He said: "The Arabs and Communist representatives accused Israel of firing the first shots. Obviously a nation that knows that it is in danger of strangulation will use its fists."[22]

Niebuhr's cohort at *Christianity and Crisis*, John Bennett, seemed to reflect the attitude of liberal American Protestantism more accurately when he differentiated between his sympathy for Israel when threatened with extinction and his withholding approval of Israel's victory unless she were to take back Arab refugees, offer compensation to unrepatriated Arabs, and build bridges to the Third World.[23] At the same time Bennett felt it would be "one sided" for the United Nations to condemn Israel as the aggressor.

Bennett later elaborated on these views in an article in which he declared it "grossly unfair" to equate Arab threats to exterminate Israel with Israeli threats against the Arab nations. He wrote: "It is obvious that Israel, having no space for retreat, is highly vulnerable, whereas the Arab nations can be defeated without being destroyed. . . . with Israel victorious, and with the question now whether she is to keep what she has gained by conquest, we find the emphasis in our own position changing."[24]

While acknowledging that the Protestant Establishment was

sensitive to the anti-Israel position of Christians in the Arab countries, Bennett refused to admit that the churches were afraid of offending Arabs because of their missionary stake among them. He did, however, express fears for the safety of Christian minorities in Arab lands were American Protestant leadership not to support the Arab cause.[25] Finally, Bennett refused to pass judgment on the moral issue of "carving a Jewish nation out of Palestine." While acknowledging the Jewish people's "right to invest their lives and their treasure in Palestine," he insisted that Israel must concern herself with the Arab refugees, even before the Arab states recognized her, and must assure the Arabs that she was not engaged in a pattern of conquest.[26]

Israel's Postwar Image

After the defeat of the Arab armies in the Six-Day War, American Protestant spokesmen began to wage a campaign against Israel's victorious image. Some statements were couched in general terms; other were very specific. What they all shared was placing the onus of responsibility for future developments in the Middle East squarely on Israel.

The mildest criticism was expressed, surprisingly, by the *Christian Century*, which under the editorship of Kyle Haseldon maintained a policy far more sympathetic to Israel than at any other time in the publication's history. Devoting an entire issue to the Middle East, the periodical dramatically noted the relative silence of its cadre of pro-Arab writers. It editorialized: "Perhaps this silence is an acknowledgment that in the present crisis the Arab world . . . was guilty of fomenting and initiating the war in which it went down to humiliating defeat before Israel's lightning strikes."[27] On the other hand, the publication recognized Israel's opportunity in the new circumstances as one of great delicacy. "Israel's advantage," it wrote, "is one that should be handled without arrogance and with great restraint and wisdom."[28]

A much sharper tone towards Israel was sounded by Alan Geyer in *Christianity and Crisis*.[29] Director of International Relations for the United Church of Christ and later editor of *Christian Century*, Geyer challenged Israel's political capacity "to respond to reasonable peace terms and to be magnanimous toward her defeated adversaries in their humiliation and appalling human need." He rationalized Hussein's entry into the war against Israel as the result of Israel's raid on the Jordanian town of Samu more than six months earlier. "Hussein's almost incredible flight to Cairo on May 30 must be seen as a political extension of the Samu raid which must be accounted now, as it was by many in November, as a major Israeli blunder." While acknowledging that the earlier partition of Jerusalem into Arab and Jewish sections "was a scandal and a failure, . . . it is beyond belief that simple acquiescence in Israeli control of all of the Holy City will really establish 'the peace of Jerusalem.' " Geyer urged Israel (and American Jewish organizations) to help relieve the plight of the Arab refugees and to avoid "double standards" by allowing United Nations forces to patrol its side of the border. Finally, the author noted "a sudden realization that most of us do not maintain any meaningful dialogue with Arabs, whether Christian or Muslim" and insisted that "new forms of communication are absolutely essential, as well as much sounder bases of understanding with Jews."[30]

Other anti-Israel Protestant spokesmen were even more violent in their attacks on Israel. Writing in *Christianity Today*, the Reverend James L. Kelso, a former moderator of the United Presbyterian Church who had worked as an archeologist in the Middle East for many years, wrote: "There is a deep horror about all this history in the fact that great numbers of Christians in the United States applaud Israel's crimes against Arab Christians and Arab Muslims. How can a Christian applaud the murder of a brother Christian by Zionist Jews?"[31]

The Reverend Willard G. Oxtoby, Presbyterian minister and assistant professor at Yale in the Department of Religious Studies, focused his criticism on the American Jewish community. He stated that the difference between Christians and Jews was not merely a lack of agreement on the role of Jesus. "To discover the heart of Judaism," he said, "we must lift the focus from the messiahship of Jesus to the peoplehood of Israel. . . . Thus while in the Christian view, the state of Israel is simply a political fact, for many Jews it is also a profoundly religious fact."[32] Oxtoby observed that for many American Jews, Zionism functioned as a defense against assimilation to modern secular culture, and that the great masses of Jews who contribute financially to Israeli causes do so for atonement reasons, i.e., for having escaped the sufferings of European Jewry. This, he asserted, explained why American Jews viewed any criticism of the state of Israel as "a blasphemous attack on their religious identity."[33]

In scathing criticism of American Jews who ensnared the sympathies of American churchmen, Oxtoby wrote:

> To assert that Israel has no moral claim to Arab land is to deny the Jewish compensation for Auschwitz and Buchenwald, and thus to question divine justice. To assert that Israel had inadequate provocation for launching its preventive attack in June is to cast doubt on the fact of Jewish suffering and thereby on the "sacramental theology" which undergirds fund drives. To suggest that Israel deserves no support from religious men because it inflicted suffering through acts of premeditated brutality is to question the concept of Jewish peoplehood. And finally, to liken Israel's militancy to the Germans, annexation of old Jerusalem to Hitler's Anschluss, is the unpardonable sin. All of which is to say that anything short of total commitment to the righteousness of Israel's cause is interpreted as antisemitism. . . . Christians clearly have more concerns besides the concern for interfaith harmony. The concern for truth and justice, in my opinion, overrides the concern for harmony.[34]

Oxtoby's attack on American Jews can better be understood in the light of other remarks in which he stressed his denomination's strong church interests and ties in the Near East. Presbyterians, he candidly said, "have for a century invested in the educational resources of Syria, Lebanon and Egypt; the good will built up over a century can vanish overnight if Americans close their ears to the Arab side."[35]

Sharp reactions against Israel came from still other Protestant spokesmen.[36] But a more typical appraisal of the official Protestant policy on Israel came from the National Council of Churches. In essence, its attitude sought to establish an "even handedness" in assessing the Israel-Arab problem. On July 7, 1967, the executive committee of the General Board of the National Council of Churches adopted a resolution which had been prepared by a task force of forty members, including churchmen involved in international affairs, Middle East overseas missions, and Christian social action.[37] The council declared that it could not "condone by silence" Israel's territorial expansion by armed force or approve her annexation of the old city of Jerusalem. But the resolution also said that recognition of Israel by the entire international community was "indispensable to peace" and called for early talks between the belligerents. Expectantly, the council urged increased effort to solve the refugee problem for which Israel, the Arab states, and other nations shared the responsibility. It also advocated free access by all nations to the Gulf of Aqaba and the Suez Canal.

The council's resolution was seemingly a balanced statement on the Near East problem, yet some critics found it wanting just because it gave equal weight to its varied components. The basic issue between the organized Jewish and Protestant communities was whether a clear moral commitment existed on the part of Christians to support Israel's survival—the survival of both its population and the state itself. A comprehensive study prepared by the American Jewish Committee concluded: "It was the unwillingness of most church organizations to declare themselves on this key question which aroused the resentment of Jewish spokesmen."[38]

A. Roy Eckardt found the Christian establishments guilty of applying a double standard when dealing with the Arabs and the Israelis:

> The Christian world has challenged no other nation's right to exist in the way it has that of Israel. . . . Why have so many Christian spokesmen condemned Israel for her alleged territorial expansion, and not arraigned the Arab nations for their relentless program to harass and annihilate Israel? Why have Protestant, Catholic and Orthodox representatives castigated the Israelis for reunifying Jerusalem, and found no sin in Jordan for her original conquest of the Old City and for abuses of religious freedom there?[39]

Eckardt concluded that "Christian anti-Zionism is the new Christian anti-Semitism. . . . The Christian death wish for Jews find[s] a new actualization" in the Arab-Israel conflict.[40]

The *Christian Century*, however, upheld the National Council's need "to take the long view" and supported its position on the Near East problem.[41] Even before the council's July 7 resolution, the periodical advised its readers that the National Council of Churches "was not and could not . . . [be] unequivocally behind Israel in the Middle East war . . . whatever the merits and demerits in the current dispute. . . . Whatever the loyalties of individual staff members of the National Council of Churches, the organization's neutrality in the present crisis is for it the only just and wise position."[42] In a further editorial the paper lauded "the sane course pursued by the National Council of Churches; captive to no pressure group, it has sought to 'speak truth to power.'"[43]

The *Christian Century* was particularly resentful of those

American Christian and Jewish spokesmen who criticized American Protestant churches for not speaking up for Israel during the trying days preceding the Six-Day War. It called their stance an "ideological flip flop" in the light of their support of the organization called Clergy and Laymen Concerned about Vietnam. "War is the enemy," proclaimed the periodical, "not this war or that, but war itself."[44]

The Protestant journal was "appalled" at the charge by Jewish leaders that the churches had deserted Israel at a perilous time. It labeled such accusations "false" in view of the mass sympathy for Israel expressed by American public opinion.[45] The periodical clearly did not differentiate between the pro-Israel public sentiment communicated through public opinion polls and the secular news media and the lack of such sympathy reflected by the relative silence of the religious press. The *Christian Century* seemed to have misunderstood the main thrust of Jewish criticism which was directed at the churches' silence *before* hostilities broke out. It advised its readers to postpone judgment about Israel's post–Six-Day War territorial integrity until matters would become more clear. Christians "will not sign a blank check," warned the publication.[46]

The *Christian Century* did not rule out the possibility of better understanding of the subject through increased dialogue with Jews. It merely refused to accept as "a condition to interfaith dialogue the notion that all Christians first become Zionists."[47] But so far as interfaith discussion was concerned, it maintained that "this is the time to increase and deepen the Jewish Christian dialogue, not to suspend it."[48]

A considered Jewish response to this plea for increased dialogue was expressed in the *Christian Century* by Rabbi David Polish of Evanston, Illinois. He maintained that Christian-Jewish dialogue thus far had been superficial. If future dialogue was to be meaningful it had to rest on a major premise, namely, that "theological conversation outside the reality of a living Jewish people is meaningless. . . . Acknowledgment of Jewish peoplehood as a human reality, not merely as a historical curiosity, is central to dialogue. . . . *These* Jews of *this* time must be confronted, not merely some shadowy descendants of the prophets."[49]

A more conciliatory approach was taken by Rabbi Marc Tannenbaum. In response to the sharp criticism of Jewish leaders against the silence of the churches and their sense of futility towards further interfaith dialogue, Tannenbaum took them to task for belittling the many years of Jewish-Christian discussions. He claimed that "the Christians by and large did well by Israel," though their official institutions did not.[50] "The dialogue may not have proven to be all that its supporters have claimed," he asserted, "but it is certainly far more than the caricature its opponents have made of it."[51]

For Tannenbaum, the most significant consequence of the Jewish-Christian dialogue to date had been "to call upon Christians to give up their designs to convert Jews."[52] The challenge facing the interfaith dialogue henceforth was to help "overcome Christian ignorance or misunderstanding of Jewish peoplehood . . . and the symbolic meaning of Israel and Jerusalem to Judaism and the Jewish people."[53]

Tannenbaum predicted a bright future for such dialogue, provided that Jews themselves clarify more fully their own understanding "of these complex questions." He declared:

> We are far from anything like a consensus on the meaning of Israel to the Jewish people. Is Israel simply a secular nation-state? Does it represent the fulfillment of messianic expectations that date back to the prophets of Israel? Is it an eschatological reality, pointing to the day of judgment which the prophets foretold would usher in . . . the Kingdom of Heaven? . . . In the main, rabbis and Jewish teachers have not clarified these fundamental issues relating to Israel, neither for themselves nor for their Jewish audience. How much less have we clarified these questions for our Christian neighbors.[54]

Tannenbaum's point clearly underscores one important reason why modern Jewry has not succeeded in guiding American Protestantism towards a more positive appreciation of Israel and the Jewish people. The terms of reference of Jews and Christians with regard to Israel are at variance with one another. Christians seem to view contemporary Israel as just another political state. The Jews view it as an expression of their people's collective will to live. The Christian has not yet digested the significance of Israel to the Jew.[55] It is little wonder, therefore, that misunderstandings on the subject continue to arise. As expressed by an American Protestant church official "known for his pro-Jewish sympathies":

> When something happens in the Middle East, Jews spark in a way we don't. For them the future of Israel is the future of their people, but I'm not part of that people and don't have that sense. I can empathize, but I can't identify. The most you can do is ask someone to react in his own way.[56]

12

Conclusion

A BASIC CONTRADICTION EXISTS BETWEEN THE AT-
titude of American Protestantism toward Jews as individuals and its
attitude toward the Jewish people as a collective entity. Modern liberal Protestantism has consistently protested overt anti-Semitic acts
against individual Jews and has labeled anti–Semitism a theological
sin. But it has remained blind to the sharp contrast which exists between its theoretical objections to anti–Semitism and the practical
injurious effects of its own subtle anti–Semitism on the destiny of the
Jewish people as a collective body. Protestantism's liberal attitude
toward Jews as individuals stands in sharp contrast to its persistently hostile attitude toward Jewish peoplehood.

The reason for this inconsistency is clear: American Protestant denominations continue to share the universal Christian view of
Jews as an amorphous mass of individuals united in their rejection of
Jesus as the Messiah and bereft of normative national attributes.
Denying the existence of a viable Jewish people, liberal Protestantism has persistently upheld the Christian theological doctrine of the
disappearance of "old Israel," the Jewish people, when "new Israel,"
the Christian church, came into being. The name "Israel" continues
to be understood by Christendom not as an ethnic-religious term
describing a corporate national body of Jews, but as a spiritual concept denoting the religious brotherhood of all Christian believers.
Jewry continues to remain an object of contempt for Christian society.[1]

This anti-Jewish bias has seldom been expressed by liberal Protestantism in theological terms. Overt theological anti-Semitism was
not appropriate to America's democratic society, nor to an "enlightened" Christianity.[2] Instead this prejudice has been projected consistently in negative policies toward concrete expressions of Jewish
collective existence. Whether through representative religious publi-

178

cations, resolutions of official church bodies, policies of ad hoc liberal Protestant organizations, or the persistent viewpoints of some of its distinguished leaders, American liberal Protestantism has fought against Jewish national and ethnic interests.

In the United States Protestant spokesmen disapproved of cultural pluralism as it related to Jewish ethnicity and fought the immigration of large numbers of Jewish refugees from the Nazi inferno.

Reacting to the European holocaust, they protested the transfer and rescue of several thousand Jewish children from Europe to Palestine and disregarded the gruesome Nazi atrocities against the Jewish people, labeling them initially as exaggerations and propaganda.

American liberal Protestantism denounced the appearance of Jewish nationalism while upholding the legitimacy of other nationalisms and campaigned against the establishment of a sovereign Jewish state in the Holy Land.

It begrudgingly recognized the existence of such a state once it was established but continually sought to reduce its boundaries and endanger its security.

It remained indifferent to the fate of the Jewish state and its two million citizens when they were threatened with extinction by hostile Arab governments in 1967.

Finally American Protestantism has refused to accept the reality of Jewish jurisdiction over Jerusalem since the Six-Day War, though it had reconciled itself to Muslim control of Jerusalem from 1948 to 1967.

The theological bias of American Protestantism against Jewish nationalism has been compounded by its support of Protestant missionary interests in the Arab world. While American Protestant missionaries were unsuccessful in converting Muslims to Christianity, they did make a major contribution to the development of Arab nationalism and the spread of Protestant educational and philanthropic institutions in the Middle East. Because the missionaries in the Arab countries provided political support for the Arab cause, they inevitably became opponents of Jewish nationalism in Palestine. Consequently, the sponsoring denominations in the United States, along with former American missionaries and children of missionaries, invariably supported the battle against Zionism. Fortuitously, the bias of Christian theology against the reemergence of Jewish nationhood blended with American Protestant support for Arab nationalism.

During the war many American Protestant leaders as individuals joined Christian groups which expressed concern for the rescue of Jews on humanitarian grounds. They supported Palestine as the major haven for Jewish refugees not because of political reasons or sympathy for Jewish nationalism, but because no other place in the world was prepared to receive these refugees. Only toward the end of the war, and especially after the war, when the United Nations began to grapple with the Palestine question, did many of these Protestant leaders endorse the Zionist goal of Jewish statehood.

The outstanding Protestant spokesman on behalf of Zionism was Reinhold Niebuhr. Unlike other Protestant leaders whose theological bias against a viable Jewish people was subtle but evident, Niebuhr viewed Jewish peoplehood in theological terms as a legitimate component of the divine plan. While not minimizing the injustice which would be meted out to the Palestinian Arabs as a result of the establishment of a Jewish state, he stressed that the Arabs had a huge hinterland into which they could be integrated. They were not faced with extinction. On the other hand, a greater injustice would be perpetrated if the Jews were to become extinct as a viable people because they were denied statehood in Palestine. Niebuhr's influence on a large sector of Protestant public opinion was seminal during the war years and after. His advocacy of Palestine first as the principal haven for Jewish refugees and later as a Jewish state was unquestionably responsible for the success of the American Christian Palestine Committee.

It would be fallacious, however, to conclude that Christian support for Jewish survival, even on humanitarian grounds, was arrived at through Christian initiative. Whenever a serious challenge existed to collective Jewish existence—the European holocaust, the struggle for a Jewish state, the threat to Israel's security in 1967—non-Jewish groups had to be prodded to express their concern. When such groups did respond to crucial issues affecting Jewish survival, they did so by and large through ad hoc Christian organizations, formed and in most instances subsidized by Jews.

The militancy of American Jewish organizations regarding the Jewish state produced a notable impact on those Protestants who initially approached the Jewish problem largely on a humanitarian basis. Without such an aggressive approach it is questionable whether many American Protestant leaders would have supported the Jewish state concept. On the other hand, Zionism's aggressive approach to Jewish statehood, as against its earlier milder policy of viewing Palestine mainly as a Jewish national home or a haven of refuge, clearly set in motion organized counterforces of American Protestants. These, however, emerged too late to change the course of history in the Middle East.

An analysis of American liberal Protestant policies regarding problems of the Near East discredits the pietistic Protestant belief that these policies have been based on purely objective, humanitarian, altruistic, or religious motivations. Like all large religious and secular groups, American liberal Protestantism has its own truths and biases. These attitudes are not devoid of political considerations nor of power-mongering.

The official Protestant treatment of the Arab refugees has been motivated primarily by political, not humanitarian, considerations. While objecting to Catholic intervention in the affairs of Jerusalem, American Protestantism did not feel discomforted in doing so itself. While strongly supporting the Arab cause in the name of self-determination, it urged the internationalization of Jerusalem against the wishes of its 100,000 Jewish residents. While heralding the universalism of Christianity against the nationalism of Judaism, it has accepted the extreme nationalism of Arab Protestants, the distinctive national traditions of European Protestants, and the pluralistic pattern of religion in American national life. While objecting strenuously to Jewish political influence in the United States, American Protestantism did not find it objectionable to promote its policies through its own Washington contacts.

American Protestantism today is confronted with the radical challenge of adjusting itself to the new reality of a living Israel. The resurrection of "old Israel" has seriously shaken its theological position on Jewish nationalism. Protestantism requires new interpretations of the meaning of "Israel"—the people, the state, the biblical term, the church. Unless it faces the need for such urgent clarifications, its own theology could be seriously undermined. By tolerating the practice of some Protestant churches in Arab lands of expunging the term "Israel" from all religious usage, lest it remind Christians of the Jewish state, Protestantism invites further weakening of its theological foundations.

Despite the fact that Christian Arabs and Protestant missionaries have lined up intransigently against the physical state of Israel, a reevaluation of the term "Israel" by Protestant thinkers the world over will undoubtedly be effected by several positive factors which have emerged since the establishment of the state.

The mere existence and functioning of a sovereign Jewish state is in itself a fact which is bound to change the views of many Christians with regard to the reality of Jewish nationalism. The hundreds of thousands of Christian tourists who visit Israel annually cannot help but be impressed with the dynamism of a viable and vibrant Jewish people which is far from extinct. The presence in Israel of a small non-Arab Protestant and Catholic population has produced a counterpoint view to the classical anti-Israel stance of Christians. Proclaimed the Christian Ecumenical Theological Research Fraternity in Israel in July 1970: "We empathize with the desire of the [Arab] Palestinians for a national homeland. However, we are grieved by the fact that they on their side do not understand the sufferings of the Jewish people and do not recognize the legitimate claims of Israel to exist. . . . There has always been a link between the Jewish people and the land of Israel. We feel that if justice is to be done to the Jews as well as to the Arabs, this link must be taken into consideration."[3]

The activities of the World Council of Churches International Committee on the Church and the Jewish People, organized in 1961, are bound to influence future Protestant thought about the state of Israel. Originally formed to help coordinate Protestant missionary activities in relation to Jews, the committee has moved away from its missionary purposes, and has played an increasingly active role in world Protestantism on behalf of Israel's national interests.[4]

Increasing, though slow, Catholic adjustment to the concept of Israel will also have a bearing on Protestant thought. In a report to the National Conference of Catholic Bishops in Washington, D.C. in November 1970, the Reverend Edward H. Flannery, executive secretary of the American Bishops Conference for Catholic-Jewish Relations, explained the rationale for the identification of the vast majority of American Jews with the state of Israel, and admitted that dialogues with Jewish spokesmen taught Christian participants about the intense bond which united Jews with Israel.[5]

Finally, American liberal Protestantism's recent acceptance of pluralistic cultural patterns in the United States is bound to lead it to develop a more sympathetic attitude toward Jewish ethnicity. While American Jews cannot assume that their emotional and psychological ties with Israel will be readily accepted by American Protestants without further Jewish crystalization and articulation of this relationship, American Protestantism is undoubtedly far more understanding of the nature of Jewish peoplehood than ever before.

A factor in this understanding has probably been the projection of the collective consciousness of the Negro population in the United States. In March 1967, in the midst of the black revolution in America, the *Christian Century* printed an editorial entitled "Evolving Negro Solidarity." In this editorial, the periodical surprisingly reversed itself on the subject of Jewish peoplehood which it had continually opposed. It now advised American Negroes to emulate the strong "Jewish sense of folk." The periodical stated:

> The story of the Negro in America is quite different from that of the Jew. We speak commonly of the Negro race, not of the Negro people. . . . The white man has not permitted the Negro to be a people, and the Negro is only at this late date beginning to develop a solid sense of folk. . . . Thus it may be that one of the chief enterprises confronting the Negro is the capturing of a sense of history, the creation of a people. . . . It may be that the Negro will have to duplicate the experience of other tightly knit minorities that were first a folk and then mainstream Americans . . . [Let] us hope that as the Negro becomes a proud, self-conscious in-group, he will not become a cultural and social enclave, but, like the Jew, will be both a people and an integral part of the nation.[6]

A thorough prolonged re-evaluation of American Protestantism's understanding of the concept "Israel," though it may prove painful, may change its long-standing negative attitudes toward Jewish nationalism and a Jewish state. It is doubtful, however, whether major progress can be expected until peace prevails between Israel and her Arab neighbors.

notes

INTRODUCTION

1. *Yearbook of American Churches*, 36th issue, 1968 (New York: Council Press), pp. 195-207. All references to American Protestantism include the Unitarian-Universalist Church which is not, however, a member of the National Council of Churches. Its membership is estimated to be fewer than 170,000 (ibid., p. 107). The book discusses only peripherally the recognized fundamentalist churches, such as the American Southern Baptists and the more extreme International Council of Christian Churches. The American Southern Baptists report a membership of eleven million, making them the largest body of American Protestants not represented by the National Council of Churches. Membership figures are unavailable for the International Council of Christian Churches, headed by Rev. Carl McIntyre.

2. Martin E. Marty et al., *The Religious Press in America* (New York: Holt, Rinehart and Winston, 1963), pp. 9-10.

3. Ibid., p. 56.

CHAPTER ONE

1. For an annotated bibliography on the Theocratic Holy Commonwealth, see James W. Smith and A. Leland Jamison, eds., *Religion in American Life* (Princeton, N.J.: Princeton University Press, 1961-), vol. 4, *A Critical Bibliography of Religion in America*, in collaboration with Nelson R. Burr (1961). See also Abraham A. Neuman, "Relation of the Hebrew Scriptures to American Institutions," *Landmarks and Goals* (Philadelphia: Dropsie College Press, 1953); W. B. Selbie, "The Influence of the Old Testament on Puritanism," in *The Legacy of Israel*, eds. Edwyn R. Bevan and Charles Singer (Oxford: Clarendon Press, 1944), pp. 408-31.

2. Robert T. Handy, "Zion in American Christian Movements," in *Israel: Its Role in Civilization*, ed. Moshe Davis (New York: Harper & Brothers, 1956), pp. 284 ff.

3. The Millennium, in Christian eschatology, is the period of a thousand years in which Christ will reign again on earth. During the earliest period of Chris-

tianity, persecuted Christians had eagerly anticipated the Second Coming of their Savior, which would inaugurate a millennium of peace. They were sustained in this belief by combining the prophecies in the Book of Daniel, especially chapters 7 to 9, with those in the Revelation of John, especially chapters 20 and 21.

However, when the church became the political power in Western society, the later church fathers sought to suppress Christian religious stirrings for any change in the earthly and natural status quo. The biblical terms "Zion" and "Jerusalem" were reinterpreted as mere symbolic names for the triumphant church itself. In no way did they bear any relationship to the Jewish people or to their messianic aspirations. See Shirley J. Case, *The Millennial Hope* (Chicago: University of Chicago Press, 1918), chaps. 4 and 5; Leroy E. Froom, *The Prophetic Faith of our Fathers*, 4 vols. (Washington: Review & Herald 1950)1: chaps. 1-20.

4. *Encyclopedia of Religion and Ethics*, 1908-1926, s.v. "Eschatology;" *New Schaff-Herzog Encyclopedia of Religious Knowledge*, 1910, s.v. "Millennium"; Froom, *Prophetic Faith*; Case, *Millennial Hope*; Loraine Boettner, *The Millennium* (Philadelphia; Presbyterian & Reformed Publishing Co., 1958); Charles C. Ryrie, *Dispensationalism Today* (Chicago: Moody Press, 1965); Elmer T. Clark, *The Small Sects in America* (New York: Abingdon-Cokesbury, 1949).

5. In 1538, Henry VIII ordered "the whole Bible of the largest volume in English" to be placed in every church in England, "in some convenient place . . . whereas . . . parishioners may most commodiously resort to the same and read it . . ." He ordered his clergy to "expressly stir, provoke and exhort every person to read the same" (Barbara W. Tuchman,*The Bible and the Sword* [New York: New York University Press, 1956], p. 52).

6. Franz Kobler, *The Vision Was There* (London: Lincolns-Prager, 1956). An example of such early proto-Zionist thinking is found in Thomas Brightman's *A Revelation of the Revelation*, published posthumously in Latin in 1609, then in English in 1615. Basing his work on the Books of Revelation and Daniel, Brightman's theme was the overthrow of the anti-Christ, whom he identified with papal Rome, as a prerequisite to Christ's Second Coming. This event was to be followed by the destruction of the Turks and by the "calling of the Jews" who, upon returning to Palestine, would become a Christian nation. "Shall they return to Jerusalem again?" Brightman asks. "There is nothing more certain: the prophets do everywhere confirm it and beat upon it" (Kobler, p. 16).

7. Tuchman, *Bible and Sword*.

8. Charles L. Sanford, *The Quest for Paradise* (Urbana, Ill.: University of Illinois Press, 1961), chap. 5; Ira V. Brown, "Watchers for the Second Coming: The Millennarian Tradition in America," *Mississippi Valley Historical Review* 39 (1952): 441-58; Truman Nelson, "The Puritans of Massachusetts: From Egypt to the Promised Land," *Judaism* 16 (1967): 193-206.

9. Sanford, *Quest for Paradise*, p. 78.

10. H. Richard Niebuhr, *The Kingdom of God in America* (Chicago: Willett, Clark & Co., 1937), pp. 47 ff.

11. A dispensation is a theological period of time in history during which man is judged by the standards of a specific divine revelation operative during that period. There are seven commonly recognized dispensations: innocence (Garden of Eden), conscience (Adam to Noah), human government (Noah to Ab-

raham), promise (Abraham to Moses), law (Moses to Jesus), grace (Jesus through the present to the final judgment), and the Millennium (Cyrus I. Schofield, ed., *Schofield Reference Bible* [New York: Oxford University Press, 1909]). Other Dispensationalists believe in fewer or more dispensations (Ryrie, *Dispensationalism Today*, p. 50). Loraine Boettner analyses Dispensationalism critically in *The Millennium*.

The Plymouth Brethren of which John Nelson Darby (1800-1882) was a leader had much to do with promoting Dispensationalism (*Encyclopedia Britannica*, 1960, s.v. "Plymouth Brethren"). Darby advocated a church so spiritual that it existed outside of history. The church in this new dispensation of grace was so much a mystery that it had been hidden even from the prophets of the Old Testament. When Israel rejected Jesus as the Messiah, God broke the continuity of history, stopped the prophetic process, and installed the church. When the church is "raptured out" of the world, the clock of prophecy will tick again, and God will return to the task of dealing with earthly Israel (Ernest R. Sandeen, *The Roots of Fundamentalism* [Chicago: University of Chicago Press, 1970], p. 67).

See also nn. 22 and 24 below.

12. Clark, *Small Sects in America*, p. 22 and especially chap. 2. Millennialism "always flourishes best in troublous times, when wickedness is rife and the poor are crying for bread" (William W. Sweet, *Religion in the Development of American Culture* [New York: Charles Scribners & Sons, 1952], p. 307).

13. Most of the Adventist and Pentecostal religious bodies have believed that Jesus would return to establish the Millennium on earth. A major Adventist group which long favored Jewish restoration to Palestine was the Jehovah Witnesses. Unlike other millennarians, they advocated that the Jews not convert to Christianity, but "realize as Jews the ideals set before them by the Lord in the Law and by the prophets." Since 1931, however, they have become increasingly anti-Zionist and pro-missionary in outlook. (See Yonah Malachy, "Jehovah Witnesses and Zionism," in *Herzl Year Book* 5 [1963]: 175-208.)

Another millennial sect, the Seventh Day Adventists, reject the concept that the Jews must be restored to Jerusalem before the Second Coming. They believe that Jesus, after his Second Advent, will reign over the kingdom of the saints for a thousand years in heaven, not on earth. The subject of a Jewish restoration to Palestine, therefore, is irrelevant to them, and their relationship to Jews has been guided by a strictly missionary goal. (See Yonah Malachy, "Seventh Day Adventists and Zionism," in *Herzl Year Book* 6 [1965]: 265-301.)

There are several smaller Adventist sects who continue to believe in Jewish restoration to the Holy Land as a prerequisite to the Millennium (ibid., pp. 292 ff).

See also Clark, *Small Sects in America*, chaps. 2 and 4.

14. Lee M. Friedman, "Cotton Mather and the Jews," *Publications of the American Jewish Historical Society* 26 (1918): 201-10.

Increase Mather wrote in 1722: "The blessed day is coming when all Israel shall be saved. . . . The miraculous manner of God's preserving the Jewish nation is an invincible proof thereof; for it is an unprecedented and incomprehensible thing that God should for two thousand years preserve this people. . . . This clearly demonstrates that God has preserved them for some great design, which can it be but their conversion?" (*Ezra Stiles and the Jews*, ed. with notes by George A. Kohut [New York: Philip Cowen, Publisher, 1902], pp. 40-41).

15. Lee M. Friedman, *Jewish Pioneers and Patriots* (New York: Macmillan Co., 1943) pp. 153-59.

16. Romans 11:26. Ezra Stiles may have been a notable exception among the leading clergymen of his generation who did not pursue an activist conversionist policy, though he may have wished for the Jews' conversion. He sought religious harmony among the Protestant denominations based on "the gentle force of persuasion and truth" which would bring men to one or another religious commitment (Alan Heimert, *Religion and the American Mind* [Cambridge, Mass.: Harvard University Press, 1968], pp. 372-73). His friendly association with Jews and his respect for Judaism have been described in Kohut, *Ezra Stiles and the Jews* and in Morris Jastrow, "References to Jews in the Diary of Ezra Stiles," *Publications of the American Jewish Historical Society* 10 (1902): 5-36. However, I find no evidence to support Selig Adler's contention that Ezra Stiles was loathe to extend full civil rights to Jews lest they "assimilate and thus counteract their destiny to pave the way to Zion" (Selig Adler, "Background of American Policy Toward Zion," in *Israel: Its Role in Civilization*, ed. Davis, p. 252).

17. Relying on Matt. 21:43, 23:38, and 1 Thess. 2:16, a modern author declares, "We want to say most emphatically that when Christ died on Calvary, the old Mosaic order died, never to be revived. . . . Judaism is a thing of the past. It is a glorious memory despite its limitations and its failings. . . . It may seem harsh to say that 'God is through with the Jews' . . . nothing has been taken from the Jews as individuals. . . . But the fact of the matter is that He is through with them as a unified national group. . . . The Old Testament era was the time of the Gentiles. . . . The Christian church is the legitimate heir and successor of Old Testament Israel. . ." (Boettner, *Millennium*, pp. 311-19). The author continues: "This does not mean, of course, that the Jews will never go back to Palestine. . . . But it does mean that as any of them go back they do so entirely on their own, apart from any covenanted purpose to that end and entirely outside of Scripture prophecy. No Scriptural blessing is promised for a project of that kind" (ibid., p. 321).

18. Samuel H. Levine, "Palestine in the Literature of the United States to 1867," in *Early History of Zionism in America*, ed. Isidore S. Meyer (New York: American Jewish Historical Society and Theodor Herzl Foundation, 1958), pp. 21-29.

19. Isaac M. Fein, "Niles Weekly Register on the Jews," *Publication of the American Jewish Historical Society*, vol. 50, no. 1, (1960): 3-22; Milton Plesur, "The American Press and Jewish Restoration During the Nineteenth Century," in *Early History of Zionism in America*, ed. Meyer, pp. 55-68.

20. Plesur, "American Press and Jewish Restoration," p. 56.

21. Extracts from Noah's speech are found in Isaac Goldberg, *Major Noah: American-Jewish Pioneer* (Philadelphia: Jewish Publication Society, 1936), pp. 139-41. Adams' reaction is found in the preface to Noah's "Discourse on the Restoration of the Jews," delivered to an interfaith audience in New York City in two parts, October 28 and December 2, 1844, published in 1845 by Harper & Brothers and reprinted in the *Maccabean* of April 1905. For extracts and framework of the "Discourse," see Goldberg, *Major Noah*, pp. 245ff.; also, Robert Gordis, "Mordecai Manuel Noah," *Publications of the American Jewish Historical Society* 41 (1952): 1-26. Noah also had requested former Presidents Thomas Jefferson and James Madison to react to the first speech at Shearith

Israel. Their acknowledgments, upholding religious freedom but omitting any reaction to the theme of Jewish restoration to Palestine, were published by Noah in the appendix to his *Travels in England, France, Spain and the Barbary States in the Years 1813-1814 and 1815* (New York: Kirk & Mercen, 1819). For extracts from their responses, see Goldberg, *Major Noah*, pp. 142-43.

22. Ernest R. Sandeen, *The Origins of Fundamentalism* (Philadelphia: Fortress Press, 1968), p. 10; see also n. 13 above; Ryrie, *Dispensationalism Today*; Sandeen, *Roots of Fundamentalism*.

23. Galatians 6:15-16. Compare with Arnold Toynbee's description of the Jews as "fossilized relics of societies now extinct," in *A Study of History* 12 vol. (New York and London: Oxford University Press, 1948-1954), vols. 1-3, 5-10 passim, and vol. 12 (1961), pp. 292-300 for his response to criticism for applying the term "fossils" to Jews. For a rebuttal to Toynbee's allegations, see Maurice Samuel, *The Professor and the Fossil* (New York: Alfred A. Knopf, 1956).

24. Daniel P. Fuller, *The Hermeneutics of Dispensationalism*, quoted in Ryrie, *Dispensationalism Today*, p. 45. Dr. Fuller is dean of Fuller Theological Seminary. Says Lewis S. Chafer, the founder of Dallas Theological Seminary and author of the eight-volume *Systematic Theology*: "Throughout the ages God is pursuing two distinct purposes: one related to the earth with earthly people and earthly objectives involved, which is Judaism; while the other is related to heaven with heavenly people and objectives involved, which is Christianity" (Ryrie, *Dispensationalism Today*, p. 45).

On the other hand, fundamentalists hostile to the dispensationalist notion of a viable Jewish people and its restoration to Palestine hold that Prophetic promises given to "the house of Israel and the house of Judah" (Jer. 31:31-34) were really addressed to the Christian church which "in its origin was an Israelitish body fully qualified to claim the promises to Israel" (Boettner, *Millennium*, pp. 315-16). Also, "the prophecies that premillennialists point to as indicating a return of the Jews to Palestine are found in the Old Testament and either were given before the return from the Babylonian capitivity and so were fulfilled by that event, or, as in the case of Zechariah 8:7,8, were given while that return still was in process, it having occurred over a period of years" (ibid., p. 321).

25. Ryrie, *Dispensationalism Today*, p. 138.

26. Sandeen, *Origins of Fundamentalism*, pp. 4-5; G. Douglas Young, *The Bride and the Wife* (Minneapolis: Free Church Publications, 1959).

27. Sandeen traces the renewal of modern Christian millennial interest in Jewish restoration to Lewis Way of England. Way vigorously supported the London Society for Promoting Christianity among the Jews, founded in 1809, which achieved its greatest success as an advocate of Protestant Zionism in England (Sandeen, *Roots of Fundamentalism*, pp. 9ff).

28. William E. Blackstone, *Jesus is Coming*, 3d ed. (Chicago: Fleming H. Revell Co., 1908).

29. Ibid., p. 160.

30. Ibid., chap. 15.

31. Ibid., pp. 236-41.

32. Anita L. Lebeson, "Zionism Comes to Chicago," in *Early History of Zionism in America*, ed. Meyer, pp. 176-77. Among the signers of the Blackstone Memorial were Melville W. Fuller, chief justice of the United States Supreme Court, Thomas B. Reed, speaker of the House of Representatives, William McKinley, congressman of Ohio and later president of the United States, the chairmen of the House Foreign Affairs and Ways and Means Committees, distinguished editors, industrialists, and bankers, including Cyrus H. McCormick, J. P. Morgan, and John D. Rockefeller.

33. Cyrus Adler and Aaron M. Margalith, *American Intercession on Behalf of Jews in the Diplomatic Correspondence of the United States, 1840-1938* (New York: Publications of the American Jewish Historical Society, 1943), no. 36, pt. 3.

34. Sandeen, *Roots of Fundamentalism*, pp. 94-95. Along with the millennarian mood which permeated American Protestant churches, other related factors influenced the religious consciousness of their congregants: the "great awakening" of the prerevolutionary era, which had brought forth a spirit of evangelism in American Protestantism, was revived in the early nineteenth century, leading to a massive religious revivalist movement which underscored the inner moral awakening and spiritual conversion of man (Smith, Jamison and Burr, *Religion in American Life*, 4:148-83); the prophecy and Bible conference movement (Sandeen, *Roots of Fundamentalism*, chap. 6); the pietistic strain in religion, emanating from Germany, which shifted man's stress from belief in creed and religious institutions to a personal striving for religious experience through Bible study, exemplary conduct, and virtuous deeds (*Encyclopedia of Religion and Ethics* 1908-1926, s.v. "Pietism"); the Zion-centered hymns of prayer, which were sung in most American Protestant denominations, reinforcing the psychological association of the participants with biblical Zion; the spread of the Holiness and Perfectionist Movements—the Keswick Conferences—helping to create the spiritual climate for man's striving for righteousness, while continuing to believe in the Millennium (Sandeen, *Roots of Fundamentalism*, pp. 178-79; Clark, *Small Sects in America*, pp. 51-84).

35. Eldin Ricks, "Zionism and the Mormon Church," in *Herzl Year Book 5* (1963): 147-74.

36. Ibid., p. 159.

37. "The Middle East held few lures for Americans in the nineteenth and early twentieth centuries. . . . Almost the sole exception was the American missionary" (William R. Polk, "A Decade of Discovery: America in the Middle East, 1947-1958," in *Middle Eastern Affairs: Number Two*, ed. Albert Hourani, St. Antony's papers no. 11 [London: Chatto & Windus, 1961], p. 50).

38. Edward Robinson, *Biblical Research in Palestine, Mount Sinai and Arabia Petraea*, 3 vols. (London and Boston: Crocker & Brewster, 1841), 1:46.

39. Russel B. Nye, *The Cultural Life of the New Nation 1776-1830* (New York: Harper, 1960), p. 152.

40. Robinson, *Biblical Research in Palestine, Mount Sinai and Arabia Petraea*.

41. William F. Albright, *The Archeology of Palestine*, rev. ed. (London: Penguin Books, 1956), p. 25.

42. Quoted in David Finnie, *Pioneers East* (Cambridge, Mass.: Harvard University Press, 1967), pp. 6, 174. Stephens produced two books about his travels in the Middle East: *Incidents of Travel in Egypt, Arabia Petraea, and the Holy Land,* 2 vols. (New York: Harper & Brothers, 1837) and *In the Russian and Turkish Empires* (London: Bentley, 1839), also published as *Incidents of Travel in Greece, Turkey, Russia and Poland,* 2 vols. (New York: Harper & Brothers, 1838).

43. William F. Lynch, *Narrative of the United States' Exploration to the River Jordan and the Dead Sea* (Philadelphia: n.p., 1849). See an excellent summary in Finnie, *Pioneers East,* pp. 262-70.

44. A. L. Tibawi, "The American Missionaries in Beirut and Bustrus al-Bustani," in *Middle Eastern Affairs: Number Three,* ed. Albert Hourani, St. Antony's Papers no. 16 (London: Chatto & Windus, 1963), pp. 137-82; Finnie, *Pioneers East,* chap. 5: Rufus Anderson, *History of the Missions of the American Board of Commissioners for Foreign Missions to the Oriental Churches,* 2 vols. (Boston: Congregational Publishing Society, 1872); Henry Jessup, *Fifty-three Years in Syria,* 2 vols. (New York: Revell, 1910).

45. Finnie, *Pioneers East,* p. 118.

46. Ibid., p. 129.

47. Ibid., p. 134.

48. For an outline of the history of the Syrian mission of the American Presbyterian Church from 1820 to 1900, see Jessup, *Fifty-three Years in Syria,* 2:809-13.

49. Stephen B. L. Penrose, *That They May Have Light* (Princeton, N.J.: Trustees of the American University of Beirut, 1941); George Antonius, *The Arab Awakening* (London: Hamish Hamilton, 1938), p. 43.

50. Penrose, *That They May Have Light,* p. 5.

51. Albert H. Hourani, *Syria and Lebanon* (London: Oxford University Press, 1946), pp. 83-84.

52. For the influence of spokesmen for American Protestant missions on the peace conference preparations, see Frank E. Manuel, *The Realities of American-Palestine Relations* (Washington, D.C.: Public Affairs Press, 1949), pp. 211ff.

Secretary of State Lansing had expressed himself clearly on the Balfour Declaration when he advised President Wilson, in December 1917, to "go very slowly in announcing a policy" with regard to Palestine. He gave three reasons, the third one being: "Many Christian sects and individuals would undoubtedly resent turning the Holy Land over to the absolute control of the race credited with the death of Christ" (ibid., p. 172).

By the end of 1918, some ten papers had been prepared for the inquiry team studying Palestine and the Arab problem. One of them included the design of Dr. James L. Barton of Boston, head of the Near East Relief Committee and former secretary of the American Board of Commissioners for Foreign Missions. In addition to Barton's design which entered the files of the American delegation at Paris, the Committee of Reference and Counsel of the Foreign Mission Conference of North America—the policy board of United States Protestant missions abroad—contributed an elaborate listing of all Protestant missionary establishments throughout the world, including, of course, the Near East (ibid., p. 212). Palestine alone had 17 Protestant missionary stations, some with more than one establishment (ibid., p. 214).

53. Ibid., p. 223.

54. In November 1918, William Yale, principal intelligence agent of the United States Department of State in the Near East, wrote of Bliss: "He is known to be anti-French. . . . The faculty of the college are as a whole opposed to French occupation of Syria and this in itself has an undoubted effect upon the people. For a number of years, the Americans have fought against French Jesuit influence in Mt. Lebanon and Syria" (ibid.).

55. Ibid., p. 224.

56. In setting forth the British government's policy toward the Near East on November 2, 1917, Foreign Secretary Balfour had declared: "His Majesty's Government view with favor the establishment in Palestine of a national home for the Jewish people, and will use their best endeavors to facilitate the achievement of this object, it being clearly understood that nothing shall be done which may prejudice the civil and religious rights of existing non-Jewish communities in Palestine, or the rights and political status enjoyed by Jews in any other country."

For a background on the wartime commitments of Great Britain, see Paul L. Hanna, *British Policy in Palestine* (Washington, D.C.: American Council on Public Affairs, 1942); Manuel, *Realities of American-Palestine Relations*; Antonius, *Arab Awakening*.

57. The Zionist presentation was made before the Big Powers, though Wilson was absent, on February 27 (Manuel, *Realities of American-Palestine Relations*, p.228).

58. For an analysis of the complicated status of former Turkish territories up to the time of the San Remo Conference (April 1920), at which time France became the mandatory power over Syria, and Britain over Palestine and Iraq, see Hanna, *British Policy in Palestine*, chaps. 1-4. The League of Nations approved the mandates only in July, 1922.

59. Frank Manuel, the historian, has labelled Crane "a man who in later years became a hysterical anti-Semite" (*Realities of American-Palestine Relations*, pp. 236-7).

60. Ibid., p. 241.

61. Ibid., p. 249.

62. Ibid.

63. Ibid.

64. The report was first published in *Editor and Publisher*, New York, 2 December 1922, and reprinted that week in the *New York Times*.

William Yale, a member of the commission's technical staff, had prepared on July 26, 1919, a more balanced report of the political factors involved in the Near East. It could be considered a minority report, though it never enjoyed any formal status. No admirer of organized religious groups, Yale did not reflect a pro-missionary bias (Manuel, *Realities of American-Palestine Relations*, p.

203). While agreeing with the King-Crane conclusion that the overwhelming majority of the indigenous population did not want a Jewish homeland in Palestine, he disputed the authenticity of Palestine Arab nationalism and felt that on balance, the national aspirations of the world Jewish people should be given serious weight (ibid., p. 250).

65. John A. DeNovo, *American Interests and Policies in the Middle East: 1900-1939* (Minneapolis: University of Minnesota, 1963), pp. 144ff.

66. The United States insisted on this provision apparently in order to secure a similar article in the treaty with France in the Syrian mandate. At Paris, Howard Bliss had written to Secretary of State Lansing, quoting a British diplomat to the effect that if France received the Syrian mandate, the United States should exact specific guarantees to protect the American University of Beirut from the incursion of French Catholics (Manuel, *Realities of American-Palestine Relations*, p. 280).

67. Ibid., chap. 7.

68. The one other area of direct concern, besides the support of missions, was Near East relief, begun after the Armenian massacres in 1915, and incorporated by a special act of Congress in 1919. In the first fourteen years of the organization's existence, cash, commodities, and supplies amounting to an estimated $108 million were collected, in large part from American Protestant churches (J. L. Barton, "The Near East Relief," *International Review of Missions* 18 [1929]: 495-502).

69. The *Christian Century*, 21 November 1918, p. 3 (hereafter cited as *CC*).

70. Ibid., 20 December 1917, pp. 8-9, 14-15.

71. Ibid., 11 August 1927, pp. 941-43.

72. Ibid., 13 December 1917, p. 718.

73. Ibid., 11 August 1927, p. 942.

74. Ibid., 11 December 1929, p. 1535.

75. Ibid., 29 October 1930, p. 1300.

76. Ibid., 11 December 1929, p. 1535.

77. Ibid., p. 1537.

78. Sandeen, *Roots of Fundamentalism*, chap. 10.

79. C. C. Morrison, editor of the *Christian Century*, spent three days in Palestine in 1935, while on a Mediterranean cruise. Though awed by the Holy Land itself—"Just to be there is to worship"—he was sharply critical of the Christian commercialism and superstition surrounding the organized exhibition of sacred things and places (*CC*, 1 May 1935, pp. 568-69).

80. John J. Holmes, *Palestine: Today and Tomorrow* (New York: Macmillan, 1929).

CHAPTER TWO

1. Both theories are attributed to Jews, the melting pot theory to an English-Jewish writer, Israel Zangwill (1864–1926), and the cultural pluralism theory

to an American-Jewish thinker, Horace Kallen (1882-   ). Zangwill wrote a novel, *The Melting Pot*, in 1908. For Kallen's views and other concepts relating to minority groups in a democracy, see the summary in Samuel Dinin's *Judaism in a Changing Civilization* (New York: Teachers College, Columbia University, 1933), chaps. 1 and 2.

2. Nathan Glazer, *American Judaism* (Chicago: University of Chicago Press, 1957); Mordecai M. Kaplan, *Judaism as a Civilization* (New York: Macmillan Co., 1934).

3. *CC*, 9 June 1937, p. 735.

4. Ibid., 7 July 1937, p. 862.

5. Ibid.

6. Ibid.

7. Ibid., p. 863.

8. Ibid., 13 March 1946, pp. 323-24.

9. Ibid., 9 June 1937, p. 735.

10. Ibid., 7 July 1937, p. 863.

11. Ibid., 1 July 1936, p. 926.

12. Ibid., 9 June 1937, p. 735.

13. Ibid., 29 April 1936, p. 625.

14. Ibid., p. 626.

15. Reviewing the period under discussion, Will Herberg concluded (in 1962): "Until about thirty years ago, America was a Protestant nation . . . Protestantism was America's established church. . . . Non-Protestants . . . experienced their non-Protestant religion as a mark of their foreignness . . . . [the] syncretism [of the democratic society and nation] was a Protestant phenomenon exclusively. Jews and Catholics, being outsiders and foreigners, did not share in this culture-religion." (*Christianity and Crisis*, 5 February 1962, pp. 3-7.)

16. *CC*, 20 December 1939, pp. 1566-67.

17. Ibid., p. 1567.

18. Ibid.

19. Ibid., 17 November 1954, p. 389.

20. The *Christian Century* was not atypical in American Protestantism regarding its views on desirable assimilation. A Princeton historian, reviewing Arthur Hertzberg's *The French Enlightenment and the Jews* (New York: Columbia University Press, 1968) in *Christianity and Crisis*, justified the assimilationist tendencies of European Jewry resulting from the emancipation period. He concluded: "The truth seems to be that 'Jewish emancipation' . . . succeeds best as in 1770 when accompanied by a degree of assimilation. If this raises special problems in Judaism, the rest of us have also had to put aside ancestral traditions" (R. R. Palmer, "At the Sources of Jewish Liberty and Equality," *Christianity and Crisis*, 28 October 1968, pp. 253-56).

21. Will Herberg, *Protestant, Catholic, Jew* (New York: Doubleday & Co., 1955).

22. An exception to this general rule was found in the minority treaties after World War I which recognized the Jews of several East European states as a nationality despite their having no modern nation. The practice of the Soviet Union also is to indicate a Jewish nationality in the passports of its Jewish citizens.

23. Kaplan, *Judaism as a Civilization.*

24. *CC*, 11 February 1942, p. 173.

25. Ibid.

26. Ibid., 28 November 1945, p. 1311.

27. Ibid., 3 January 1945, p. 5.

28. Ibid., 25 June 1947, p. 789.

29. Ibid., 9 June 1937, p, 736.

30. Ibid., 13 June 1945, p. 702.

31. Ibid., 27 June 1945, p. 702.

32. Ibid., 3 May 1933, pp. 582-84.

33. Ibid.

34. Ibid., 10 May 1933, pp. 659-62.

35. *Judaism* 20, (January 1971). The major feature of *Judaism's* winter 1971 issue is a symposium of distinguished scholars on the trial of Jesus. Robert M. Grant of the University of Chicago asserts that though the idea of kingship preached by Jesus was religious in nature, it was interpreted by Jews and Romans alike as having political overtones and, therefore, carried within it the seeds of rebellion against Rome. S. G. F. Brandon of the University of Manchester argues that Jesus was a nationalist patriot, a member, or at least a sympathizer, of the zealots. He maintains that the Gospels alter these facts in order for the early Christian church to win favor, or at least toleration, in the Roman Empire. Israel Supreme Court Justice Haim Cohen believes that at the hearings before the Jewish authorities, the latter sought to save Jesus from execution, but his insistence on proclaiming himself the Christ rendered their attempt futile.

36. *CC*, 3 November 1937, p. 1351. The editorial arbitrarily equated Christian nationalism with German nationalism.

37. Other Protestant periodicals published similar views. Warned a leading British Protestant, the principal of New College, London: "If Jewish nationalism were arrogant and aggressive, as it is probable it might be, it would become a danger to the world as German communities dominated by Nazi sentiment are proving to be" (A. E. Garvie, "The Jewish Problem," *International Review of Missions,* 30 [1941], p. 222).

38. The religious explanation for anti-Semitism was that the Jews were responsible for Jesus' crucifixion and that they had rejected Jesus' role as the Messiah. The psychological explanation for anti-Semitism was that the Gentiles had rejected Jesus' Jewishness in favor of their pagan background. The sociological explanation was that the Jews retained their separate identity within the American society.

39. This adamant isolationist stand on the part of the *Christian Century* brought forth *Christianity and Crisis* in 1941. In December of 1940 the *Christian Century* published an article by Dr. Reinhold Niebuhr in which he analyzed the error of liberal Protestants who upheld a policy of neutrality and non-involvement in war. The thrust of Niebuhr's argument was that it was wrong for Christians to believe that Christianity would shame the enemy into goodness so that he will cease to imperil them (*CC*, 8 December 1940, pp. 1578-80). Niebuhr was particularly incensed at the *Christian Century's* stubborn isolationist policy affecting the possible survival of Western European democracies.

Subsequently, Niebuhr was instrumental in launching a nondenominational, biweekly journal, *Christianity and Crisis*. In its first issue of February 10, 1941, Dr. Niebuhr again analyzed the fallacies which he saw in the *Christian Century's* position. As an example of such an error he wrote: "I think it dangerous to allow [Christian] religious sensitivity [about the imperfection of the Western position] to obscure the fact that Nazi tyranny intends to annihilate the Jewish race" (*Christianity and Crisis*, 10 February 1941, p. 6).

Undaunted by Niebuhr's criticism, the *Christian Century* invited him to review *The Christian and the War*, a book written by its editor, Charles C. Morrison. (See *CC*, 23 December 1942, pp. 1589-93.) The review denounced Morrison's brand of nationalism, calling it "immoral." Morrison responded in two consecutive installments (*CC*, 23 December 1942, pp. 1590-93; ibid., 30 December 1942, pp. 1620-23).

40. *CC*, 8 January 1941, p. 47.

41. Ibid., 18 June 1941, pp. 796-97. In a letter published in response to this editorial, a rabbi asked: If the majority of American Jews agree with Roosevelt and Willkie "should they then give expression to a contrary view in order to forestall the possibility that otherwise they may be used as scapegoats at some future date?" (ibid., 23 July 1941, p. 937).

42. Ibid., 18 June 1941, pp. 796-97.

43. Ibid., 24 September 1941, pp. 1167-69.

CHAPTER THREE

1. *CC*, 29 November 1933, p. 1491.

2. Ibid.

3. See p. 29.

4. *CC*, 12 November 1930, p. 1376.

5. Ibid., p. 1377.

6. Arthur D. Morse, *While Six Million Died* (New York: Random House, 1968), chaps. 6-10.

7. The 1936 immigration dropped because of the outbreak of the Arab riots in April of that year (Robert R. Nathan, Oscar Gass, Daniel Creamer, *Palestine: Problem and Promise* [Washington, D.C.: Public Affairs Press 1946], p. 137).

8. Jacob C. Hurewitz, *The Struggle for Palestine* (New York: W. W. Norton & Co., 1950), pp. 27ff. Of the 968,000 Palestine Arabs, some 95,000 were Christian. The latter consisted largely of Greek Orthodox (about 47,000) and Roman Catholic (approximately 41,000), with more than half of the latter affiliated with the autonomous Jerusalem Patriarchate of the Latin Church. The Greek Catholic, or Melkite, adherents numbered about 15,000 and the Maronites 3,700. The remaining Christian Arabs were attached to the Syrian Orthodox, or Jacobite, Church, or to the various Protestant churches founded by European missionaries.

9. Ibid., chap. 5.

10. *Survey of International Affairs* (London: Oxford University Press, 1936), pp. 97-98. The Palestine Arab reaction was to institute an economic boycott against the Jewish community, and gradually the campaign developed from sporadic acts of violence and sabotage against the Jews into open rebellion against the British mandatory regime. Trains were derailed, roads mined, telephone wires cut, and the oil pipe line from Iraq (to Haifa) punctured. The British High Commissioner in Palestine enacted drastic police regulations against the Arab rebels, but refrained from offensive military action against them.

The Arab revolt inadvertently consolidated the Palestinian Jewish community. While the immigration of Jews was sharply curtailed, the British High Commissioner permitted the gradual expansion of the Jewish community's civilian police force, and allowed vessels to be unloaded at the all–Jewish city of Tel Aviv rather than at the Arab city of Jaffa. Because of the Arabs' economic strike against Jewish agricultural, commercial, and industrial enterprises, Jewish workers learned to replace Arabs. Also, when Arabs refused to sell agricultural produce to Jewish markets, Jewish farmers were forced to increase production.

By early fall, Arab violence had not diminished. The mandatory regime brought new British troops into the country to assume an offensive against the rebellious Arab bands. Militarily, the Arabs could not withstand a determined British drive, and economically, the Arab Palestinian community was on the verge of collapse. In mid-October, therefore, the strike was called off officially, and by early November, organized Arab resistance was temporarily suspended.

11. Great Britain, *Parliamentary Papers*, vol. 14 (1936/37) (*Reports from Commissioners, Inspectors, and Others*, vol. 6), "Report of the Royal Commission on Palestine," Cmd. 5479, p. vi.

12. *Minutes of Evidence of the Palestine Royal Commission* (London: His Majesty's Stationery Office, 1937), p. 358.

13. Great Britain, *Parliamentary Papers*, vol. 14 (1936/37) (*Reports from Commissioners, Inspectors, and Others*, vol. 6), "Report of the Royal Commission on Palestine," Cmd. 5479, p. 325.

14. Ibid., p. 381.

15. Ibid., p. 387.

16. Great Britain, *Parliamentary Papers*, vol. 14 (1936/37) (*Reports from Commissioners, Inspectors, and Others*, vol. 6), "Palestine: Statement of Policy by His Majesty's Government of the United Kingdom," Cmd. 5513.

17. Within Zionist circles some objected to partition because, in their view, the Jews had an "inalienable right" to all of Palestine, while others, mainly left-

wing and pacifist Zionist elements, were against partition because they believed that Jews and Arabs could coexist peacefully within a single sovereign jurisdiction. The "propartition" groups in Zionism, while accepting the principle of a sovereign Jewish state, were unhappy with the size of the projected state and concerned about its economic viability. Thus, the twentieth World Zionist Congress, meeting in August 1937 in Zurich, by majority vote (249 to 160) endorsed the principle of partition, but bound the Zionist executive to negotiate further with the mandatory power without committing itself to a final plan before prior approval by a newly elected Zionist congress (Hurewitz, *Struggle for Palestine*, chap. 5).

The Arab community, though weakened by internecine quarrels, was more uncompromising in its opposition to the partition scheme than were the Zionists (ibid.). The Arab National Defense Party, controlled by the Nashashibi family, was somewhat milder in its criticism than the truncated Arab High Committee controlled by the Husseini family under the leadership of the Mufti of Jerusalem. Both Arab factions were, however, committed to the partition plan's failure. Under the direction of the Arab High Committee, Arab acts of terrorism were renewed with growing intensity following the publication of the royal commission's report. Only after the assassination in late September of a high British mandatory official who had served as the government's liaison officer with the commission, did the mandatory regime begin an intensive campaign against Arab terror. The earlier guerrilla tactics of 1936 remained largely unchanged, except that the Arab community was no longer united—the Arab High Committee having been outlawed and its leaders exiled. The terrorist groups, under the overall direction of the Mufti who escaped to Lebanon, intimidated the murdered Arab "dissidents" who disagreed with them, while continuing their attacks on British forces and Jews. Arabs killed more Arabs during this second phase of the revolt than Jews or Englishmen.

The Arab revolt gradually ground to a halt not only because of superior British forces and an improved Jewish defense organization, but due to a worsening of the European political situation (and a correlative British no-nonsense strategy towards the Arab rebels), and a sharp negative change in British policy towards Jewish rights in Palestine (ibid., chaps. 6 and 7).

18. *CC*, 14 July 1937, p. 892.

19. Ibid., 21 July 1937, pp. 917-20.

20. Great Britain, *Parliamentary Paper*, vol. 25 (1923) (*Accounts and Papers*, vol. 13), "Mandate for Palestine," Cmd 1785; reprinted in Paul L. Hanna, *British Policy in Palestine* (Washington, D.C.: American Council on Public Affairs, 1942), pp. 162-69.

21. *CC*, 21 July 1937, p. 920.

22. Ibid.

23. "The Palestine Commission's Report: From the Point of View of the Church," *International Review of Missions* 36 (1937): 468.

24. Ibid., p. 469.

25. Ibid., p. 470.

26. *CC*, 17 November 1937, p. 1412.

27. Albert Vitton, "Palestine Chaos Without End," ibid., 2 October 1938, p. 1292.

28. Ibid., 26 October 1938, p. 1283.

29. Ibid., 11 September 1929, p. 1108.

30. Morse, *While Six Million Died*, chap. 12.

31. *CC*, 23 November 1938, p. 1420.

32. Ibid.

33. Dr. Bliss' grandfather's involvement in the subject of Palestine during the peace negotiations following World War I has already been noted.

34. The author knew Dr. Bliss personally during the 1950s when both men served as clergymen in Greenwich, Connecticut.

35. *CC*, 25 January 1939, p. 115.

36. Ibid., p. 116.

37. Judah L. Magnes (1877-1948), an American Reform rabbi who came to Palestine in 1921, was the first president of the Hebrew University in Jerusalem. His pacifist ideas led him to oppose official Zionist policies as threatening a conflict with the Arabs. An example of his Zionist thinking may be found in an article, "Like All the Nations," published after the 1929 Arab riots, and reprinted in *The Zionist Idea*, ed. Arthur Hertzberg (New York: Doubleday, 1959), pp. 443-47. For a resume of Magnes' activities on behalf of binationalism, see Norman Bentwich, *For Zion's Sake* (Philadelphia: Jewish Publication Society, 1954), chap. 8.

Martin Buber (1878-1965), professor of the sociology of religion at the Hebrew University, immigrated to Palestine from Germany in 1938. His Zionist views were similar to those of Magnes (Hertzberg, *Zionist Idea*, pp. 453-65). In 1942, both men founded the Ihud Party with the object of fostering greater cooperation between Jews and Arabs in Palestine and the country's conversion into a binational Arab–Jewish state. Under this formula, both communities would govern on a parity basis, while retaining internal autonomy.

38. *CC*, 1 September 1937, p. 1061.

39. Ibid.

40. Ibid., 8 September 1937, p. 1094.

Herbert Samuel (1870-1963), a British Jew, was first British High Commissioner in Palestine (1920-25). Following the publication of the royal commission's report on partition, he advocated a plan wherein the Jews would constitute a permanent minority in Palestine, at no time to exceed forty per cent of the population, to be ruled in self-governing cantons (ibid., 18 August 1937, p. 1014).

By contrast, the plan proposed by Judah Magnes and several influential Jewish leaders in Palestine, would have limited the Jewish population only for the ensuing ten years (Bentwich, *For Zion's Sake*, p. 191).

41. Great Britain, *Parliamentary Papers*, vol. 27 (1938/39) (*Accounts and Papers*, vol. 12, May 1939), "Palestine: Statement of Policy," Cmd. 6019, pp. 597-608.

42. *CC*, 31 May 1939, p. 695-96.

CHAPTER FOUR

1. *CC*, 5 April 1933, p. 443.

2. Morse, *While Six Million Died*, chap. 1; Henry L. Feingold, *The Politics of Rescue* (New Brunswick, N.J.: Rutgers University Press, 1970), chap. 7.

3. *CC*, 9 December 1942, pp. 1518-19.

4. Ibid., 23 December 1942, p. 1597.

5. Ibid., 30 December 1942, p. 1611.

6. Ibid., 13 January 1943, p. 53.

7. Based upon the research of Morse, *While Six Million Died*, and Feingold, *Politics of Rescue*, one would suspect that the reply may have been written by one of the many State Department officials who were unsympathetic to the Jews.

8. Wise refused to become further involved in the *Christian Century* episode. He also refused to be interviewed by *Time* magazine about the matter, but sent a letter to the publication, in which he said: "I do not care to enter into any further controversy with the *Christian Century*. If I had to make a statement I would say that I took exception to the statement of the *Christian Century* because it set out not to deal with the guilt of Hitler in perpetuating crimes, but with my own sin of exaggeration. I have no hesitation in saying that his indictment of me for reporting, rather than of Hitler for committing the most awful crime in history, is of a piece with the distorted and thwarted mind of Dr. Morrison touching every Jewish question that is brought up for discussion in the pages of the *Christian Century*" (*Servant of the People: Stephen S. Wise, Selected Letters*, ed. Carl H. Voss [Philadelphia: Jewish Publication Society, 1969], pp. 255-56).

9. *CC*, 5 May 1943, p. 533.

10. Ibid., 13 September 1944, p. 1045.

11. Ibid., 9 May 1945, pp. 575-76.

12. Fred Eastman, "A Reply to Screamers," ibid., 16 February 1944, pp. 204-06.

13. Feingold, *Politics of Rescue*, p. 168. The author concludes that the period between September 1939 and January 1942 offered "the best opportunity to save the Jews of Europe."

14. Ibid., chaps. 2, 7; Morse, *While Six Million Died*, chaps. 3, 11.

15. Morse, *While Six Million Died*; Feingold, *Politics of Rescue*. Both books are replete with references to such officials.

16. *CC*, 28 June 1939, p. 813. See Morse, *While Six Million Died*, pp. 270-88 for the story of the *St. Louis*.

17. *CC*, 6 April 1938, p. 421.

18. Morse, *While Six Million Died*, p. 205.

19. *CC*, 31 August 1938, pp. 1030-31.

20. Ibid., 27 July 1938, p. 907.

21. Ibid., 23 November 1938, pp. 1422-23; see also p. 49, above.

22. Ibid., 30 November 1938, pp. 1456-58.

23. Ibid., p. 1457.

24. Ibid., p. 1458.

25. See for example, ibid., 18 January 1939, pp. 80-81, in which it fallaciously compared the possible transfer of six million European Jews with the evacuation of all Chinese from Japanese-held territories.

26. Ibid., 7 December 1938, p. 1485.

27. Ibid., 20 July 1938, pp. 885-86.

28. Ibid., 29 March 1939, pp. 407-08.

29. Ibid., 1 February 1939, p. 141.

30. Ibid., 29 March 1939, p. 408.

31. Ibid., 1 March 1939, pp. 270-72.

32. Ibid., 25 January 1939, p. 116.

33. An October 1936 meeting of sixty leaders of Protestant churches "emphasized the general misapprehension existing in the United States that German refugees are of the Jewish faith alone," with the result that some 14,000 Christian exiles are left to their own resources. Says the *Federal Council Bulletin:* "They cannot turn their steps towards a Christian homeland as the Jews have towards Palestine." (*This, incidentally, was the only mention of Palestine by the Bulletin during the prewar and war periods.*) The Federal Council of Churches endorsed a national appeal for funds for Christian refugees, which was sent to 100,000 Protestant ministers (*Federal Council Bulletin*, November 1936, p. 9).

After Germany annexed Austria in 1938, the *Bulletin* again reminded its readers that the percentage of Christians among the exiles has "especially increased" and the "prevalent impression that these people are nearly all Jews is now known to be gravely erroneous" (*Federal Council Bulletin*, September 1938, p. 304). In its September 23, 1938 call for a Day of Prayer for victims of racial and religious oppression, it again distinguished between those of Jewish and Christian faith—though both groups were of "Jewish blood" (*Federal Council Bulletin*, November 1938, p. 9; ibid., December 1938, p. 9). At no time did the Federal Council of Churches ask Protestants to contribute funds specifically for Jewish refugees. It repeatedly praised American Jews for caring for their coreligionists, and the president of the council was pleased to receive a contribution from the United Jewish Appeal in January 1940, for the rehabilitation of Christian refugees (*Federal Council Bulletin*, February 1940, p. 7).

34. *Federal Council Bulletin*, January 1943, p. 12.

35. Ibid., April 1943, p. 4.

36. Ibid., June 1943.

37. *CC*, 2 June 1943, p. 669. Letter from Rev. Karl Chworowsky of Brooklyn, New York.

38. Ibid., 30 September 1942, p. 1184.

39. Ibid., 10 March 1943, p. 284.

40. Ibid., 30 June 1943, p. 772.

41. Ibid., 8 September 1943, pp. 1004-5.

42. Ibid., 24 May 1944, p. 636.

CHAPTER FIVE

1. Only periodically, however, was the theme of Jewish restoration explicated, for example, by the president of the fundamentalist Moody Bible Institute of Chicago. See Will H. Houghton, "Zion: Sole Solution for Israel," *Pro-Palestine Herald*, vol. 3, nos. 9-11, (1934): 16-17.

2. A. B. Elias, "Christian Cooperation in the Restoration of Zion," *Pro-Palestine Herald*, vol. 3, nos. 3-4 (1934): 17-18.

3. Reuben Fink, *America and Palestine* (New York: American Zionist Emergency Council, 1944), pp. 59-60.

4. Writing to the World Zionist Organization's London office in January 1934, the president of the ZOA noted that his organization had "from time to time utilized non-Jewish agencies in connection with our political work," but the tenor of the times, at the height of the Depression, was not favorable to intensified Zionist activity in America (Samuel Halperin, *The Political World of American Zionism* [Detroit: Wayne State University Press, 1961], pp. 178ff).

5. Ibid., p. 179.

6. The active honorary president of the Pro-Palestine Federation was Rev. Charles Edward Russell, a retired minister, journalist, and socialist from Chicago, who resided in Washington. Its less active president was George L. Scherger, a professor of history at the Lutheran Evangelical Seminary in Chicago, and its national board members included John Haynes Holmes, S. Parkes Cadman, a Congregationalist minister of New York City, and author Pierre Van Paasen, a former Dutch pastor. The federation operated on a shoestring budget which was met largely by the personal efforts of its secretary. Elias' bitterness at the official Zionist Organization of America for not supporting the federation's efforts is revealed in his correspondence, housed in the Zionist Archives in New York City.

7. John H. Holmes, "Zion: A Romance and Adventure," *Pro-Palestine Herald*, vol. 1, (1932).

8. Ibid., p. 2.

9. "If this daring order, built on the pattern of common ownership and common life, dedicated to the far ideal of 'each for all and all for each,' eliminating completely the traditional property concepts, and substituting therefor creative spiritual concepts of human welfare—if this order, I say, succeeds under the peculiarly trying conditions of the new Palestine, why may it not succeed elsewhere?" (ibid., vol. 2, no. 1, [1933]: 2-3).

10. Ibid., vol. 1, (1932): 2.

11. Holmes to Elias, 23 November 1933, Papers of the Pro-Palestine Federation, Zionist Archives, New York.

12. *New Palestine*, 4 June 1936, p. 9.

13. Its chairman was Francis J. McConnell, Methodist bishop of New York City. Other speakers included Ralph W. Sockman, pastor of Christ Church in New York City, and Henry Smith Leiper, executive secretary of the Universal Christian Council on Life and Work. Among the sponsors of the conference were Ivan Lee Holt, president of the Federal Council of Churches of Christ in America; Henry A. Atkinson, secretary of the Church Peace Union; Arthur L. Swift, professor of religion, Union Theological Seminary; Clarence E. Pickett, secretary, American Friends Service Committee; Frederick M. Smith, first president, Church of Jesus Christ of Latter Day Saints; J. Henry Carpenter, secretary, Brooklyn Church and Mission Federation; William J. Manning, Protestant Episcopal bishop of New York; F. J. Clark, the National Council, Protestant Episcopal Church in the United States of America; Conrad Hoffman, International Missionary Council; and Henry Emerson Fosdick, Riverside Church, New York City.

14. *New Palestine*, 18 December 1936, p. 1.

15. John H. Holmes, "The Palestine Mandate is Workable," *Pro-Palestine Herald*, vol. 6, nos. 6-11, (1937): 6-7.

16. John H. Holmes, *Palestine: Today and Tomorrow*.

17. Ibid., chap. 5. Holmes believed that Palestine could become the bridge of conciliation between East and West, the central focus for Jewish peoplehood throughout the world, and the world's laboratory for peace. On the other hand, he felt that a Jewish society as a political entity, built under the protection of British bayonets, would inevitably clash with Arab national interests. "Zion is too high a dream, too fine a spirit . . . it were better than she perish utterly than by such survival bring mockery to a sublime tradition" (ibid., p. 254).

18. Holmes reaffirmed these views in a 1957 interview, in which he criticized the Zionist movement for becoming too involved in international politics (D. M. Leith, "American Christian Support for a Jewish Palestine" [Senior Thesis, Princeton University, 1957], pp. 140-45).

He felt that the Balfour Declaration and the mandate were "mistakes" because they diverted the concept of Zionism from a "cultural concept of society" to a political one. He reiterated his position that Zionism was peoplehood, not statehood, "a culture and not a government, a commonwealth and not a power." Holmes was not in favor of the United Nations resolution of November 29, 1947, which promulgated a Jewish state, and stuck to his binational theme even when other Christian pro–Zionists felt that his idealistic attitude was unrelated to reality (ibid., p. 145).

However, though disinterested in the goal of a Jewish state, Holmes refused to turn his back on it, once it was established. He wrote in 1949: "I seek peace and prosperity for Israel, and do all that my poor help may avail to secure these ends" (*Christianity and Crisis*, 21 February 1949, p. 31).

19. The Pro–Palestine Federation continued as a paper organization long after the establishment of the state of Israel. Its influence waned considerably with the organization of larger pro–Zionist American Christian groups supported by the American Zionist movement. It continued to play an independent, though

minor, role until 1954, the last year of any recorded correspondence from its secretary. Aaron B. Elias Papers, Zionist Archives, New York.

20. *CC*, 30 December 1936, pp. 1741-43.

21. Ibid., 25 October 1939, p. 1302. See also chap. 2, n. 39, above.

22. *The Nation*, 21 February 1942, pp. 214-16; ibid., 28 February 1942, pp. 253-55.

23. Ibid., 21 February 1942, p. 216.

24. Ibid., p. 215.

25. Louis D. Brandeis, "The Jewish Problem and How to Solve It," (1915), in *Zionist Idea*, ed. Hertzberg, pp. 517-18.

26. *The Nation*, 21 February 1942, p. 215.

27. Ibid., 28 February 1942, p. 254.

28. Ibid., p. 255.

29. Robert Silverberg, *If I Forget Thee O Jerusalem* (New York: William Morrow & Co., 1970), pp. 183-84.
   Sharett's view was shared by several leading American Zionists who, however, were not at the helm of the movement. As expressed by one of them, Dr. Emanuel Neumann, the concept of a " 'Jewish State' became taboo. . . . The national home, interpreted as a spiritual and cultural center, was deemed a nobler and loftier conception . . . a 'spiritual center' required little space, no Jewish majority, and no political sovereignty. . . . The accent was upon patience, caution, and restraint, and the avoidance of risk" (Joseph B. Schechtman, *The United States and the Jewish State Movement* [New York: Herzl Press, 1966], p. 59).

30. Silverberg, *If I Forget Thee O Jerusalem*, p. 186.
   By 1945, at the end of World War II, the American Zionist membership totaled 486,000 (Schechtman, *United States and the Jewish State Movement*, p. 63).

31. *CC*, 7 May 1941, pp. 612-13. It is interesting to contrast the periodical's concern for Britain's difficult task when applied immediately to Palestine, and the pressures it demanded be applied against Britain with regard to her long-range postwar international policies, before the United States considered aiding her against Germany; see ibid., 5 February 1941, pp. 174-76.

32. For an account of the Biltmore conference, see Yehuda Bauer, *From Diplomacy to Resistance* (Philadelphia: Jewish Publication Society, 1970), pp. 224ff.

33. While many Jews began to take a more active interest in the official Zionist program following the Biltmore conference, the militancy of Zionism also elicited a reaction of Jewish anti-Zionism. An activist anti-Zionist organization called the American Council for Judaism was formed in 1942 and led by a small group of Reform rabbis.
   The American Council for Judaism received support from powerful Jewish laymen such as Lessing Rosenwald, chairman of the board of Sears Roebuck, and Arthur Hays Sulzberger, publisher of the New York Times. The purpose of the organization was to offset the pro–Zionist resolutions of the American

Jewish Conference (see p. 72 below). The council made every effort to spread the impression that Zionism endangered the status of American Jewry by raising the prospect of "dual loyalties," one to the United States and another to a Jewish State. (See the *New York Times*, 31 August 1943.)

The appearance of the American Council for Judaism gave an unexpected boost to the Protestant anti–Zionist forces in America. (See *CC*, 17 June 1942, p. 722; ibid., 18 November 1942, p. 1413.) Support for the council came principally from a small group of Reform Jews. The initial "Statement of Principles" of the council was endorsed by 92 Reform rabbis. By contrast, a pro–Zionist statement was issued in November 1942 signed by 818 rabbis of all three branches of American Judaism—Orthodox, Conservative, and Reform—including 215 Reform rabbis (Halperin, *Political World of American Zionism*, pp. 287-88).

After the American Jewish Conference sessions in the early fall of 1943, and with the increasingly areligious and political programs of the American Council for Judaism, the latter's rabbinical support waned rapidly. Numerous public withdrawals from the council were announced. In 1946 one of the founders and provisional chairmen of the council, Rabbi Louis Wolsey of Philadelphia, resigned publicly from the post of vice-president, in protest against the organization's policy of blocking Jewish immigration to Palestine. (See Louis Wolsey, *Sermons and Addresses* [Philadelphia, 1950], pp. 14-15.)

By 1946 fewer than a dozen rabbis remained on the council's roster and withdrawals continued well into the 1950s (*New York Times*, 22 July 1956, p. 43).

34. *Christianity and Crisis*, 27 July 1942, pp. 7-8.

35. Halperin, *Political World of American Zionism*, p. 183.

36. Silverberg, *If I Forget Thee O Jerusalem*, pp. 219-231.

37. See n. 33, above, and chap. 6.

38. Carl H. Voss, "Christian Ministers Speak Out," *New Palestine*, 31 March 1944, pp. 339-40.

39. Ibid. Voss then listed four specific subjects of concentration: "The Jewish problem as a Christian problem"; the validity of the Balfour Declaration; opposition to the 1939 British White Paper; and a description of Palestine's development which benefited both Jews and Arabs.

40. Halperin, *Political World of American Zionism*, p. 184.

41. Carl H. Voss, "Christians and Zionism in the United States," *Palestine Year Book* 1 (1946): 497.

42. Halperin, *Political World of American Zionism*, pp. 181-83.

43. Voss, "Christians and Zionism in the United States," p. 500.

44. Speeches from the Papers of the Christian Council for Palestine, Zionist Archives, New York.

45. *Christianity and Crisis*, 28 June 1943, pp. 3-4.

46. Ibid. Atkinson even suggested that a "competent international Christian commission" be sent to Palestine, to study the situation on the spot and offer concrete solutions. "This is not a 'Protestant Zionism,'" he concluded. "It is an

attempt to answer what is basically not a Jewish problem but rather a Christian problem."

47. Waldo Frank, *The Jew in Our Day* (New York: Duell, Sloan and Pearce, 1944).

48. Ibid., pp. 12-13.

49. Silverberg, *If I Forget Thee O Jerusalem*, pp. 231-42.

50. *Christian Voice for a New Palestine* (New York: American Christian Palestine Committee, and Washington, D.C.: World Committee for Palestine, 1946).
The National Christian Conference in Washington further voted to coordinate the work of the American Palestine Committee and the Christian Council on Palestine. This resolution resulted in April 1946 in the merger of both bodies into the American Christian Palestine Committee. Meanwhile, both groups established local American Christian Palestine Committees throughout the country, convened city and regional conferences, and in November 1945 sponsored an international Christian Conference for Palestine, held in Washington, D.C.

51. Papers of the Christian Council on Palestine, Zionist Archives, New York.

52. *CC*, 29 March 1944, p. 389.

53. *Christianity and Crisis*, 3 April 1944, p. 2.

54. "It is very likely that efforts will be made by some of the Zionist leaders to obtain from you at an early date some commitments in favor of the Zionist program which is pressing for unlimited immigration into Palestine, and the establishment there of a Jewish state. As you are aware, the Government and people of the United States have every sympathy for the persecuted Jews of Europe and are doing all in their power to relieve their suffering. The question of Palestine is, however, a highly complex one and involves questions which go far beyond the plight of the Jews in Europe" (Silverberg, *If I Forget Thee O Jerusalem*, p. 268).

55. Ibid., p. 277.

56. Few American Jews were happy about the establishment of the Anglo-American Committee of Inquiry. The Zionist groups felt it was merely a stalling device. Even Jewish non–Zionists were disappointed that masses of Jewish refugees were not being moved immediately to Palestine. (Only the anti–Zionist American Council for Judaism endorsed the committee.)
The strength of pro–Zionist feeling in the United States motivated American Zionist leadership to reintroduce their previously aborted resolution in Congress, and despite President Truman's reluctance to approve this move pending a report from the joint Anglo–American Committee of Inquiry, both houses passed the following resolution in the week before Christmas 1945:

Resolved by the Senate (the House of Representatives concurring) That the interest shown by the President in the solution of this problem is hereby commended and that the United States shall use its good offices with the mandatory power to the end that Palestine shall be opened for free entry of Jews into that country to the maximum of its agricultural and eco-

nomic potentialities, and that there shall be full opportunity for coloniza-
tion to develop so that they may freely proceed with the upbuilding of
Palestine as the Jewish national home and, in association with all elements
of the population, establish Palestine as a democratic commonwealth in
which all men, regardless of race or creed, shall have equal rights.

(U.S., Congress, House, *Congressional Record*, 19 December 1945, 79th Cong.,
1st sess., 1945, 91, pt. 9: 12396.)

Evidently, the voice of grass-roots America had been heard in the capital,
though the resolution was more circumspect in its advocacy of a Jewish commonwealth than the Zionist sponsors had hoped for.

57. The minutes of the hearings of 14 January 1946 reveal that when the chairman called, "Dr. William Hocking. Is he present?" there was no response. There
was similar silence when he asked for Dr. Henry Sloan Coffin (U.S., Department
of State, *Hearings of the Anglo-American Committee of Inquiry*, 14 January
1946, p. 127).

58. Their testimony will be discussed in chap. 6.

59. Carl H. Voss, executive secretary of the Christian Council on Palestine, to
Leslie L. Root, secretary of the Anglo–American Committee of Inquiry, 3 January 1946, Papers of the Christian Council on Palestine, Zionist Archives, New
York. The memorandum criticized the 1939 White Paper as an "inhuman document," stressed that the Jewish development of Palestine would prove beneficial
to Arabs, argued that whereas the mandates for the Arab countries were "more
fully kept," the pledge to the Jewish people in the mandate for Palestine "has
not been kept," and urged that "we should support the individual decisions on
Palestine by the same measures that we support other international decisions.
Only such a solution would be in accord with international conscience and with
the Christian concept of justice." The covering letter to the memorandum advised the committee of inquiry that Reinhold Niebuhr, treasurer of the Christian
Council on Palestine, would give "the oral presentation of our case."

60. U.S., Department of State, *Hearings*, p. 101.

61. This testimony will be discussed in chap. 6.

62. "The body didn't refuse to commit itself on whether we should regard
Palestine as the homeland of the Jews. It refused to authorize a statement that
we did not favor Palestine as a homeland for the Jews" (U.S., Department of
State, *Hearings*, p. 124).

63. Ibid., p. 122.

64. Ibid., p. 130.

65. Ibid., pp. 141-42. When a member of the committee told Niebuhr that a
previous witness, a well-known demographer, had said that it would not be
possible to attain a Jewish majority in Palestine because the Arabs increase twice
as rapidly as the Jewish population, Niebuhr replied: "If that is true, why then
stop your immigration for fear of establishing a Jewish majority?" (ibid., p. 147).

66. Ibid., pp. 147-48.

67. Ibid., p. 155.

68. Great Britain, *Parliamentary Papers*, vol. 26 (1945/46) (*Accounts and Papers*, vol. 12), "Report of the Anglo-American Committee of Inquiry Regarding the Problems of European Jewry and Palestine," CMD. 6808, pp. 81-164; see also, Hurewitz, *Struggle for Palestine*, chap. 18.

69. It would appear from the report that the committee members would have had the United Nations prepare the country for a binational state, with a government to be based on equal rather than on proportional representation. "Jew shall not dominate Arab and Arab shall not dominate Jew in Palestine," asserted the report.

70. Foreign Secretary Ernest Bevin told a Labour Party conference in England on June 12: "Regarding the agitation in the United States, and particularly in New York, for 100,000 to be put into Palestine, I hope it will not be misunderstood in America if I say, with the purest of motives, that that was because they do not want too many of them in New York." The Arabs were unhappy with the recommendations affecting Jewish immigration and the political status of the country. The Zionists, while welcoming the immigration recommendation, saw themselves again denied a Jewish state in Palestine. While the British government continued to stall, the organized Jewish community in Palestine began a showdown with the mandatory regime by stepping up its acts of violence against government property and in the case of the extremist groups, against British personnel (Hurewitz, *Struggle for Palestine*, pp. 253-57).

71. While welcoming the immigration recommendation and commending President Truman's statement approving the recommendation abrogating the 1939 White Paper, the ACPC claimed in its detailed analysis of the report that final authority would rest with Great Britain who could make "arbitrary decisions on any issues that may arise and at the same time maintain themselves as rulers of Palestine indefinitely" (*Analysis of Report of Anglo-American Committee of Inquiry on Palestine*, American Christian Palestine Committee, May 1946, Papers of the American Christian Palestine Committee, Zionist Archives, New York).

72. Ibid.

73. Yehuda Bauer suggests that the term "commonwealth" became popular in Zionist ranks to stress the democratic nature of the projected Jewish state, "since the connotations of the word 'state' in English smacked of the German–Nazi *staat* during the war period" (Bauer, *From Diplomacy to Resistance*, p. 405, n. 10).

For an analysis of the serious conflicts between Weizmann and Ben-Gurion, see ibid., chap. 6. Ben-Gurion, for example, was insistent upon an immediate mass transfer to Palestine of at least two million Jews, thereby transforming the Arab majority in the country into a minority, while Weizmann was thinking about a gradual migration of 100,000 each year. In Palestine proper, the Zionist Action Committee, the body responsible for Zionist policy and activity between World Zionist Congresses, had adopted Ben-Gurion's policy by approving the Biltmore Program in November 1942, by a vote of 21 to 3, with 5 abstentions (ibid., p. 250). The minority represented the views of those Palestinian Zionist factions which indeed would allow for free Jewish immigration, but in which Jews and Arabs would not dominate one another.

In December 1943, the British government returned to the subject of partitioning Palestine into Arab and Jewish states, but the formal Zionist attitude, though not yet declared by an international Zionist Congress, could be summed up in the Biltmore Program: the whole of Palestine. Only a sufficiently large territory could absorb the expected mass transfer of Jews (ibid., chap. 7). The Biltmore Program was subsequently modified by Jewish Agency leaders, against the strenuous opposition of Rabbi Silver (Schechtman, *United States and the Jewish State Movement*, pp. 180-86; Silverberg, *If I Forget Thee O Jerusalem*, p. 315). Silver's viewpoint, however, prevailed at the World Zionist Congress in Basel, which in December 1946 affirmed the Biltmore policy, leading to Dr. Weizmann's defeat as president of the World Zionist organization.

74. *Analysis of Report*, p. 5.

75. Ibid.

76. The public actions of the American Zionist groups in arousing public opinion were matched by the public relations campaign of Ben Hecht on behalf of the major Palestine dissident underground group, the *Irgun*. Hecht sparked the *Irgun*'s fund raising campaign in the United States with a series of dramatic newspaper advertisements and pageant-like mass meetings. The American Zionist groups denounced him and his sponsoring American group, called the American League for a Free Palestine, as irresponsible. But as a result of Hecht's skillful portrayal of dissident underground heroism in Palestine, many American Jews ignored the more moderate Zionist leaders and supported the dissident cause. On the other hand, the official American Zionist movement did not explicitly condemn the militant acts perpetrated by the Jews of Palestine, though individual Zionist groups did so (Silverberg, *If I Forget Thee O Jerusalem*, pp. 323ff).

The statements of the American Christian Palestine Committee followed the American Zionist Emergency Council line of neither condemning nor condoning the militant activities of Palestinian Jewry, but of explaining them. In a memorandum to its membership in July 1946, the ACPC held that Jewish violence in Palestine was not the cause of the chaotic situation there, but an effect of it. The memorandum stated: "What else but an outburst of violence would be expected in view of six million Jews killed by Nazism, of repeated promises and resultant betrayals, of the pitiful sight of 'visa-less' refugees driven away from the shores of the Promised Land to still another concentration camp" (Leith, "American Christian Support for a Jewish Palestine," p. 116).

CHAPTER SIX

1. Virginia C. Gildersleeve, *Many a Good Crusade* (New York: Macmillan, 1954), p. 412.

2. For the story of the American Council for Judaism, see Halperin, *Political World of American Zionism*, pp. 71-101, 282-92; see also chap. 5, n. 33, above.

3. E.g., *CC*, 19 November 1947, pp. 1401-22.

4. E.g., Ibid., 17 December 1947, pp. 1555ff.

5. E.g., Ibid., 8 November 1944, pp. 1274-75; ibid., 2 January 1946, p. 18.

6. E.g., ibid., 25 June 1947, p. 789.

7. Gildersleeve, *Many a Good Crusade*, p. 409.

8. Roosevelt was later exposed as a CIA agent who worked closely with President Nasser of Egypt (David Wise and Thomas G. Ross, *The Invisible Government* [New York: Random House, 1964], pp. 114-17). In 1958, Roosevelt became vice-president in charge of governmental relations of Gulf Oil Corporation in Washington.

9. Gildersleeve, *Many a Good Crusade*, p. 409.

10. Ibid.

11. Ibid., pp. 177, 407. In her earlier years Miss Gildersleeve had been deeply impressed with ancient Egyptian culture as portrayed in James H. Breasted's *The Dawn of Conscience*, and "realized how very early in man's history the Egyptians had evolved ideals of ethical conduct. Over a thousand years before the Ten Commandments were proclaimed, wrote Breasted, the Egyptians had formulated a standard of morals far superior to that of the Decalogue" (ibid., p. 178).

12. Ibid., pp. 184-85.

13. Ibid., p. 409.

14. The Committee for Justice and Peace in the Holy Land had powerful support in Washington. Among its members were James Terry Duce, influential lobbyist of the Arabian American Oil Co. (Aramco); Secretary of Defense James Forrestal; Harold B. Minor, chief of the State Department Office of Middle Eastern Affairs in 1946 and 1947, later United States ambassador to Lebanon, and then an official of Aramco; William A. Eddy, son of a missionary family, who had been minister to Saudi Arabia (1944-46), chief of a diplomatic mission to Yemen (1946), a special assistant to the Secretary of State for research and intelligence (1946-47), and a consultant to Aramco (1947-57); Wallace Murray, for many years chief of the State Department's division of Near Eastern affairs, who had urged President Roosevelt in 1942 to curb the Zionists lest they cause the Allies to lose the war in the Near East (*Near East Report, Special Survey* (October 1964): B14).

15. In June 1948, after the establishment of the state of Israel, the Committee for Justice and Peace in the Holy Land warned that "American Zionists, Christians as well as Jews, gravely consider the great growth of feeling in this country against the extreme Zionist pressure here, with its insistence on separate Jewish nationalism, as causing danger of disruption of our national unity and encouraging anti–Semitism" (Press release, 18 June 1948, Papers of the Committee for Peace and Justice in the Holy Land, Zionist Archives, New York). Eleven days later, a month and a half after the state of Israel had been in existence, and eight months after the United Nations had rejected a resolution to refer the Palestine question to the Court of International Justice for an advisory opinion, the committee again urged the United States government "to change its stand regarding the reference by the Security Council of the Palestine question to the Court of International Justice. . . . Forty millions of people of the Arab world feel that their case has not had a fair and just hearing" (Press release, 29 June 1948, Papers of the Committee for Peace and Justice in the Holy Land, Zionist Archives).

If the problem of Palestine could not be resolved to the satisfaction of the Arabs in the arena of international politics, it was only "just" that it be given a chance to succeed in an international legal forum. No other modern state had undergone this process of being passed on by an international tribunal before being admitted to political and legal sovereignty. Only a Jewish state was expected to do so. But it was too late. The state of Israel already existed and had been recognized by several of the major world powers.

16. See, for example, the assertions of Wilbert B. Smith, former senior secretary of the Egyptian YMCA, in *Christianity and Crisis*, 9 August 1943, pp. 6-7, and the response by Carl H. Voss, executive director of the Christian Council on Palestine; see also the views of Dr. Jabir Shibli, a Protestant of Arab extraction who taught at Pennsylvania State College, ibid., 10 January 1944, pp. 5-6 and *Christian Century*, 2 June 1943, p. 640, and the reply by Dr. Simon Greenberg, vice-chancellor of The Jewish Theological Seminary of America, in *Christianity and Crisis*, 21 February 1944, pp. 6-7.

17. *CC*, 1 November 1944, pp. 1244-45. The periodical went on to question the wisdom of certain church leaders in lending their names to the support of appeals or political proposals connected with the Zionist movement. It continued: "Such mild words of warning have been written not because the *Christian Century* is either pro–Zionist or anti–Zionist (although it has at different times been accused of being both), but because the problem of Palestine's future is so involved." One must ask: whoever accused the *Christian Century* of being pro–Zionist?

18. *Truth About Palestine* (New York: Christian Council on Palestine, 1946), p. 5.

19. Such statements include: "A prominent member of the [Palestine] Protestant community, since deceased, stated that his people felt the economic and cultural pressure of Zionism, and feared a materialistic domination unsympathetic to Christianity" (*Information Service*, 7 October 1944, p. 4); "it is well to keep in mind that the welfare and economic health of Palestine and of the Jewish colonies . . . are separate questions from the rescue of war refugees. It has been urged that a slower and steadier expansion might produce a more stable future" (ibid., p. 8); quotations from the *Information Bulletin* of the American Council for Judaism, like, "The [Peel] Royal Commission noted that the Arabs detected, too, in some of these young newcomers an arrogance which seemed to suggest that they felt themselves to be members of a superior race, destined before long to be masters of the country" (ibid., p. 8). Such charged expressions were not likely to validate the claim of lack of bias, nor did the report's complete silence about the holocaust and the pressing refugee problem. Were it not for the urgency of the latter issue, the subject of Palestine undoubtedly would have been played in a lower key by everyone concerned.

20. *Bulletin* no. 6, (Foreign Missions Conference, November 1944): 8.

21. *CC*, 7 November 1945, p. 1227; see also the statement of the Foreign Missions Conference on p. 1236.

22. *Truth About Palestine*, p. 5.

23. S. A. Morrison, American secretary of the Egyptian Inter–Missionary Council, actually stated in 1945: "It may be necessary to establish under international protection a small Jewish state in part of Palestine with the rest of Palestine attached to an enlarged Syria. . . ." (*Christianity and Crisis*, 23 July 1945, pp. 3-5). This unusual admission—later to be reversed—by a spokesman of the

missionary movement can be understood only in the context of his somewhat naive belief, based on wishful thinking, that regardless of political framework, Christianity could penetrate the lives of citizens of any state, and contribute to molding them into a harmonious society. Said Morrison: "The Christian church in Palestine appears to have been the only body which has succeeded hitherto in uniting the Jew by birth with the Arab by birth in a simple community."

For the most part, however, missionaries operating in Palestine to convert Jews were not in favor of Jewish national aspirations. G. L. B. Sloan, chairman of the Near East Christian Council, who was affiliated with the Church of Scotland in Tiberias, Palestine, has accused the Palestinian Jewish leadership of "spreading a spirit of intolerance and narrow jingoism in many respects hardly to be distinguished from the Nazi race doctrine" (*International Review of Missions*, 34 [1945]:406-11).

In the same issue of the *International Review of Missions* that carried his article, Rev. Sloan also reviewed Maurice Samuel's *Harvest in the Desert* (Philadelphia: Jewish Publication Society, 1944), a book describing the Jewish development of Palestine in favorable terms. Said the reviewer: "If the narrow, domineering nationalism evident in this book is to prevail in Zionist counsels, then we stand not at the birth of a new era of promise for the Jewish people, but at the graveside of an abortive hope" (ibid.:443-44).

Israel, the mystical concept of spiritual peoplehood, was acceptable to the missionary movement in Palestine as long as it did not mean peoplehood "in the flesh," that is, Jewish nationalism. The latter was a serious stumbling block on the road to Israel's conversion to Christianity.

24. *CC*, 21 November 1945, pp. 1284 ff.

25. U.S., Department of State, *Hearings of the Anglo-American Committee of Inquiry*, 10 January 1946, pp. 147-71.

26. Ibid., p. 164.

27. Ibid., p. 151.

28. Ibid., p. 156.

29. Ibid., 12 January 1946, p. 74.
    Later, Bridgeman projected the *Christian Century* line when he answered his own question, whether a Jewish state in Palestine was the best solution to the Jewish problem. He said: "The answer can be 'yes' only if the people of Jewish faith, here and elsewhere, insist that they are an unassimilable, permanently alien race which must be segregated" (Charles T. Bridgeman, "Why No Peace in the Holy Land?", in *Papers on Palestine II* [New York: Institute of Arab American Affairs, 1947], p. 72).
    A similar argument, with a state-church-separation twist, was raised by Rev. Charles R. Watson, president of the American University of Cairo from 1922 to 1945. In discussing how the Zionist proposal "appears to Protestants," he said: "Is Judaism a race or religion? If it is a religion, have we given up the idea of separating church and state? . . . We have regarded the political side of Roman Catholicism as irregular and undesirable. . . . Do we mean now to abandon this policy and give our approval to a Jewish state? . . . Are we to accept today the blood and ráce standards of Judaism for its national requirements? These all are questions . . . relevant to our consideration of the Jewish state, of the Vatican assumption, and in a lesser degree, of the Arab-Moslem state" (ibid., in "Jew and Arab in the Holy Land," p. 55).

30. U.S., Department of State, *Hearings of the Anglo-American Committee of Inquiry*, 23 March 1946, pp. 304.

31. Ibid., p. 306.

32. Ibid., p. 9.

33. "The Tragic Fallacy of Political Zionism" in *Papers on Palestine II*, p. 61.

34. Leiper to Howard M. LeSourd, director of ACPC, 11 June 1946, Papers of the American Christian Palestine Committee, Zionist Archives, New York. The letter began: "Dear Hank." LeSourd's response, 18 June 1946, began: "Dear Paddy."

35. Walz to Voss, 11 February 1947, Papers of the American Christian Palestine Committee. The letter was addressed "Dear Carl." Specifically, Walz recalled Churchill's statement in the House of Commons on 15 February 1945 in which the prime minister is quoted as saying: "We did not press the Egyptian Government at any time to come into the war, and indeed upon more than one occasion in the past, our advice has been to the contrary."

36. Voss to Walz, 3 March 1947, Papers of the American Christian Palestine Committee. The letter was addressed "Dear Humphrey."

37. Chworosky to Walz, 20 February 1947, Papers of the American Christian Palestine Committee.

38. Voss's argument was similar: "Time and again I have asked for donations from Christians, from men who, like yourself, profess what I presume is a genuine concern about the future of European Jewry; but I am sorry to say the contributions have been meager and all too few. Fortunately, our Jewish friends, in accord with their traditional generosity, are willing to aid. But until the Christian conscience is awakened, we shall have to rely, albeit reluctantly, on contributions from our Jewish friends as well" (3 March 1947, Papers of the American Christian Palestine Committee).

39. *CC*, 30 July 1947, p. 917.

40. Ibid., 12 March 1947, p. 323.

41. Ibid., 23 April 1947, p. 515.

42. *Christianity and Crisis*, 4 August 1947, pp. 5-6.

43. Once the partition resolution was adopted, the *Christian Century* found a new rationale for its opposition to a Jewish state: the Jews in Palestine would be subjected to the danger of extinction at the hands of the Arabs (*CC*, 17 December 1947, pp. 1541-43). Without spelling out his own reasoning, the Anglican bishop in Jerusalem, W. H. Stewart, also declared partition to be "wrong in principle and unworkable in practice" (ibid., 14 January 1948, p. 57).
     There did not seem to be any unusual interest in the partition resolution by other American Protestant bodies. At a meeting in Kansas City on December 29, 1947, the hundred delegates from forty states of the Methodist Federation for Social Action merely urged the United States government "to work through the United Nations for justice to both groups" (ibid., p. 61).

44. *Christianity and Crisis*, 2 February 1948, p. 2.

45. Ibid. Van Dusen's more vehemently expressed feelings about the Arab–Israel conflict will be cited later, in connection with the June 1967 Six–Day war.

46. *Christianity and Crisis,* 15 March 1948, pp. 27-30.

47. United Nations, Security Council, *Official Records, Special Supplement No.* 2 (S/676), 16 February 1948, pp. 10-20.

48. *CC,* 21 January 1948, p. 94.

49. *Christianity and Crisis,* 15 March 1948, p. 28. In point of fact, Arab conversions to Christianity, and especially to Protestantism, had been relatively few since the beginning of the modern missionary movement in the Near East (Walton Wynn, "Joining Hands with Arab Christendom," *CC,* 4 July 1951, pp. 792-94; W. M. Watt, "The Missionary Task of the Church in Palestine and Syria," *International Review of Missions* 36 (1947): 153-62; Paul E. Scherer, "The Near East Kaleidoscope," *Christianity and Crisis,* 21 September 1953, pp. 114-20; Gabriel Gersh, "Christians in Arab Lands," *CC,* 22 June 1960, pp. 747-48). The overwhelming majority of Near Eastern Christians—all told fewer than two million in number—belong to the ancient monophysite and uniate churches. When Protestant missionaries sought converts, their principal though minor success was in "converting" some of these Christians to Protestantism. Very few Moslems joined Christianity. The contemporary upsurge of Arab nationalism in the region has been dominated largely by Islamic loyalties, and pragmatic Protestant spokesmen have begun to minimize the need for formal conversion to Christianity. Instead they have rather called for coexistence and patience with Islam. See Kenneth Cragg, *The Call of the Minaret* (New York: Oxford University Press, 1956), especially pt. 3. For an acknowledgment that the "spirit of Christ" pervades non–Christians, too, see John Bennett, "Christ and non–Christians," *Christianity and Crisis,* 15 May 1961, pp. 73-76.

50. *Christianity and Crisis,* 15 March 1948, p. 30. Niebuhr objected to resubmitting the question to the United Nations because there was "little prospect that an agreement could be reached on any alternative proposal, thus making confusion worse confounded." Other reactions to Dodge's position were published in *Christianity and Crisis,* 26 April 1948, p. 56.

51. *CC,* 25 February 1948, pp. 241-42. Hopkins was so disturbed about this possibility that, in an attempt to make Christianity more appealing to Arab Moslems, he headed an organization in the late 1950s seeking to increase Christian–Moslem understanding by deliberately playing down the distinctive features of Christianity.

52. Robert Root, "Whose Holy Land?" *CC,* 14 January 1948, pp. 45-48.

53. Ibid., p. 47.
　　Rev. W. Clark-Kerr, moderator of the Church of Scotland's Presbytery of Jerusalem, had given Cardinal Spellman of New York City credit for getting the United Nations Special Committee on Palestine to refer specifically to Christian interests in its terms of reference, but was "despondent" over the lack of American Protestant concern for Palestine's Holy Places. The correspondent quotes him as saying that American Protestant leaders "seem to be completely dominated by Zionism, and have no realization that there is a Christian interest in this land" (ibid., p. 48).
　　A sharp retort to Mr. Root's article was published in the *Christian Century* on 25 February 1948 in a letter from Rabbi Gerson Hadas of Kansas City.

The rabbi wrote: "The Near East Christians . . . are apparently chiefly preoccupied with churches and buildings and missions and vested interests and expediency, especially expediency. A large part of the article deals with the 'question of sacred spots,' not a word about poverty, disease, illiteracy. . . . 'Whose Holy Land?' Theirs who will make it blossom once again" (p. 241).

54. *CC*, 26 May 1948, p. 500.

55. 9 June 1948, Papers of the Committee for Justice and Peace in the Holy Land, Zionist Archives, New York.

56. *CC*, 14 July 1948, p. 701.

57. Ibid., 8 September 1948, p. 910.

58. *Newsweek*, 17 April 1950, p. 92.

59. *CC*, 5 April 1950, pp. 422-23.
In a subsequent editorial entitled "A Billion to Make more Trouble," the paper expressed the hope that American Jews would not contribute any additional funds to Israel lest the immigration of more Jewish refugees require expansion into Arab territory. The editorial noted: "Some . . . [Jews] should be brave enough to ask how much of this amount is to be used to help resettle Arab refugees in their old homes" (ibid., 27 September 1950, p. 1125). Hopkins also accused "many bookshops throughout the country" of deliberately not stocking an anti–Israel book by Mrs. W. S. Ethridge, *Going to Jerusalem* (New York: Vanguard, 1950), (ibid., 9 August 1950, p. 950). This was vigorously denied by the president of Vanguard Press (ibid., 20 September 1950, p. 1110).

60. Ibid., 19 April 1950, p. 501.

61. Ibid., 3 May 1950, pp. 563-64.

62. Ibid., 30 January 1952, p. 117.

63. *Near East Report, Special Survey*, (October 1964): B14. In 1949, two other pro–Arab organizations emerged on the American scene, but they were short-lived. One of them, the Holy Land Emergency Liaison Program (HELP), was subsidized in part by the Arabian-American Oil Co. (ARAMCO), and its sponsors included practically the same members as the Committee for Justice and Peace in the Holy Land: Gildersleeve, Coffin, Kermit Roosevelt, and Garland Hopkins. William E. Hocking, professor emeritus of philosophy at Harvard, served as chairman, and William A. Eddy, former United States minister to Saudi Arabia and later a consultant to Aramco, was its first executive director. Ostensibly, its purpose was to coordinate American volunteer interests for the Arab refugee problem, but in fact it tried to serve as a public relations agency for the Arab cause with respect to Palestine.
The other organization, Middle East Relief, Inc., sought to raise funds to aid Arab refugees, and its meetings invariably whipped up anti–Israel sentiment (ibid.).

64. Among the distinguished names on the council were William E. Hocking; William Eddy; W. F. Stinespring, professor of Old Testament, Duke University; Millar Burrows, chairman, Department of Near Eastern Languages, Yale University; Alford Carleton, who, upon leaving Syria, became executive vice-president, American Board of Commissioners for Foreign Missions; Carleton Coon, professor of anthropology, University of Pennsylvania; James Farley, for-

mer Democratic Party national chairman; Harry E. Fosdick, minister emeritus, Riverside Church, New York City; Virginia Gildersleeve; Philip Hitti, Department of Oriental Languages, Princeton University; Douglas Horton, dean, Harvard Divinity School; Rabbi Morris Lazaron, listed as "author, pioneer in interdenominational understanding"; Wallace Murray, formerly chief, Division of Near Eastern Affairs, Department of State; Henry Regnery, publisher; Ovid Sellers, former dean, McCormick Theological Seminary, Chicago; and Lowell Thomas, the newscaster.

65. *Third Annual Report of the American Friends of the Middle East* (1953-54), p. 5.

66. Ibid., p. 6.

67. Garland Hopkins actually told a Jewish journalist that the immediate aim of AFME was to redress the balance between Jewish and Arab public opinion in the United States, in view of the fact that the public media were under Jewish control (report of a conversation with Hopkins by Samuel Margoshes, editor of the Yiddish *Jewish Day*, 11 February 1953, Papers of the American Friends of the Middle East, Zionist Archives, New York).

To James Sheldon, administrative chairman of the Non-Secretarian Anti-Nazi League, Hopkins confided, "If the American people ever find themselves losing in another war in the Middle East and begin to ask why, and discover what the cause has been, you will find the same thing happening here to the Jews as happened in Germany. I hesitate to think what might happen in New York" (*American Zionist*, 5 April 1953, p. 10). When Sheldon complained to Hopkins that AFME had never invited Israel's viewpoint to be represented in his group, Hopkins replied that Israel already had too much representation on the American scene, that Arabs would not sit down with Jews, and that the overriding concern of American policy in the Middle East was to cater to the Muslim majority and save them from going Communist.

68. *Third Annual Report of the American Friends of the Middle East* (1953-54), p. 13. An early AFME strategy was to concentrate on American college youth. Winners of essay contests about the Middle East were provided with free trips to the region.

69. *Fifth Annual Report of the American Friends of the Middle East* (1955-56), pp. 54-56.

70. Ibid., pp. 56-58. Aparently the local committees' representatives were volunteers. The report described a wide range of activities and publications. Its budget for the year was $516,000 (ibid., p. 48).

71. Ibid., pp. 6-7.

72. *Proceedings of the First Annual Conference of the American Friends of the Middle East* (held in New York, January 29-30, 1953), p. 6.

73. Ibid.

74. The author's efforts to obtain the names of representative Jewish groups who had been invited but who had refused the invitation have been in vain.

75. *Proceedings of the Second Annual Conference of the American Friends of the Middle East* (held in New York, January 28-29, 1954), pp. 39-41.

76. *Facts* (New York: Anti-Defamation League of B'nai B'rith, March 1954), pp. 1-2; *New York Times,* 29 January 1954.

77. *New York Times,* 29 January 1954.

78. *Proceedings of the Second Annual Conference of the American Friends of the Middle East,* pp. 57-58.

79. *Near East Report, Special Survey* (October 1964): B15.

80. Ibid.: B16-B17. Replying to Howard's criticism, the Department of State advised the Senate's committee: "There is no factual basis for Mr. Howard's charge that United States officials support an anti–Israel organization."
     Another foundation that contributed substantially to AFME was the San Jacinto Fund of Texas, and a third one (unnamed) assisted the organization's department of student affairs. The Arabian American Oil Co. had been AFME's principal corporate contributor (*Fourth Annual Report of the American Friends of the Middle East* [1954-55], p. 43). In the organization's fifth annual report Hopkins notes: "Contrary to belief in some circles, contributions from American oil companies amounted to only seven percent of our total receipts" (*Fifth Annual Report of the American Friends of the Middle East,* p. 46).

81. One cannot accurately determine the role of any agency or corporation in financing the AFME, for the Internal Revenue Service has not allowed the records of this tax-exempt organization to be opened for public inspection (*Near East Report, Special Survey* (October 1964): B15. But AFME's very reluctance to publish its sources of income tends to arouse suspicion about its financial backers. It is natural to suppose that corporations affiliated with Arabian oil production would contribute to AFME's operations. One could surmise that the CIA has been interested both in fighting the advance of Communism in the Near East—a constant topic of AFME literature—and in trying to help the United States retain an image of "even handedness" with respect to Israel. It is certainly reasonable to assume that there are many Americans who would want to establish a genuine pattern of mutual exchange with the Arab world (though AFME never claimed more than a few thousand members). But the fact remains that, despite all the ancillary activities concerned with strengthening America's ties with the Middle East, the principal activity of AFME has been to focus attention on the injustice inflicted upon the Arab world by Israel's very existence.

82. *Fifth Annual Report of the American Friends of the Middle East,* p. 7.

83. *Near East Report, Special Survey* (October 1964): B15; *Fifth Annual Report of the American Friends of the Middle East,* p. 7.

84. In 1959 it looked back on its first eight years of activity, reiterated its belief that the Palestine question was the "very core of the problems in the Arab heartland of the Middle East," and reasserted America's responsibility for creating it ("Story of a Purpose," American Friends of the Middle East, Washington, D.C., 1959).
     The organization's income, earmarked for the pursuit of its goals, passed the million dollar mark in 1955-56 (*Fifth Annual Report,* p. 26).

85. Membership figures have not been released. In 1953-54 the organization claimed six hundred new members (*Third Annual Report,* p. 39). Its receipts from membership fees and individual donations are listed as over $55,000 (ibid., p. 41). The following year's receipts from the same sources are listed as only over

$23,000 (*Fourth Annual Report*, p. 45), while the *Fifth Annual Report of the American Friends of the Middle East*, claiming a membership increase of about 3,000 (p. 46), cites an income of over $66,000 from the "individual contributions and membership fees" category (p. 48).

CHAPTER SEVEN

1. General Assembly Resolution 181 (11), part IIIA, *Yearbook of the United Nations* (1947-48), pp. 778-79. Under this resolution, the United Nations was to "ensure that order and peace, and especially religious peace, reign in Jerusalem," and "promote the security, well being and any constructive measures of development of the residents." The resolution also provided for "a special police force of adequate strength . . . to assist in the maintenance of international law and order."

2. Ibid., pp. 778-81.

3. A/530, ibid., p. 257.

4. General Assembly Resolution 187(S-2), ibid., p. 267.

5. *Official Records*, Third Session, Supplement no. 1, A/565, p. 8.

6. *Yearbook of the United Nations*, (1947-48) pp. 271-73.

7. General Assembly Resolution 186(S-2), ibid., p. 281. The vote on the resolution was 31 to 7 with 16 abstentions. During the General Assembly's second special session debate, the United States representative announced, on May 14, United States recognition of the Provisional Government of Israel, which was proclaimed that day at Tel Aviv, as the *de facto* authority of the new state of Israel. On July 29, 1948, the Trusteeship Council decided to postpone indefinitely consideration of a statute for the city of Jerusalem (ibid., p. 781).

8. General Assembly Resolution 194(III), ibid. (1948-49) pp. 174-76.

9. The mediator, Count Bernadotte, was murdered in Jerusalem on September 17, 1948.

10. The conciliation commission consisted of representatives of the United States, France and Turkey.

11. A/973 and A/973/Add 1, *Yearbook of the United Nations* (1948-49), p. 199. The area would be divided into two autonomous zones, one Jewish (encompassing the new city of Jerusalem with its 100,000 Jewish inhabitants), and the other Arab (encompassing the rest of the territory). Israeli and Jordanian authorities would provide municipal administration for the respective zones in matters not reserved for the authority of the United Nations. Such reserved authority would function under

   a) a United Nations commissioner, responsible to the United Nations General Assembly, who would, *inter alia*, ensure the protection of and free access to the Holy Places (article 6), supervise the permanent demilitarization of the area and ensure the protection of human rights therein (article 8);

   b) a general council of fourteen members (five each appointed by the authorities of the Arab and Jewish zones, and four by the commissioner) which would deal with general public services in the area (article 11);

c) an international tribunal elected by the General Assembly, which would enjoy supreme judicial authority for the entire international area (including disputes regarding Holy Places) (article 12); and

d) a mixed tribunal (an Arab, an Israeli, and a neutral appointed by the president of the international tribunal), which would handle all civil and criminal cases involving residents of the two zones (article 13).

Before presenting the plan to the assembly, the conciliation commission prepared a series of progress reports. In its second report (A/838), it indicated that on April 7, 1949 Israel's Foreign Minister had advised the commission of his government's intent to seek a revision of part of the General Assembly's December 11, 1948 resolution, to wit, to place only the Holy Places under United Nations control, but not the city of Jerusalem itself.

12. General Assembly Resolution 303(IV). *Yearbook of the United Nations* (1948-49), p. 196.

13. T/427, ibid., p. 197.

14. T/475, *Yearbook of the United Nations* (1950), p. 335.

15. Trusteeship Council document, T/457, 31 January 1950, p. 18.

16. T/564, *Yearbook of the United Nations* (1950), p. 337.

17. A/1286, ibid.

18. A/1724, ibid., p. 341. The vote was 30 for, 18 against, and 11 abstentions. A Swedish resolution upholding the principle of functional internationalization of Holy Places was not put to a vote at the General Assembly plenum when it was removed from the agenda by a 25 to 18 vote with 12 abstentions. For a summary of the debate, see ibid., pp. 335-41.

19. *CC*, 17 September 1947, p. 1100.

20. Ibid., 16 June 1948, p. 387.

21. Ibid., 4 May 1949, pp. 548-49.

22. When, in January 1957, President Eisenhower asked for congressional standby authority to send troops into the Middle East, the *Christian Century* reported on an interview with John McCormack, in which the Massachusetts congressman declared he intended to vote for the President's request although he knew of no crisis to warrant it (*CC*, 16 January 1957, p. 70). The paper asked: "Could he have been moved by the passage in the President's message concerning the Holy Places in which the Roman Catholic church claims a special interest?" The paper also noted that the heaviest congressional applause followed mention of the Holy Places in the presidential address. It likened the president's appeal to that of the Crusades, "to deliver the Holy Places from the hands of the infidel," and wondered whether such an appeal was the best justification for adopting the government's new policy.

23. Ibid., 11 January 1950, p. 36. Such a conclusion had been reached earlier by Edward Robinson, the archeologist, who rejected the site of the Church of the Holy Sepulchre as the spot where Jesus is buried. He believed that it could have been located only outside the city walls. (Finnie, *Pioneers East*, pp. 178-79.) See also chap. 1, n. 79.

24. Ibid., 11 January 1950, p. 36.

25. Ibid., 9 August 1950, pp. 939-40.

26. Ibid.

27. Ibid., 11 January 1950, p. 36.

28. Ibid.

29. For a brief historical account of the development of Christian interests in the Holy Land, see Saul P. Colbi, *Christianity in the Holy Land* (Tel Aviv: Am Hassefer, 1969).

The struggle between the Greek Orthodox and the Roman Catholics for control over the Holy Places is as old as the split between Rome and Constantinople in the eleventh century. Since the "capitulations era" of the sixteenth century, when an increasingly feeble Turkish government had to accede to the demands of European powers that their subjects living in the Ottoman Empire be placed under the jurisdiction of their respective consuls, the religious rivals in Palestine found support in powerful secular states. The Catholics had France in their corner, while Russia supported the Greek Orthodox. The latter also enjoyed the tacit support of the Ottoman authorities who preferred their own Greek Orthodox subjects to the Latin nationals of European states. Thus, for example, despite the superior status with respect to the Holy Places, granted to the Catholics in the 1740 capitulations treaty with France, the Greek Orthodox in the Holy Land not only forcefully dispossessed the Catholic Franciscans from one of the shrines, but influenced the Sultan in 1757 to issue a new firman restoring the preeminent rights of the Greek Orthodox to the Holy Places (ibid., p. 70). This position was confirmed in 1852 (ibid., p. 75), and has served as the prevailing status of the Holy Places ever since.

30. Ibid., pp. 89-92. Since 1840 the British Anglicans in association with the German Lutherans had been actively converting Greek Orthodox Christians to Protestantism in addition to providing medical and educational services in the Holy Land. The period of Anglican and Lutheran cooperation ended in 1888 when Emperor William II created the Jerusalem Evangelical Association of Berlin to support Lutheran institutions in Palestine. The Anglicans continued to carry on their own missionary activities.

31. Sandeen, *Roots of Fundamentalism*, pp. 10-12.

32. Frederick Jones Bliss, *The Religions of Modern Syria and Palestine* (New York: Charles Scribner's Sons, 1917), p. 320.

33. *CC*, 16 November 1949, p. 1347.

34. Ibid., 26 April 1948, p. 456.

35. Walter W. VanKirk, "Shall Jerusalem Be Internationalized?" mimeographed (New York: Federal Council of Churches, 21 October 1949), p. 6.

36. Ibid.

37. Trusteeship Council document T/457, 31 January 1950, p. 18.

38. *International Review of Missions* 39 (1950):34.

39. Trusteeship Council document T/457, 31 January 1950, pp. 19-21. In submitting the same memorandum of the Commission of the Churches on International Affairs to the president of the Trusteeship Council on January 3, 1950, its

director, O. F. Nolde, also attached a private statement of the Archbishop of Canterbury, dated October 31, 1949, in which the British clergyman proposed a modified single Jerusalem enclave without division into Jewish and Arab zones (ibid., pp. 23-27). Still another private version of an internationalized Jerusalem was submitted to the president of the Trusteeship Council by Rev. Charles T. Bridgeman on January 6, 1950 (ibid., pp. 32-45). He felt that the proposed division of the city into predominantly Israeli and Arab sections was highly inequitable to the Arab Christians, some 24,000 of whom, in his estimate, lived in the new sector of Jerusalem.

40. Ibid., p. 20.

41. Ibid.

42. Evan M. Wilson, "The Internationalization of Jerusalem," *Middle East Journal* 23 (1969):2. The mutual suspicions among the Christian ecclesiastical leaders in old Jerusalem were so strong that it took seven years of negotiations (1954-61) to agree to carry out necessary repairs in the church.

43. The CCIA also felt that it was not the most appropriate agency to deal with the Arab refugee problem on the spot. It stated: "The primary role of CCIA has been to make representation to governments regarding issues of Christian concern in international affairs." Papers of the International Missionary Council, Missionary Library, Union Theological Seminary, New York.

44. Statement of the National Executive Council of 30 December 1948, Papers of the American Christian Palestine Committee, Zionist Archives, New York.

45. Press release, 20 October 1949, Papers of the American Christian Palestine Committee, Zionist Archives.

46. *A Proposal for an International Curatorship for the Holy Places,* Zionist Archives, November 1949.

47. Niebuhr to Nolde, Papers of the Commission of Churches on International Affairs, New York.

48. Niebuhr followed up his letter with further comments on the subject of internationalization, in *Christianity and Crisis,* 9 January 1950, pp. 178-79. He indicated that while most American Protestant churches had passed resolutions favoring the internationalization of Jerusalem, there was no agreement among their leaders as to the nature of "internationalization" except that they all accepted the principle of free access to the Holy Places. In his view, the reason why the Arab states were fighting for the *corpus separatum* status of Jerusalem was that they believed the internationalized city would become a buffer zone against further Israeli territorial expansion.

49. Press release, 19 January 1950, Papers of the American Christian Palestine Committee, Zionist Archives. The investigation commission included Rev. Samuel Guy Inman, a member of the Federal Council of Churches Commission of Justice and Goodwill; Charles J. Turck, president of Macalester College and president of the National Council of Presbyterian Laymen; John W. Bradbury, editor of the National Baptists' magazine, *The Watchman-Examiner*; Ralph W. Riley, president of the American Baptist Theological Seminary; Professor Victor Obenhaus of the University of Chicago and national chairman of the Council of Social Action, Congregational Christian Church of America; and Mrs. M. E. Tilly, member of President Truman's Commission on Civil Rights.

50. *New York Times*, 26 January 1950.

51. *CC*, 25 January 1950, p. 187.

52. Press release, 17 September 1953, files of the National Council of Churches, New York.

53. In December 1952 in the General Assembly, the representative of the Philippines proposed an amendment to the Ad Hoc Committee's report on the question of Jerusalem's status, which had urged the governments concerned—Jordan and Israel—to enter into direct negotiations on the Jerusalem question, bearing in mind the "religious interests of third parties" (*Yearbook of the United Nations* (1952), p. 252). The proposed amendment added: "and in particular the principle of the internationalization of Jerusalem." Neither the Ad Hoc Committee's formula nor the amendment received the necessary two-thirds majority.

54. The relevant paragraph of the Soviet draft resolution of 18 June 1967 (A/L.519) was defeated on 4 July 1967 by 36 votes in favor, 57 against, and 23 abstentions. On the same day, an Albanian draft resolution (A/L.521), also condemning Israel as an aggressor, lost by even a larger vote: 22 in favor, 71 against, and 27 abstentions (*Yearbook of the United Nations* [1967], p. 209).

55. General Assembly Resolution 2253 (ES-V). The vote was 99 in favor, 0 against, and 20 abstentions (ibid., p. 211).

56. Elihu Lauterpacht, *Jerusalem and the Holy Places* (London: Anglo-Israel Association, 1968), pp. 50-51.

57. *Interchurch News*, August-September 1967, p. 4.

58. In late fall 1969, following the fire ignited in the Al-Aksa Mosque in Jerusalem by a deranged Christian tourist, the *Christian Century*, while absolving the Israelis from direct responsibility, "understood" the Arab rage over the incident—because Israel continued to occupy portions of Egypt, Jordan, and Syria! The paper claimed: "the tangle of religious claims at stake in the city of Jerusalem continues to argue for some kind of authoritative international presence in that city. In the face of bitter criticism from some American Jewish leaders, the National Council of Churches has, since 1967, wisely and steadfastly supported such an international authority" (*CC*, 3 September 1969, p. 1129).
  While the American Protestant establishment was toying with the concept of an "international presence" in Jerusalem, the Roman Catholic Church was pushing for the territorial internationalization of the entire city (*New York Times*, 24 June 1967, p. 3). The Pope explicitly urged this policy at a secret consistory in Rome in which he elevated twenty-seven prelates, including four Americans, to the College of Cardinals (ibid., June 26, p. 1). The Vatican spokesman was reported to have made clear that assurances of free access to all faiths by Israel, which now controls the entire city, are not sufficient (ibid., p. 3).

59. *New York Times*, 12 July 1967.

60. Kirster Stendahl, "Judaism and Christianity, II—after a Colloquium and a War," *Harvard Divinity Bulletin*, autumn 1967, p. 7.

61. *New York Times*, 18 June 1967, p. 6; ibid., 22 June 1967, p. 12.

62. Ibid., 18 June, 1967.

63. Ibid., 22 June, 1967.

CHAPTER EIGHT

1. *Christianity and Crisis*, 3 October 1949, pp. 122-26.

2. For another version of the Dir Yassin episode, see Menachem Beigin, *The Revolt* (London: W. H. Allen, 1951), pp. 162ff.

3. *CC*, 27 June 1951, pp. 763-65.

4. Ibid., 16 May 1956, p. 614.

5. See above, chap. 6.

6. *Christianity and Crisis*, 3 October 1949, p. 123.

7. *International Review of Missions* 39 (1950): 33.

8. General Assembly Resolution 194 (III), *Yearbook of the United Nations* (1948-49), pp. 174-75.

9. General Assembly Resolution 394 (V), ibid., (1950), p. 334.

10. *CC*, 22 August 1951, p. 967. Among the signers were Walter VanKirk, executive director of the Department of International Justice and Goodwill of the National Council of Churches, and Glora M. Wysner, executive secretary of the International Missionary Council.

11. Ibid., 18 July 1952, p. 838.

12. Ibid., 13 January 1954, p. 39.

13. Ibid., 16 May 1956, p. 611.

14. Ibid., 10 October 1956, p. 1158.

15. *A Christian Report on Israel*, (New York: American Christian Palestine Committee, 1949), foreword by Carl Voss.

16. Ibid., p. 8. This statement was made by John P. Jones, president of the Brooklyn division of the Protestant Council.

17. *CC*, 10 October 1956, p. 1159.

18. *International Review of Missions* 47 (1958):36.

19. *Christianity and Crisis*, 3 October 1949, p. 124.

20. Ibid., 20 February 1956, p. 13.

21. *CC*, 10 October 1956, p. 1159.

22. See chap. 9.

23. *Christianity and Crisis*, 6 February 1961, p. 7.

24. Ibid., p. 8.

25. Ibid., 16 May 1955, p. 60.

26. Ibid.

27. A. Roy Eckardt, *Christianity and the Children of Israel*, (New York: Kings Crown Press, 1948), p. 170.

28. Some 15,000 young people among the refugees were trained during the first ten years of the United Nations Relief and Work Agency's existence in trades, or were helped to establish themselves in different occupations (*CC*, 2 April 1958, p. 399). In place of thousands of tents overlooking Amman, modern stone built villages arose in the late 1950s (*CC*, 11 May 1960, p. 567). A correspondent wrote to the *Christian Century*: "A visit to the camps [in West Jordan] soon dispels long held visions of fragile tents, bedraggled children and begging adults. The camps have become settlements with individually designed abodes and stone houses, small gardens and orchards, schools, shops, restaurants, post offices, clinics and mosques. The villagers appear infinitely better off than the Arabs one sees in the slums of old Jerusalem" (*CC*, 20 September 1967, p. 1183).

29. Elfan Rees, *We Strangers and Afraid* (New York: Carnegie Endowment for International Peace, 1959), p. 42.

A Middle Eastern correspondent of *Christian Century* wrote: "As long as they [the refugees] see a hope of returning, the problem will continue" (*CC*, 11 May 1960, p. 567).

30. Elfan Rees, "Middle East Mission: October–November 1949," 15 November 1949, pp. 4-5, Files of Commission of Churches on International Affairs, New York.

31. Ibid., p. 6.

32. Ibid., p. 7.

33. Ibid., p. 8.

34. Ibid., p. 9.

35. *CC*, 21 November 1956, p. 1366.

36. Elfan Rees, *The Refugee Problem: Today and Tomorrow*, (Geneva: World Council of Churches, 1957).

37. Ibid. An American Protestant leader, Stewart W. Herman, director of the Resettlement Division of the Lutheran World Federation, concurred with Rees's principal thesis of refugee integration rather than repatriation. Writing in the *Christian Century* after the 1951 Beirut Conference, Rev. Herman asserted that the "ideal solution" of returning the refugees to their former homes "disregards political realities." He advocated instead finding new homes for them elsewhere, and specifically mentioned the rich Jezira area of the fertile crescent, where only fifty percent of the soil was being cultivated (*CC*, 6 June 1951, pp. 680-82).

38. Rees reiterated his position in *We Strangers and Afraid*.

39. The United Nations Relief and Work Agency was established by a General Assembly Resolution in December 1949, and began to function in May 1950. By 1959, only thirty-three of the eighty-two governmental members of the United Nations had contributed to UNRWA's budget—the United States and the United Kingdom providing ninety percent of the funds. Its 1959 budget was over $37 million (ibid., p. 43).

40. Ibid., p. 42.

41. Ibid., pp. 42-43.

42. Ibid., p. 59.

43. *CC*, 15 September 1948, p. 950; ibid., 24 November 1948, p. 1261.

44. Ibid., 22 September 1948, p. 964.

45. These spokesmen included the American Friends of the Middle East. See the excerpts of the sermon "Let My People Go," by Dean Francis B. Sayre of the Washington Cathedral Church (*CC*, 19 December 1962, pp. 1553-54).

Said Walter W. VanKirk, executive director of the Department of International Justice and Goodwill of the National Council of Churches, in 1954: "It is not in harmony with the New Testament concept of charity for Christians to stand knee-deep in the tears of anguished refugees, and there debate the pros and cons of the political or military circumstances related to their plight." In the same address, however, Rev. VanKirk admitted that "the problem of the Arab refugees cannot be solved in terms of relief." What was needed, therefore, was "for the United States to display toward the Arab peoples a larger measure of human concern expressed in political understanding and goodwill" (from an address delivered on January 29, 1954 in *The Proceedings of the Second Annual Conference of the American Friends of the Middle East* [1954]).

Again, the only "political understanding" that one could reasonably infer from Rev. VanKirk's address was to be developed at Israel's expense.

46. *CC*, 9 January 1952, p. 37.

47. Ibid., 19 February 1952, p. 195.

48. In 1937 members of the indigenous churches were invited to join the council as "corresponding members" ("Quarterly Notes," *International Review of Missions* 47 [July 1935]. In 1939 they became constituent members "on the same footing as missions" (ibid., 64 [October 1939]). In September 1965 an Egyptian Coptic pastor, educated at Hartford Theological Seminary in the United States, became the first Arab executive of the Near East Council of Churches (*CC*, 7 September 1966, p. 1090).

49. *Palestine Refugees: Aid with Justice* (Geneva: World Council of Churches, 1970), p. 5.

50. Ibid., p. 6. Of the nineteen, fourteen represented local Orthodox churches and five represented local Evangelical Protestant churches.

51. Ibid. For practical purposes, the NECCCRW acted as an independent organization, meeting every six weeks, and reporting annually to the Near East Christian Council. The World Council of Churches' share in its budget was covered by the Service Program of the Division of Interchurch Aid, Refugee and World Service (DICARWS).

52. Ibid.

53. Ibid.

54. *Christianity and Crisis*, 11 June 1951, pp. 78-79.

55. *Palestine Refugees: Aid with Justice*, p. 44.

56. Ibid., p. 43.

57. Ibid., p. 45.

58. Horace M. McMullen, *International Review of Missions* 46 (1957):56. Dr. McMullen was president of missionary-sponsored Aleppo College, Syria.

59. *Palestine Refugees: Aid with Justice* p. 45.

60. Ibid., pp. 76-77.

61. In connection with the subject of Jerusalem, noted earlier (e.g. pp. 121-22), Nolde, director of the CCIA, also represented that part of the Protestant establishment whose policy advocated the territorial internationalization of Jerusalem.

62. The sequel to our analysis of the Protestant attitude toward the Arab refugee problem falls beyond the period considered here. In the fall of 1969 a Consultation on the Palestine Refugee Problem was held at Nicosia, Cyprus. It was sponsored by the member churches of the World Council of Churches in the Middle East and the World Council's Division of Inter-Church Aid, Refugee and World Service (DICARWS), into which the International Missionary Council had been integrated in 1961 (*Palestine Refugees: Aid with Justice,* p. 5). Whereas the first Beirut conference in 1951 had a predominantly Anglo-Saxon group of participants, the Cyprus meeting was dominated by members of the Middle Eastern churches themselves. Its resolutions, therefore, reflected a strong pro–Arab militancy which was not bound by the ambivalence caused by conflicting forces, pro- and anti–Israel and political in purpose.

The consultation asserted the need to redress the injustice meted out to the Palestine Arabs by recognizing their right to self determination. This right, the meeting held, had not been recognized when the state of Israel was established (though in fact the Palestinians themselves had tacitly rejected a state of their own when they discarded the 1947 UN partition plan). The consultation agreed to promote among Christians throughout the world a deeper understanding of the "inalienable nature of the fundamental rights of the Palestinian people" and a recognition of the reality of a Palestinian identity as shown in the Palestine liberation movement ("Report of the Consultation on the Palestine Refugee Problem," mimeographed [Geneva: World Council of Churches, 1969]).

CHAPTER NINE

1. Note the debates between David Ben-Gurion and representatives of American Zionism, e.g. *CC,* 26 September 1951, pp. 1092-93; ibid., 18 January 1961, pp. 35-36.

2. *Christianity and Crisis,* 21 February 1949, pp. 9-10.

3. Ibid., 21 March 1949, pp. 30-32.

4. The conclusion which Eckardt said could be drawn from Coffin's position was that "thus, the possible legitimacy of such a state is ruled out *a priori*" (ibid., p. 32).

5. William E. Hocking, *The Spirit of World Politics* (New York: Macmillan, 1932), pt. 5; idem, *Rethinking Missions* (New York: Harper & Brothers, 1932).

6. *CC,* 19 September 1951, pp. 1072-74.

7. Responding to Hocking's article, Rabbi H. J. Wilner of Maryland wrote in

a letter in the *Christian Century*: "In looking through the index of my copy of Professor Hocking's *Meaning of God* . . . I find no listing of Jews, Judaism, Moses or any of the Hebrew prophets, but I do find entries for Islam and Mohammed. Under the line entry for 'Hebrew religion,' which has two skimpy listings, I find such derogatory remarks as 'the god (sic, small letter) of the Jews,' and 'in the Hebrew religion the imaginative elements are little in evidence'. . . . Must professional missionary spirit or *odium theologicum* always obsess you? . . . Can't you find a single good thing to say [about Israel] even at this late date, when [other] publications . . . have undergone significant changes of heart for a people committed to practical religion whose metaphysics differ from yours?" (*CC*, 24 October 1951, p. 1225).

8. *CC*, 16 March 1949, pp. 327-29. Little did it realize how difficult the victory was. See David Ben-Gurion's *Israel* (New York: Funk and Wagnalls, 1971).

9. For a lengthier analysis of this editorial, see *The Reconstructionist*, 1 April 1949.

10. 2 Samuel 23:3. See Solomon Mandelkorn's *Concordance*, (Berlin: Margolin Publishers, 1925), pp. 993-4, for numerous biblical references of "Rock" meaning "God."

11. *CC*, 9 June 1948, p. 565.

12. Ibid., 14 July 1948, p. 701.

13. Ibid., 8 September 1948, p. 901. The periodical was correct in asserting that the term "Rock of Israel" was used in the text of the Declaration of Independence to win approval of the few professed ideological atheists among the signers of the document, who represented a small political constituency which would have felt uncomfortable with the term "Almighty God."

14. *International Review of Missions* 37 (1948): 433.

15. *CC*, 28 February 1951, p. 260.

16. Ibid., 1 November 1950, p. 1286.

17. Ibid., 6 January 1954, pp. 5-7.

18. Ibid., 13 January 1954, p. 38.

19. Ibid., pp. 38-40.

20. Ibid., 20 January 1954, p. 73.

21. Ibid., 27 January 1954, p. 115. Shulman further reminded Fey that Rabbi Lazaron, though an anti-Zionist, was not permitted to enter Jordan because he was Jewish.

22. Ibid., 10 February 1954, p. 180.

23. Ibid., 17 February 1954, p. 210.

24. Ibid., 6 December 1950, p. 1445.

25. Ibid., 10 October 1956, p. 1155.

26. On a different level, the *Christian Century* felt that Israel was being too harsh towards Germany when in 1951 it negotiated for German financial rep-

arations. "While it is reported," stated the periodical, "that Israel stands ready to accept goods in lieu of cash settlement, even this amount ($600 million) of restitution may seriously impede the economic recovery of Germany. We hope that Israel will be more moderate and forgiving in its demands" (ibid., 17 October 1951, p. 1180). In fact, the amount of the reparations was much higher, and the German economy continued to boom.

27. Ibid., 5 December 1951, p. 1396.

28. *International Review of Missions* 39 (1950): 64.

29. *CC*, 2 January 1957, p. 4.

30. Ibid., 3 September 1958, p. 989. In fact, only in late 1964, after Kyle Haseldon became the new managing editor of the publication, did the *Christian Century* come to terms with Israel's reality.

31. Ibid., 9 November 1955, p. 1293.

32. Ibid., 14 September 1955, p. 1043.

33. Ibid., 16 January 1957, p. 69.

34. Ibid., 30 October 1957, p. 1276.

35. *Christianity and Crisis*, 2 April 1956, p. 34.

36. Ibid., 28 May 1956, p. 65.

37. Ibid., 26 November 1956, p. 158.

38. Ibid., pp. 158-59. Niebuhr was supported in his thesis by a contributing editor to *Christianity and Crisis*, Kenneth W. Thompson, who had moved from a professorship of international relations at Northwestern University to the Rockefeller Foundation. Thompson wrote: "Christian sectarian thought has felt impelled to picture political action in terms of radically simple moral absolutes. Peace, anti-colonialism and the United Nations currently are invested with absolute ethical value. They are the new triad of international values which have become the American standard against which we are asked to judge every event. . . . [Yet] we must concede that today as in the past, peace is attainable only by risking war. . . . While we have strong, bold visions of the end of international life, we falter in the realm of means. . . . In the interest of national security, we must prevent further Russian expansion, assure that the Suez Canal is kept open beyond blackmail by any nation, and press for a settlement of Arab–Israeli problems that will establish a *status quo* worth being preserved. . . . We and our allies have obscured this community of interests, they by acting with a reckless and unfortunate impatience, we by choosing to view our friends rather than the Russians as the real threat. . . ." (ibid., 7 January 1957, pp. 181-86).

In an article written a year later, Thompson reiterated his theme that the confusion in United States policy lay in "the bankruptcy of the moralistic tradition in American thinking. . . . [which] calls essentially for an all or nothing approach." He suggested instead that political morality "demands the wisdom and courage to pursue an intelligent, accelerated arms program at the same time that we seek limited political solutions to concrete problems" (ibid., 17 February 1958, pp. 11-15).

39. Ibid., 24 December 1956, pp. 172-74.

40. Ibid.

41. Ibid., 7 January 1957, p. 187.

42. Ibid., 18 March 1957, p. 26.

43. Ibid.

44. Ibid., 15 April 1957, p. 43.
    Niebuhr wrote: "Something has certainly gone wrong with the 'moral influence' theory of diplomacy. . . . The moral is that idealism in politics is ineffective if it is not implemented in detailed policy. . . . There is a good historical analogy for the present situation in the history of the Roman Empire. . . . Marcus Aurelius wrote some very idealistic moral meditations. . . . But he was too vague to be interested in any specific problems which vexed the Empire. Consequently, most historians mark his reign as the beginning of Roman decay. . . ."

CHAPTER TEN

1. At the end of 1964, the new managing editor of *Christian Century*, Kyle Haseldon, began to modify radically that paper's policy with regard to such subjects as Jewish nationalism, Israel, and the "melting pot" desideratum for America. Haseldon's more flexible stance on these issues was reflected in the editorials of the publication from the time he assumed his position as managing editor through the end of the period of our investigation. In late 1967, Haseldon was stricken with cancer, and died shortly thereafter.

2. *CC*, 30 August 1967, pp. 1091-92.

3. Modern Jews have not helped very much in clarifying the theological term 'Israel.' Reporting on a 1966 interfaith dialogue in England, a *Christian Century* correspondent wrote that one of the participants, Professor Uri Tal of the Hebrew University in Jerusalem, told the gathering that the character of contemporary Israel had not yet been fully articulated. Tal, personally an observant Jew, was purported to have said that though Israel appeared to be a politically secular society it was essentially a religious state and had a theological, but not an eschatological, significance. Commented the reporter, Cecil Northcott: "No messianic vision for Professor Tal! His Israel seems to be an Anglican type, church-state compromise, which perhaps explains why Anglicanism seems to be able to live so happily with Israel on the dialogic frontier" (*CC*, 31 August 1966, p. 1049).

4. *Christianity Today*, 15 October 1956, pp. 7ff.

5. Ibid., 21 July 1967, pp. 1044-45.

6. Ibid., 7 June 1968, pp. 870-73.

7. CC, 9 January 1957, pp. 41-42.

8. Ibid., 24 March 1965, pp. 360-61.

9. A. Roy Eckardt, *Elder and Younger Brothers* (New York: Charles Scribners' Sons, 1967), p. 147.

10. The principal question at the 1951 meeting of the German branch of the

International Missionary Council's Commission on the Christian Approach to the Jews was not the *sui generis* nature of the Jewish people—which was acknowledged—but the uniqueness of the land of Israel. One reporter wrote: "The only question was whether one could now say, in the same [*sui generis*] sense, that even the land of Israel, the Holy Land, is 'no mere country among countries,' on the same plane as them, but that it had the character of a 'sacrament,' that the Land of Israel acquires 'consecrated dignity' " (Gerhard Jasper, "The State of Israel and Christendom," *International Review of Missions* 40 [1951]:313-21). The meeting spent time studying Martin Buber's appraisal of the land of Israel in the divine design, which can be found in Martin Buber, *Israel and Palestine* (London: East and West Library, 1952).

The meeting reached no conclusions. It affirmed that the state of Israel had not emerged without God's will, but it could not agree on whether this was a new stage in the eschatological process.

11. *CC*, 2 November 1966, pp. 1359-62.

12. Ibid., 30 March 1949, pp. 400-02. See chap. 2, note 35. Karl Baehr of the American Christian Palestine Committee responded to Burrows as follows: "If they had done so—i.e. if they had accepted Jesus—there would have been no Jews, either in the religious or in the ethnic sense of the word. . . . While it may be that Christianity ('Judaism denationalized') is theoretically incompatible with nationalism, it is also true that the Christian world is divided into nations, that these nations have been most intensely nationalistic, and that Jews—both religious and secular—have been the victims of this nationalism." Why, asked Baehr, begrudge the Jews their own national security? (ibid., 27 April 1949, p. 530).

13. Ibid., 16 March 1949, pp. 327-29.

14. Ibid., 7 May 1958, p. 550. Karl G. Rengstorf, a Lutheran professor of theology at the University of Munster, Germany, denied any theological significance to the ingathering of Jews in Israel. While acknowledging that what is happening in Palestine is "surely not without God's guidance," he maintained that the exiled existence of the Jewish people will be continued in Palestine. "This will of course take place in a quite new form of exile; namely, not an outward, but in a spiritual exile . . ." ("The Jewish Problem and the Church's Understanding of its own Mission," in *The Church and the Jewish People*, ed. G. Hedenquist [London: Edisburgh House Press, 1954], pp. 36-37).

15. *Christianity Today*, 24 December 1956, pp. 6ff.

16. *Collection of Statements Made by the World Council of Churches and Representatives Bodies of its Member Churches* (Geneva: World Council of Churches, July 1964), p. 15.

17. For example: "God's revelations of His faithfulness to His promises was given in His dealings with Israel." (ibid., p. 19.)

18. *International Review of Missions* 44 (1955): 199.

19. Ibid., pp. 198-204.

20. The delegate from the Egyptian Coptic Church wrote to the *Christian Century*: "We felt that whatever the theological motivation towards 'the ultimate fulfillment of God's promise to the people of ancient Israel' [was, it] . . . carried political implications, and would be so interpreted throughout the Mid-

dle East to the detriment of the Christians of the area. . . . it would be an embarrassment even though modified by the description 'New Testament concept of' " (*CC*, 29 September 1954, p. 1182).

21. *Collection of Statements*, p. 20.

22. Bishop Stewart, in a letter to the *International Review of Missions*, defended himself as follows: "The title of Bishop of Jerusalem . . . should make a man a champion of truth, justice, and a dedicated servant of the spiritual Israel, the Christian church. . . . But it does not and should not make him a champion of any race, any state or any political creed. Similarly, to describe a vote against the particular proposal that was before the Assembly as a vote 'on the anti–Israel side' is to beg the whole question. . . . To suggest that our attitude was . . . anti–Semitic is simply untrue and frankly insulting. . ." (*International Review of Missions* 44 [1955]:369).

23. *Collection of Statements*, pp. 22-23.

24. Ibid., p. 21.

25. *International Review of Missions* 44 (1955): 203.

26. Ibid., 46 (1957): 54.

27. Ibid.

28. Ibid. 44 (1955):369.

29. Ibid. 23 (1934):201.
   In 1934 the *International Review of Missions* stated: "In Europe, in a Christian gathering, one can assume that there is no question as to the validity of the Christian approach to the Jew; in America, no such assumption can be made. On the contrary, one must assume that the validity of such an approach must first be proved."
   In the United States the home mission boards of various denominations and the Department of Evangelism of the National Council of Churches pursued their conversionist activities among American Jews, but it appears that their success was limited (Jacob Gartenhaus, "Evangelizing the Jews," *Christianity Today*, 14 April 1958, pp. 8-10; G. E. Sweazy, "Are Jews Intended to be Christians," ibid., 29 April 1959, pp. 514-16). They tended to go to great lengths to justify their activities, while resenting the attitudes of other Protestants who considered them "fruitless."
   Noted American Protestant theologians were either ambivalent or outright antagonistic to their conversionist policies. Paul Tillich believed that the function of Judaism was to criticize "those tendencies in Christianity which drive toward paganism and idolatry . . . and perhaps it is the meaning of historical providence that this shall remain so as long as there is history" (*Christianity and Crisis*, 4 April 1955, pp. 35-38).
   Even more strongly than Tillich, Reinhold Niebuhr vigorously opposed the conversion of Jews by Protestant missionary forces. (See *Central Conference of American Rabbis Journal*, April 1958, pp. 18-32; see also *Christianity and Crisis*, 12 December 1966, pp. 279-83.) Niebuhr believed that the Jewish tradition possessed a unique civic virtue which served "as a corrective for the irrelevant individualism and perfectionism of Protestantism." He called for a "religio-political partnership" between the two faiths.
   David Stowe, assistant general secretary for Overseas Missions of the Na-

tional Council of Churches, felt that Niebuhr's position was based on his ambivalence about Christianity's origins. (See *Christianity and Crisis,* 6 February 1967, p. 12; for Niebuhr's response to Stowe, see ibid., p. 14.)

A. Roy Eckardt asserted that "conversion as a policy is a theological impossibility" (*Elder and Younger Brothers* [New York: Charles Scribners' Sons, 1967], p. 157).

30. E.g., *CC,* 1 November 1950, pp. 1285-87.

31. Compare the views of the advisor to the Anglican bishop in Jerusalem who wrote, in 1966: "The particular ethos of Judaism strikes a non–Jewish visitor to Israel perhaps more than any religious feature of the modern state . . . the Jewish emphasis [is] upon 'doing' rather than 'believing' " (Peter Schneider, *The Dialogue of Christians and Jews* [New York: Seabury Press, 1967], p. 126).

32. E.g., *International Review of Missions* 47 (1958): 67.

33. *Christianity Today,* 8 August 1961, p. 973.

34. R. Clephane Macanna, "The Emergence of the State of Israel and its Significance," *The Church and the Jewish People,* no. 2 (1970): 77-91; Hans Kosmola, "State and Religion in the State of Israel," ibid., pp. 91-101; Carl Henry, "Israel: Marvel among the Nations," *Christianity Today,* 11 September 1961, pp. 1029-31, and 25 September 1961, pp. 1079-82; *International Review of Missions* 47 (1958): 67.

35. *CC,* 16 March 1949, pp. 327-29; ibid., 1 November 1950, pp. 1285-87; ibid., 14 December 1960, pp. 1466-68.

36. *Christianity Today,* 13 October 1961, p. 12; ibid., 23 November 1962, pp. 171-73.

37. *International Review of Missions* 38 (1949): 197-202.

38. Ibid. 39 (1950): 64.

39. Ibid. 43 (1954):63. In 1955, the Southern Baptist Mission had a total membership of 75. Its staff of four families was responsible for the Children's Home in Petah Tikvah and the Mission School for 360 pupils in Nazareth (*CC,* 21 September 1955, pp. 1092-94).

40. *Christianity Today,* 31 July 1961, p. 937,

41. *CC,* 26 July 1961, p. 891.

42. Ibid., 1 November 1961, pp. 1308-09.

43. Ibid., 23 September 1964, p. 1186.

44. *Christianity Today,* 31 July 1961, p. 935.

45. Ibid., 22 December 1958, p. 8.

46. Ibid., 15 October 1956, p. 29.

47. Ibid., 31 July 1961, pp. 934-35; ibid., 8 August 1961, pp. 969-73.

48. Ibid., 8 August 1961, p. 973.

49. Ibid., 2 March 1962, p. 530.

50. Ibid., 24 November 1961, p. 207.

51. Schneider, *Dialogue of Christians and Jews,* pp. 174-75.

52. The case of Brother Daniel involved a Jew who had converted to Catholicism abroad. The Court held that the tenor of the times was not yet ripe for the Israeli society to consider such a person Jewish under the Law of Return. Brother Daniel, however, did become an Israeli citizen under the regular citizenship law of the country.

53. Roy Kreider, "A Review of Recent Anglican and Ecumenical Happenings in Israel," *Christian News from Israel* 21, no. 2 (1970):24.

54. Colbi, *Christianity in the Holy Land,* p. 189; Herbert Weiner, "Israel and Religious Freedom," *CC,* 26 July 1961, pp. 1003-06.

55. Weiner, "Israel and Religious Freedom," p. 1004.

56. In 1968 six American Protestant denominations in Israel—Baptists, Lutherans, Nazarenes, Pentecostals, Mennonites, and Christian and Missionary Alliance—applied to the Israel government for religious "community status" recognition (*Christianity Today,* 24 May 1968, p. 860). In 1970, with the appointment of a new bishop, the Israeli Anglicans, almost all of them Arabs, became the first Protestant group to be accorded official "community" recognition in Israel. This new status allowed it to set up its own ecclesiastical courts on matters of personal status of its congregants, including divorce and the admission of converts. Before 1970 the Anglican Church had enjoyed only the right to perform marriages between members (*The Church and the Jewish People,* no 2 [1970]: 14).

57. In January 1951 the Swedish Theological Institute in Jerusalem opened its doors to Protestant students from different parts of the world. The curriculum emphasized subjects of Judaica (*Christian News from Israel* 7 [June 1956]: 33-36). During its first ten years of existence over 79 students enrolled in the Institute from as far away as Japan (ibid. 10 [December 1959]: 13). Maintained by Swedish funds and governed by a board of trustees in Stockholm, students attended its lecture courses for semesters of three to nine months.

58. Ibid.:31-34.

59. Ibid.

60. Ibid.:32.

61. Ibid. 12 (May 1961): 12-15. Pentecostalism is a movement in Protestantism which believes in the religious experience of baptism through the Holy Spirit, as described in Acts 2:4. The religious revivals in American history reflect this movement.

62. *Christianity Today,* 27 March 1964, p. 615. Cf. Isaiah 11:10.

63. *Jerusalem Post Weekly,* 26 December 1966, p. 11.

CHAPTER ELEVEN

1. Judith H. Banki, *Christian Reactions to the Middle East Crisis* (New York: The American Jewish Committee, 1968), p. 2.

2. David Polish, "Why American Jews are Disillusioned," *CC*, 26 July 1967, pp. 965-67.

3. Marc H. Tannenbaum, "Israel's Hour of Need and the Jewish-Christian Dialogue," *Conservative Judaism*, vol. 22, no. 2, (1968): 7. Rabbi Tannenbaum did, however, distinguish between the private views of several key churchmen who spoke up for Israel's survival, "at some personal risk and in the face of some institutional pressures," and the official church bodies who remained silent (ibid.: 8).

4. Banki, *Christian Reactions*, p. 3.
   In a letter to the *Christian Century*, a leading Washington rabbi, Stanley Rabinowitz, wrote that Jews had hoped for some sort of reassurance during the tense days before the outbreak of hostilities from their Christian friends. Instead, the recurrent response was that Christian concern extended to all the peoples in the Middle East. Rabinowitz wrote: "The man who proclaims his impartiality when he sees another accosted by a man with a gun is neither impartial nor neutral; he is siding with the man with the gun." (*CC*, 6 September 1967, pp. 1128-30).

5. News release, Files of the International Affairs Commission, World Council of Churches, New York.

6. News release, Files of the World Council of Churches, Geneva. The June 8 statement of the United States Conference of Catholic Bishops also asked for "a crusade of prayer for peace," and expressed the "fervent hope" that the United Nations would be successful in halting the fighting (Tannenbaum, "Israel's Hour of Need," p. 8),

7. Ibid.

8. Polish, "Why American Jews are Disillusioned," p. 961. A Lutheran theologian, Aarne Siirala, later admitted how ashamed he felt when a rabbi friend had to plead for support from the Christian community ("Symposium: Lutheran Reactions to the Arab-Israel War," *Lutheran Quarterly*, August 1968, pp. 285-86).

9. This information comes from a conversation between the writer and Professor Abraham Joshua Heschel. The signers included: John C. Bennett, president, Union Theological Seminary; Robert McAfee Brown, professor of religion, Stanford University; Martin Luther King, Jr., president, Southern Christian Leadership Conference; Franklin H. Littell, president, Iowa Wesleyan College; Reinhold Niebuhr, professor emeritus, Union Theological Seminary; Daniel Poling, chaplain, Interfaith Memorial of the Four Chaplains; Lloyd C. Wicker, former president, Methodist Council of Bishops; S. G. Spottswood, chairman, national board of directors, NAACP; and the dean of St. Vladimir's Russian Orthodox Seminary.

10. Several other individual Protestant churchmen lent their names to statements of conscience in favor of Israel's survival, but they were so relatively few in number as to underscore the validity of our thesis (Banki, *Christian Reaction*, p. 2; and for the period after the Six–Day War, ibid., pp. 12-13). On June 1, for example, nine Washington, D.C. staff members of the Division of Peace and World Order of the General Board of Christian Social Concerns of the Methodist Church, apparently at their initiative and speaking only for themselves, recommended a strong United Nations presence in the area, free passage through

the Gulf of Aqaba, and support of the territorial integrity of all states in the Middle East. (News release.)

11. Banki, *Christian Reactions*, p. 3.

12. Ibid., p. 17.

13. A. Roy and Alice Eckardt, "Again, Silence in the Churches," *CC*, 26 July 1967, p. 973.

14. Ibid., 2 August 1967, p. 993.

15. Ibid.

16. Ibid., pp. 992-993.

17. Ibid., p. 993. A similar analysis of the silence of the churches was made by Franklin H. Littell, professor of religion at Temple University ("Israel and the Christian-Jewish Dialogue," in *The Religious Dimension of Israel*, ed. Henry Siegman [New York: Synagogue Council of America, 1968], pp. 41-46).

18. *CC*, 4 October 1967, p. 1259.

19. Ibid., 6 September 1967, p. 130.

20. *New York Times*, 26 June 1967.

21. Ibid., 13 July 1967.

22. *Christianity and Crisis*, 26 June 1967, pp. 141-42.

23. Ibid., p. 142.

24. Ibid., 18 September 1967, pp. 204-05.

25. Ibid., p. 205.

26. Ibid. Bennett's article came in response to the views of Rabbi Balfour Brickner of the Union of American Hebrew Congregations. Brickner had criticized Rev. Howard Schomer, director of the Specialized Ministries Department of the National Council of Churches, for circulating a polemical tract sent to him by Coptic Bishop Samuel of Cairo (ibid., pp. 203-04).

27. *CC*, 26 July 1967, p. 955.

28. Ibid., 21 June 1967, p. 804.

29. *Christianity and Crisis*, 10 July 1967, pp. 160-64.

30. In a vehemently anti–Israel article in 1970, the editor of *Christianity and Crisis*, Wayne H. Cowen, reiterated Geyer's thesis: "Even today few Americans know any Arabs . . . let alone take them seriously as human beings, and therein lies the tragedy" (*Christianity and Crisis*, 11 May 1970, p. 96).

31. *Christianity Today*, 21 July 1967, p. 1052.

In an obvious allusion to Kelso, Horace D. Hummel of the Lutheran School of Theology in Chicago wrote: "It is no secret that the vast majority of Christian intellectuals who have worked in the Arab world as archeologists or the like, champion the Arab cause." Hummel compared their language to the extreme expressions used with regard to the Vietnam issue: "The unquestionable good of Arab nationalism and self-determination is thwarted by Israeli imperialism or aggression; Israel even becomes a fascist and racist state, guilty of genocide, of all things" ("Symposium: Lutheran Reactions," *Lutheran Quarterly*, August 1968, pp. 279-80).

32. Willard G. Oxtoby, "Christians and the Mid-East Crisis," *CC*, 26 July 1967, p. 963.

33. Ibid., p. 964.

34. Ibid. Responding to Oxtoby, Rabbi David Lieber of the University of Judaism in Los Angeles wrote: "What I find especially offensive about this article is its condescension and self-righteousness" (Ibid., 20 September 1967, pp. 193-94).

35. Cited in Solomon M. Bernards, "The Arab-Israel Crisis and the American Christian Response," *Lutheran Quarterly*, August 1968, pp. 271-72.

36. On Israel's uniting of Jerusalem, J. A. Sanders, professor of Old Testament at Union Theological Seminary, stated that "it must be effectively resisted, else there will be another and more serious Arab crusade." He anticipated the Old City "reverting to Jordanian administration under massive United Nations presence," and called for Christians to support this move (*CC*, 26 July 1967, p. 970).

    Rev. Dana E. Klotzle, director of the United Nations Office of the Unitarian–Universalist Association, condemned "unequivocally the apparent expansionist policy of the present Israeli government, which cannot help but lead to more violence and bloodshed in the area." He also accused the Arab leaders of inciting their people to violence against Israel (Banki, *Christian Reactions*, p. 11).

    Dr. Alford Carleton, executive vice president of the United Church of Christ Board for Homeland Ministries, in an open letter to pastors and leaders of his church, warned that if the Arabs "in their frustration and bitter disappointment . . . now turn angrily against us, we should not be surprised" (ibid.).

    Perhaps the most extreme anti–Israel presentation was made by Rev. A. C. Forrest, editor of the *United Church Observer*, family magazine of the United Church of Canada, that country's largest Protestant denomination. In a special issue appearing on October 1, 1967, the editor condemned Israel for her "treatment of the Arab people in occupied territory in the weeks that followed the war, and the harsh, inhumane treatment of the refugees now, and the nineteen-year-old record of inhumanity to Palestinian refugees."

37. Banki, *Christian Reactions*, pp. 6-7.

38. Ibid., p. 17.

39. A. Roy Eckardt, "The Reaction of the Churches," in *Proceedings of the Annual Conference of American Academic Association for Peace in the Middle East* (New York: 1969) p. 80. Eckardt also points out that Christian leaders deplored the Israeli raid on the Beirut airport in December 1968, while saying nothing about the Arab terrorist acts which ostensibly provoked the Israeli reaction (ibid., p. 81). In support of his thesis, he also chastised the National Council for approving a report of three clergymen dispatched to study the Arab refugee problem in the summer of 1968, without any attempt to give perspective to the subject (ibid., p. 75).

40. Ibid., pp. 83, 84.

41. *CC*, 21 June 1967, p. 804.

42. Ibid., pp. 804-05.

43. Ibid., 26 July 1967, p. 954.

44. Ibid., 12 July 1967, p. 883.

45. Ibid., p. 884.

46. Ibid.

47. Ibid.

48. Ibid.

49. Ibid., 26 July 1967, pp. 966-67.

50. Tannenbaum, "Israel's Hour of Need," p. 10.

51. Ibid., p. 12.

52. Ibid., p. 13.

53. Ibid., p. 17.

54. Ibid., pp. 17-18.

55. "The truth . . . is that the Christian community has never understood that Israel, so far as Jews are concerned, is a symbol in some sense analogous to the Christian symbol of resurrection: after death (Auschwitz), God miraculously raised His people to life (Israel) in the midst of the nations" (Alan T. Davies, *Anti-Semitism and the Christian Mind* [New York: Herder and Herder, 1969], pp. 179-80).

56. *New York Times*, 29 March 1970, section 4, p. 11.

Martin E. Marty, an editor of the *Christian Century*, acknowledged that he grasped the notion of Israel's significance to the Jew, but admitted that he could not accept it (*CC*, 12 February 1969, p. 207).

CHAPTER TWELVE

1. Jules Isaac, *The Teaching of Contempt* (New York: Holt, Rinehart and Winston, 1962).

2. M. E. Marty et al, eds., *Religious Press in America* (New York: Holt Rinehart and Winston, 1963), p. 55.

3. *The Church and the Jewish People*, World Council of Churches Newsletter no. 3 (September 1970), p. 3.

4. *The Ecumenical Courier*, November-December 1969, World Council of Churches.

For the newly defined functions of the Committee on the Church and the Jewish People, as determined in Geneva in December 1969, one of which was "to urge the churches to study the theological implications of the continued existence of the Jewish people," see the quarterly newsletter of the World Council of Churches Division of World Mission and Evangelism, *The Church and the Jewish People*, March 1970. See also, Eckardt, *Elder and Younger Brothers*; H. Berkhof and Jakob J. Petuchowski, "Israel as a Theological Problem in the Christian Church," *Journal of Ecumenical Studies* 6, no. 3 (Summer 1969) pp. 329-53.

5. "Survey of Catholic-Jewish Relations, 1970," Secretariat for Catholic-Jewish Relations, Seton Hall University, South Orange, New Jersey. See also, Edward H. Flannery, "Anti-Zionism and the Christian Psyche," *Journal of Ecumenical Studies* 6, no. 2 (Spring 1969); Friedrich Heer, "The Catholic Church and the Jews Today," *Midstream* 17, no. 5 (May 1971), pp. 20-31; Robert F. Drinan, "The State of Israel: Theological Implications for Christians," *Conservative Judaism* 22, no. 3, (Spring 1968) pp. 28-35.

6. *CC*, 29 March 1967, pp. 395-396.

selected bibliography

Agus, Jacob G. "Israel and the Jewish-Christian Dialogue." *Journal of Ecumenical Studies* 6:18-36.

American Christian Palestine Committee. *A Christian Report on Palestine.* New York, 1949.

————. *Analysis of Report of Anglo-American Committee of Inquiry on Palestine.* New York, 1946.

————. *Christian Voice for a Jewish Palestine.* New York, 1946.

————. *Truth About Palestine.* New York, 1946.

American Friends Service Committee. *Search for Peace in the Middle East.* Philadelphia, 1970.

Anderson, Rufus. *History of the Missions of the American Board of Commissioners for Foreign Missions to the Oriental Churches.* 2 vols. Boston: Congregational Publishing Society, 1872.

Antonius, George. *The Arab Awakening.* Philadelphia: Lippincott, 1939.

Badeau, John S. *The American Approach to the Arab World.* New York: Harper and Row, 1968.

Baly, Denis. *Multitudes in the Valley.* Greenwich, Connecticut: Seabury Press, 1957.

Banki, Judith H. *Christian Reactions to the Middle East Crisis.* American Jewish Committee, 1968.

Baron, Salo W. *Modern Nationalism and Religion.* New York: Harper, 1947.

Barth, Markus. "Shall Israel Go it Alone?" *Journal of Ecumenical Studies* 5:346-52.

Bentwich, Norman. *For Zion's Sake.* Philadelphia: Jewish Publication Society, 1954.

Berkhof, H. and Petuchowski, Jakob J. "Israel as a Theological Problem in the Christian Church." *Journal of Ecumenical Studies* 6:329-53.

Blackstone, William E. *Jesus is Coming.* 3rd edition. Chicago: Fleming H. Revell Co., 1908.

Bliss, Frederick Jones. *The Religions of Modern Syria and Palestine.* New York: Charles Scribner's Sons, 1917.

Boettner, Loraine. *The Millennium.* Philadelphia: Presbyterian and Reformed Publishing Co., 1958.

Bokser, Ben Zion. *Judaism and the Christian Predicament.* New York: Knopf, 1966.

Bridgeman, Charles T. "Why No Peace in the Holy Land?" *Papers on Palestine II,* pp. 69-73. New York: Institute of Arab-American Affairs, 1947.

Selected Bibliography

Buber, Martin. *Israel and Palestine*. New York: Farrar, Straus & Young, 1952.

Burton, William L. "Protestant America and the Rebirth of Israel." *Journal of Social Studies* 26:203-14.

Case, Shirley J. *The Millennial Hope*. Chicago: University of Chicago Press, 1918.

Clark, Elmer T. *The Small Sects in America*. New York: Abingdon-Cokesbury, 1949.

Colbi, Saul P. *Christianity in the Holy Land*. Tel Aviv: Am Hessefer, 1969.

Cragg, Kenneth. *The Call of the Minaret*. New York: Oxford, 1956.

Davies, Alan T. *Anti-Semitism and the Christian Mind*. New York: Herder & Herder, 1969.

Davis, Moshe, ed. *Israel: Its Role in Civilization*. New York: Harper, 1956.

DeNovo, John A. *American Interests and Policies in the Near East, 1900-1939*. Minneapolis: University of Minnesota Press, 1963.

Diamond, Malcolm L. "Christian Silence on Israel: An End to Dialogue?" *Judaism* 16:410-22.

Eckardt, A. Roy. *Christianity and the Children of Israel*. New York: Kings Crown Press, 1948.

———. *Elder and Younger Brothers*. New York: Charles Scribners Sons, 1967.

———. "The Reaction of the Churches." In *Proceedings of the Annual Conference of American Academic Association for Peace in the Middle East*, p. 80, New York: 1969.

Farah, Rafiq A. "Arab Church in Israel." *Muslim World* 42:245-48.

Federal Council of Churches of Christ. *Conflict Over Palestine*. New York, 1944.

———. *Shall Jerusalem be Internationalized?* New York, 1949.

Fein, Isaac M. "Niles Weekly Register." *Publications of the American Jewish Historical Society* 50:3-22.

Feingold, Henry L. *The Politics of Rescue*. New Brunswick, N.J.: Rutgers University Press, 1970.

Finnie, David H. *Pioneers East*. Cambridge, Massachusetts: Harvard University Press, 1967.

Fink, Reuben, ed. *America and Palestine*. New York: American Zionist Emergency Council, 1944.

Flannery, Edward H. and Harcourt, Hugh R. "Anti-Zionism and the Christian Psyche." *Journal of Ecumenical Studies* 6:173-84, 634-40.

Foreign Missions Conference of North America, Committee of Reference and Counsel. *The Palestine Question: A Christian Position*. New York, 1945.

Gildersleeve, Virginia C. *Many a Good Crusade*. New York: Macmillan, 1954.

Goldberg, Isaac. *Major Noah: American-Jewish Pioneer*. Philadelphia: Jewish Publication Society, 1936.

Graves, Philip. *Palestine: The Land of the Three Faiths*. London: Jonathan Cape, 1923.

Halalenbach, John W. "Christian Stance on the Arab-Israeli Conflict." *Reformed Review* 22:10-17.

Halkin, Abraham S., ed. *Zion in Jewish Literature*. New York: Herzl Press, 1961.

Halperin, Samuel. *The Political World of American Zionism*. Detroit: Wayne University Press, 1961.

Handy, Robert T. "Zion in American Christian Movements." In *Israel: Its Role in Civilization*, edited by Moshe Davis, pp. 284-97, New York: Harper & Brothers, 1956.

Hauer, Christian E. *Crisis and Conscience in the Middle East*. Chicago: Quadrangle, 1970.

239

Selected Bibliography

Hedenquist, Gote, ed. *The Church and the Jewish People*. London: Edisburgh House, 1954.

Heer, Friedrich. "The Catholic Church and the Jews Today." *Midstream* 17:20-31.

Herberg, Will. *Protestant, Catholic, Jew*. New York: Doubleday & Co., 1955.

Hertzberg, Arthur, ed. *The Zionist Idea*. New York: Doubleday & Co., 1959.

Heschel, Abraham J. *Israel*. New York: Farrar, Straus and Giroux, 1969.

Hilberg, Raul. *Destruction of the European Jews*. Chicago: Quadrangle, 1961.

Hitti, Philip K. *History of the Arabs*. 5th edition. New York: Macmillan, 1950.

Holmes, John J. *Palestine: Today and Tomorrow*. New York: Macmillan, 1929.

Homrighausen, Elmer G. "Christianity and the Israel-Arab World." *Theology Today* 24:375-78.

Hurewitz, Jacob C. *The Struggle for Palestine*. New York: W. W. Norton & Co., 1950.

Institute of Arab-American Affairs. *Papers on Palestine, I*. New York, 1945.

———. *Papers on Palestine, II*. New York: 1947.

Isaac, Jules. *The Teaching of Contempt*. New York: Holt, Rinehart & Winston, 1962.

Katz, Shlomo. "The Oswald Rufeisen (Brother Daniel) Case." *Midstream* 9:78-96.

King, Michael C. Preface to *Palestine Refugees: Aid With Justice*. Geneva: World Council of Churches, 1970.

Klausner, Joseph. *The Messianic Idea in Israel*. New York: Macmillan, 1955.

Knight, George A. F. "Israel: A Theological Problem." *Reformed Theological Review* 17:33-43.

Kobler, Franz, *The Vision Was There*. London: Lincolns-Prager, 1956.

Lauterpacht, Elihu. *Jerusalem and the Holy Places*. London: Anglo-Israel Association, 1968.

Leith, David M. "American Christian Support for a Jewish Palestine." Senior thesis, Princeton University, 1957.

Levine, Samuel H. "Palestine in the Literature of the United States to 1867." In *Early History of Zionism in America*, edited by Isidore S. Meyer, pp. 21-29. New York: American Jewish Historical Society and Theodor Herzl Foundation, 1958.

Lichtenstein, Aharon; Frimer, Norman E.; Wyschograd, Michael. "Brother Daniel and the Jewish Fraternity." *Judaism* 12:260-80; 13:102-07, 107-10, 110-16.

Littell, Franklin H. "Politics, Theology and the Jews," *Journal of Ecumenical Studies* 2:475-77.

Malachy, Yonah. "Jehovah Witnesses and Zionism." *Herzl Year Book* 5, pp. 175-208. New York: Herzl Press, 1963.

———. "Seventh Day Adventists." *Herzl Year Book* 6, pp. 265-301. New York: Herzl Press, 1964-65.

Manuel, Frank E. *The Realities of American-Palestine Relations*. Washington, D.C.: Public Affairs Press, 1949.

Maritain, Jacques. *A Christian Looks at the Jewish Question*. New York: Longmans, Green & Co., 1939.

Marty, M. E.; Deedy, J. C.; Silverman, D. W.; Lekachman, R.; eds. *The Religious Press in America*. New York: Holt, Rinehart and Winston, 1963.

Meyer, Isidor S., ed. *Early History of Zionism in America*. New York: American Jewish Historical Society, 1958.

Morse, Arthur D. *While Six Million Died*. New York: Random House, 1968.

Near East Report: Special Survey. October 1964.

Selected Bibliography

Niebuhr, Reinhold. "Jews After the War." *The Nation*, 21 February 1942, pp. 214-16.

———. "The Relations of Christians and Jews in Western Civilization." *Central Conference of American Rabbis Journal*, April 1958, pp. 18-32.

———. Introduction to *The Jew in Our Day*, by Waldo Frank. New York: Duell, Sloan and Pearce, 1944.

Parkes, James. *A History of Palestine from 135 A.D. to Modern Times.* London: Gollancz, 1949.

———. "Jewry, Judaism, Israel." *Congregational Quarterly* 27: 18-26.

Polk, William R. "America in the Middle East, 1947-1958." In *Middle Eastern Affairs: Number Two*, edited by Albert Hourani, pp. 49-80. St. Antony's Papers, no. 11. London: Chatto & Windus, 1961.

Rees, Elfan. *We Strangers and Afraid.* New York: Carnegie Endowment for International Peace, 1959.

Ricks, Eldin. "Zionism and the Mormon Church." *Herzl Year Book* 5, pp. 147-74, New York: Herzl Press, 1963.

Roosevelt, Kermit. "Partition of Palestine: A Lesson in Pressure Politics." *Middle East Journal* 2:1-16.

Ryrie, Charles C. *Dispensationalism Today.* Chicago: Moody Press, 1965.

Sandeen, Ernest R. *The Origins of Fundamentalism.* Philadelphia: Fortress Press, 1968.

———. *The Roots of Fundamentalism.* Chicago: University of Chicago Press, 1970.

Scharper, Philip. "Israel the Modern State and Contemporary Christian Points of View." *Lutheran Quarterly* 20:255-59.

Schechtman, Joseph B. *The United States and the Jewish State Movement.* New York: Herzl Press, 1966.

Schneider, Peter. *The Dialogue of Christians and Jews.* New York: Seabury Press, 1967.

———. "Torah and State in Israel." *Lutheran World* 10:430-35.

Schwadron, Benjamin. "Jordan Annexes Arab Jerusalem." *Middle Eastern Affairs* 1:99-111.

Siegel, Seymour. "Jews and Christians: The Next Step." *Conservative Judaism* 19:1-11.

Siegman, Henry, ed. *The Religious Dimensions of Israel.* Synagogue Council of America, 1968.

Silverberg, Robert. *If I Forget Thee O Jerusalem.* New York: William Morrow & Co., 1970.

Smith, Reuben W. "American University of Beirut." *Middle Eastern Affairs* 7:329-33.

Solheim, Magne. "Israel: People, Land and State." *Lutheran World* 10:423-30.

Stendhal, Kirster. "Judaism and Christianity: After a Colloquium and a War." *Harvard Divinity Bulletin*, Autumn 1967, pp. 2-9.

Tannenbaum, Marc. "Israel's Hour of Need and the Jewish-Christian Dialogue." *Conservative Judaism* 22: 1-18.

Tibawi, Abdul L. "The Genesis and Early History of the Syrian Protestant College." *Middle East Journal* 21: 1-15.

———. "The American Missionaries in Beirut and Butrus Al Bustani." In *Middle Eastern Affairs: Number Three*, edited by Albert Hourani, pp. 137-82. St. Antony's Papers, no. 16. London: Chatto & Windus, 1963.

Toynbee, Arnold J. and Zeitlin, Solomon. "Jewish Rights in Palestine." *Jewish Quarterly Review* 52:1-11, 12-34, 367-69, 369-81.

Tuchman, Barbara W. *The Bible and the Sword*. New York: New York University Press, 1956.

Voss, Carl H. "Christian Indecision on Zionism." *Churchman* 160:16-17.

————. "Christian Ministers Speak Out." *New Palestine* 34, pp. 339-40.

————. "Christians and Zionism in the United States." In *Palestine Year Book* 2, pp. 497-500.

Wilson, Evan M. "The Internationalization of Jerusalem." *Middle East Journal* 23:1-13.

Wise, Stephen. *Challenging Years*. New York: Putnams, 1949.

World Council of Churches. *Collection of Statements Made by the World Council of Churches and Representative Bodies of its Member Churches*. Geneva, 1964.

————. *Palestine Refugees: Aid With Justice*. Geneva, 1970.

index

Dr. Hertzel Fishman has been a White House appointee to the National Advisory Council on Education Professions Development, and a consultant to the Appalachian Regional Commission, the U.S. Office of Education, and the Agency for International Development. He currently serves as an advisor to the Israel Ministry of Education in Jerusalem. A graduate of the Jewish Theological Seminary of America (1946), he also holds a Ph.D. degree from New York University (1971).

Anne Meyering edited the manuscript. The book was designed by Don Ross. The text typeface is Linotype Caledonia designed by W. A. Dwiggins about 1938; and the display face is Americana designed by Richard Isbell in 1967.

The text is printed on Bradford Book text paper and the book is bound in Interlaken's Arco Vellum over binders' boards. Manufactured in the United States of America.